D0702224

Diversity in Single-Parent Families:
Working from Strength

Diversity in Single-Parent Families: Working from Strength

**Cathryne L. Schmitz, Ph.D., ASCW and
Susan Steiger Tebb, Ph.D., LSW Editors**

Families International, Inc. Milwaukee, Wisconsin

ISBN 0-87304-304-9

© Copyright 1999 Families International, Inc.
Publishing in association with the Alliance for Children and Families, Inc.
11700 West Lake Park Drive
Milwaukee WI 53224

Diversity in Single-Parent Families:
Working from Strength

Table of Contents

About the Authors

Faye Y. Abram, Ph.D.

Faye Abram is an Associate Professor at Saint Louis University, School of Social Service. Her professional practice experience includes work in substance abuse treatment, administration of community programs for preschoolers and their parents, and involvement with elderly residents in low-income housing. As an African-American mother and member of a large, very-connected inter-generational family system, Dr. Abram is committed to practice capitalizing on the strengths of family systems, as well as practice which unites systems in their struggle to solve problems within their families and communities.

Linda Anderson, M.S.

Linda Anderson is a non-Indian therapist. She was raised in rural Wyoming and has lived in the Puget Sound area for over twenty years. She has worked in the mental health field for approximately eighteen years with children, adults and families. Her work has occurred in several contexts, including an American-Indian/Alaskan-Native agency, an African-American agency, a drop-in center for homeless youth and a private agency.

Janice H. Chadha, Ph.D., MSW

Janice Hays Chadha is an Associate Professor of Social Work, Columbia College, Columbia, Missouri. A native of the area studied, she has worked over twenty years in health systems social work with diverse rural and urban populations in Missouri and Illinois. In 1973, she helped develop and staff the first Child Protection Team at the University of Missouri Health Sciences Center as part of a statewide child abuse prevention program aimed primarily at rural areas. Her research interests include equity in the delivery of health care services, catastrophic health issues and managed care and health care delivery to diverse populations.

Viqui E. Claravall, MSW, ACSW

Viqui Claravall received her Masters Degree in Social Work from the University of Washington in 1974 and also completed post-graduate training in Marriage and Family Therapy in 1988. She has twenty-one years experience as a certified Minority/Children/Geriatric Mental Health Specialist for the state of Washington and has a specific interest in cross-cultural issues providing training on culturally responsive service delivery with Asian/Pacific populations. She is currently employed part time as the Mental Health Specialist for the City of Seattle, Early Childhood Education and Assistance Program. She worked for many years as a Clinical Manager/Program Developer for the Children, Youth and Family Services at Asian Counseling and Referral Service (ACRS), a multi-cultural, multi-lingual agency which she co-founded twenty-one years ago. As a Filipino, Ms Claravall is an active volunteer in her community and in the broader Asian/Pacific Islander community. Currently she is serving as co-founder and co-chair of the Asian Pacific Islander Women and Family Safety Center.

Fransing Sinclair-Daisy, Ph.D.

Fransing Daisy has a doctorate in clinical psychology from the University of Washington. She has over fifteen years of experience in crisis intervention and adult/adolescent substance abuse counseling. Dr. Daisy's research interests include the area of substance abuse looking at the interaction of substance use/abuse with emotional disorders in the American Indian population. She currently provides in-service training and consultation to the staff of the Thunderbird Treatment Center. She has worked with the Nisqually IHS Service Unit and provides training and technical assistance to community mental health centers and university programs. She has performed numerous community activities including serving on the Indian Child Welfare Advisory Committee. She has authored numerous publications on Indian cultural issues and crisis intervention.

Geoffrey L. Greif, DSW

Geoffrey Greif is an Associate Dean and Professor, School of Social Work, University of Maryland, Baltimore. He is the author of over sixty articles as well as five books on single parents, including Single Fathers and the recently published, Out of Touch: When Parents and Children Lose Contact After Divorce.

Pauline Jivanjee, Ph.D.

Pauline Jivanjee is an Assistant Professor at the Portland State University Graduate School of Social Work and a Research Associate at the University's Research and Training Center on Family Support and Children's Mental Health. Her twenty-five-year career in social work practice and education has focused on providing support and services to vulnerable families, many of them single-parent families. A native of England, Pauline worked for a time as a social worker in a school for children with serious mental and physical disabilities. She and her husband, Saj, are the parents of three sons and a daughter.

Sue Pearlmutter, Ph.D., MSW

Sue Pearlmutter is an Assistant Professor at the Mandel School of Applied Social Sciences, Case Western Reserve University. She teaches in the areas of macro social work practice and diversity. Her research interests include poverty and welfare, organizational behavior and leadership issues involving low-income women and children, lesbian and gay families and lesbian elders.

Janese Prince, MSW

Janese Prince has a Masters in Social Work from Saint Louis University. She has worked with high-risk, low-income families in the City of Saint Louis. Many of the families were low income, with few resources and little sense of their own power leading her to explore supportive, empowering models of collective practice. Her own experiences as a successful African-American single parent intensifies her interest in understanding the empowerment needs of vulnerable populations. She has interests in multi-dimensional research/evaluation with high-risk, inner-city youth and families, particularly single-parent families. She currently serves on the Board of the Center for Social Justice Education and Research at Saint Louis University.

Julia Putnam, MSW, DCSW

Julia Putnam has had a longstanding interest in cross-cultural issues with specific experience in Indian and Alaska Native and multi-ethnic projects. She currently works at Seattle University and maintains a private practice in psychotherapy. Additionally, she is on the Board of Advisors for Antioch University Seattle and assists in teaching interpersonal therapy to psychiatric residents of the University of Washington's School of Medicine.

Marjorie Sable, Ph.D, MSW

Marjorie Sable is an Assistant Professor of Social Work at the University of Missouri-Columbia. From 1989-92 she was Chief of the Bureau of Perinatal and Child Health for Missouri Department of Health which administered the Healthy Mothers/Healthy Fathers/Healthy Babies project. Her research interests include understanding and reducing barriers of prenatal care and improving pregnancy outcomes.

Cathryne L. Schmitz, Ph.D., ASCW

Cathryne Schmitz recently joined the faculty of the Graduate School of Social Work at the University of Denver after several years at Saint Louis University. Her teaching focuses on children/families, community-based practice, diversity and poverty. She spent many years in practice with families and children and has a rich history of experience with single-parent families. Her understanding of the issues is enriched through her own enjoyable experience as the single parent of two grown, successful, happy adults. She continues an active commitment to and involvement with a diverse range of vulnerable children and families.

Annette Squetimkin-Anquoe, M.A.

Annette Squetimkin-Anquoe lives in Seattle and is a member of the Colville Confederated Tribes of Washington state. She has a masters in Psychology Counseling and has worked in the field of alcoholism and substance abuse prevention, intervention and treatment for over twelve years. Annette is the prevention director for the National Association for Native American Children of Alcoholics and has developed numerous substance abuse prevention materials for a handbook about Native-American children of alcoholics. Annette has provided training on a variety of health and wellness topics including alcoholism and substance abuse prevention and intervention, adult children of alcoholics, cross-cultural awareness and sensitivity, personal growth and recovery and related health care issues.

Susan Steiger Tebb, Ph.D., L.S.W.

Sue Tebb, Dean of the School of Social Service at Saint Louis University, has centered her research interests around family caregiving. She has been a social worker for over twenty-five years working with many diverse family configurations in adoptions, medical social work, court mediation and caregiving situations.

Maria R. Vidal de Haymes, Ph.D., MSW

Dr. Vidal received her Masters Degree from the University of Chicago in 1987 and her Ph.D. from Ohio State University in 1993. Dr. Vidal taught at the University of Wisconsin in Milwaukee before joining the faculty of School of Social Work at Loyola University in 1992. She teaches in the area of social welfare policy, community organizing and race, ethnicity and culture. Her research interests focus on the economic incorporation of immigrants in the United States, Latino family structure and process, Latino political participation, welfare reform and child welfare with Latino families. Dr. Vidal is a consultant to numerous local and state organizations and serves on the boards of several Latino community-based agencies.

J. Wilson Watt, Ph.D., MSW

J. Wilson Watt is an Assistant Professor of Social Work at the University of Missouri-Columbia. Prior to entering academic social work, he spent almost twenty-five years in practice in family services and child welfare. His research interests include development of effective interventions in child abuse and neglect treatment, the role of the father in the development on sexually predatory behavior in males and international social work and its impact on social values and the development of democratic institutions. He has been a Fulbright recipient for his international work.

Dedication

We would like to dedicate this book to the children who have brought us wisdom — our children, grandchildren, and for some, nieces and nephews. They are from diverse communities, heritages, experiences and family structures. They are all thriving and bringing us great pleasure. We want to thank them for their lessons.

Stacey, Joshua, Hayley
Nealee, Zachary
Maseo, Gabriela
Sonia, Jahmel
Sibby, Washie
Saroj, Rajinder
Joel, Emily
Stephanie
Neal, Steve, Josh, Lina
Peter, Michael, Sara, Nick
Jennifer, Alissa
Alex, Bram
Karen, Jeffrey, Jerald, Asher
Nina, Jim, Debbie, Brownie, Gwynne, and their children

Preface

THE IDEA FOR THIS BOOK came out of the editors' personal and professional experiences with Single-Parent families. Professionally we have worked with widowed, divorced and never-married Single-Parent families across ethnic, racial and socioeconomic status. Personally, we have experienced the loss of a spouse through death or divorce and the reconfiguration of family life as a result. This professional as well as personal experience helps us understand the importance of well informed, strength based, community oriented services.

In spite of the many strong positive Single-Parent families, negative stereotypes abound. Successful Single-Parent families receive inadequate attention. Rather, Single-Parent families have been ill defined, stigmatized and demonized in ways which make it difficult for them to get the support and recognition they need. Arising from this reality, we had two main goals in mind when we conceptualized this book. First, we wanted to expand the availability of knowledge about a diverse range of Single-Parent families while decreasing assumptive biases about a family structure increasing nationally and internationally. Second, we wanted to select authors for the book who could contribute to this body of scholarship from many backgrounds and geographic regions. As such, the authors (including the editors) all have personal and/or professional experience with multicultural, economically diverse communities; and all are knowledgeable about the strengths and needs of Single-Parent families. Most importantly, each has expertise in and experience with the communities that are the focus of her/his chapter.

While there are a number of books on practice with Single-Parent families, most are written for practice with white, middle-class families. This book is designed to fill the gaps in the literature particularly as relates to interventions with diverse Single-Parent families. Each chapter focuses on service delivery to populations of Single-Parent families which have been underrepresented in research, education, and the literature. Knowledge is provided about a wide range of communities by race/ethnicity, gender, economic status, sexual orientation, structure and disability. The unique as well as common strengths and needs faced are presented with examples of appropriate service responses. The programs and interventions reviewed are as diverse as the populations, reflecting the diversity of resources and needs. Individual, family, group and community practice responses are addressed.

The authors articulate that the two most common problems faced by the Single-Parent families are the impact of stigmatization and inadequate income due to the economic inequality of women. Both increase stress, thereby making the job of parenting more difficult. This book suggests that what Single Parents need most is support – social and financial – and respect. Because of our combined belief in these basic understandings, only approaches respecting the Single-Parent family as a viable system and working with families from a perspective of strength are included in this book.

The authors of the chapters offer insight into many of the issues faced by Single Parents. In covering the commonalties, stressing the strengths and discussing the needs; the authors impress upon us the need to understand the uniqueness experienced due to community and family context as well as individual difference. The extended family and community support offered by communities of color become apparent in the reading. So also do the needs arising when community is not available. For some families such as the gay/lesbian families and families with a child with disabilities, there are unique legal, advocacy and support needs which require the social worker to increase her/his knowledge of these issues. Social workers must understand not only the individual family but also the community and historical context faced by the family. The social worker must listen to the strengths and needs of each family and individual, then work within the community to help families build on their strengths.

The process of editing this book confirmed our belief in the importance of reframing our understanding of Single-Parent families. All families, including Single-Parent families, need support, a sense of community, respect and adequate financial resources. The kind of support and the resources available will vary with the community, history and heritage. Social workers who are knowledgeable and enjoy the diversity of these families will be able to listen, view the strengths as well as the difficulties and help Single-Parent families rewrite their story in a way that supports them. This leads to the creation of a climate which empowers parents and children, strengthening their resolve to succeed on their own terms.

The authors and editors share a commitment to the future of our children. We each believe it is important to invest in the plight of children facing risk due to the lack of financial, social and societal support. Therefore the dilemma of equity in the use of profits arising from the sale of this book was an easy one. Collectively, the authors and editors have agreed to donate the proceeds to the Children's Defense Fund, an organization advocating nationally in the United States on behalf of children, youth, and families.

Introduction

The Multiple Faces and Realities of Single Parenthood: Support, Diversity, and Shifting Demographic Patterns

Cathryne L. Schmitz, Ph.D., ASCW
and Susan C. Tebb, Ph.D., L.S.W.

NATIONALLY AND INTERNATIONALLY, economic and social trends have shifted resulting in an increase in Single-Parent households (Schmitz, 1995). Two-parent, married families decreased from 44% in 1960 to 26% in 1990 (Miller, 1992) while Single-Parent families almost tripled between 1970 and 1990 (Miller). The number of children living in Single-Parent families increasing from one in twelve in 1960 (Garfinkel, 1987) to one in four in 1988 (Ellwood, 1988). Estimates indicate 50% (Garfinkel, 1987) to 60% (Norton & Glick, 1986) of all children in the United States will spend at least part of their lives in a Single-Parent family.

The formation and structure of Single-Parent families is changing as well. Between 1970 and 1985 the number of children living with widowed mothers decreased by 40% while the number living with divorced mothers more than doubled and the number living with unmarried mothers increased by a factor of six (U.S. Children, 1989). Prior to World War II, widows made up the largest percentage of mother-only households (Hansen & Lindblad-Goldberg, 1987). Since that time, divorce rates have climbed and the number of children born outside of marriage has increased (Bane, 1988; Danziger, 1988; Gribschaw, 1985). The divorce rate has more than doubled over the last several decades (Miller, 1992). Between 1980 and 1990, there has been a 64% increase in the number of children born to unmarried women (Miller).

The rapid social and cultural changes resulting both in and from shifting values, norms and lifestyles (Miller, 1992) have left us confused (Schmitz, 1995) and

13

without adequate knowledge and understanding. Amidst this rapid change, Single-Parent households, particularly those headed by women, have been blamed for multiple social problems (Schmitz). Although Single-Parent families have been negatively stereotyped as a group, they are not a homogenous group. Great diversity exists among Single-Parent families. While some result from divorce and widowhood, others occur outside marriage – some by choice. According to Kamerman and Kahn (1988):

> Describing someone as a "single parent " or a "single mother" provides very little information except that the family is not headed by a legally married, cohabiting husband and wife. The label does not, by itself, give a picture of the economic situation of the family, the health or well-being of the mother and children, the way the parent discharges her or his parenting and job responsibilities, or the threat the single parent may present to established social norms. All the label does is to serve as a kind of indicator of a possible problem. Moreover, the definition of "the problem" varies depending on who is involved, who is carrying out the analysis, and current societal preoccupations with the concept of the single parent (p. 1).

Except for its common family structure, much of the diversity in Single-Parent families goes unrecognized. Although some share poverty, isolation and stigmatization; others are secure and self-directing (Kamerman & Kahn, 1988).

Differences exist along ethnic, racial, class and gender lines among Single-Parent households. While there is a higher percentage of female-headed, Single-Parent families among African Americans than European Americans, the rates of growth are same (Garfinkel & McLanahan, 1986). The proportion of Single-Mother families resulting from widowhood and separation were similar (Kamerman & Kahn, 1988). Beyond widowhood, differences in formation patterns exist. Divorce accounts for half of the European-American mother-only families; only 17% result from never-married families. Among African Americans, half the mother-only families were headed by never married women. Some studies examining causes indicate the primary causal factors also differ across racial groups. The rising income of women may be the biggest influence in the rise of Single-Mother families for European Americans; while male unemployment may be a significant additional contributing factor in African-American families (Garfinkel & McLanahan, 1986; Hansen & Lindblad-Goldberg, 1987). This hypothesis needs further study.

Economic Risk

Poverty is a major risk factor faced by female-headed, Single-Parent families. "Some, perhaps most, of the problems of families headed by single women with children stem from their very low incomes" (Garfinkel, 1987, p. 2). The poverty rate for female-headed families is 55.4% while the poverty rate for married-couple households is only 10.6% (Children's Defense Fund [CDF], 1992). Female-headed, Single-Parent families have half the income of Single-Father households (Schorr & Moen, 1984). According to Schiller (1989), low-income, female-headed families have a different pattern of income. These families have less earned income and are more dependent on income assistance than low-income, male-headed families. Women enter the job market at lower wages relative to the wages of men (Danziger, 1988)and women's incomes are significantly lower than men's even in the same occupational categories (Bernard & Nesbitt, 1981).

There are three major contributors to the high level of poverty in female-headed, Single-Parent households. Female-headed families experience the low earning power of women as well as coping with insufficient child support and a welfare system which is inadequate and counterproductive (Ehrenreich & Piven, 1984; Ellwood, 1988; Garfinkel, 1987). Women enter the labor market in a disadvantaged position (Mihaly, 1989)and many of the jobs open to women are in the low-income sector (Pearce, 1989). An insufficient pool of jobs is available at wages which could bring women and children out of poverty.

Overall, African-American families are twice as likely to live in poverty as European-American families while Hispanic families face an even higher rate of poverty. The "differences in poverty rates show up most strikingly in single-mother families….Poverty rates are significantly worse in minority single-mother families, and median incomes are lower" (McChesney, 1989, p. 2). The interaction between race, ethnicity, and gender results in higher rates of poverty for female-headed, African-American and Hispanic families (Pearce, 1989). In female-headed households; 42% of European-American, 63% of African-American and 64% of Hispanic families live in poverty (CDF, 1992).

Poverty in female-headed, Single-Parent households is complex (Garfinkel, 1987). The interaction between the economy and the family system results in stereotyping of occupations by gender thus creating unequal power relations which are institutionalized by the state (Abramovitz, 1989). Globally, women are poorer than men while also being responsible for the majority of unpaid household work (Nichols-Casebolt, Krysik, & Hermann-Currie, 1994). This interaction occurs is such diverse areas as Malaysia (Stivens, 1985), Costa Rica (Yudelman, 1987), Britain (Nichols-Casebolt et al.) and many third world countries studied by Chant & Brydon (1989). While the issues are global, Wong, Garfinkel and McLanahan's (1993) comparison of Single Mothers in the United States with those of eight European countries found a lower relative economic status of Single Mothers in America.

Challenging Perception

Theoretical assumptions presume two-parent families are the norm and therefore the only healthy model. The perception of "two parent families as the norm results in a focus on single parent families as harmful by definition" (Schmitz, 1995, p. 432). "Defining single parent families as deviant maintains the unity and position of two parent families as primary in society" (Schmitz, p. 431) resulting in the treatment of Single-Parent families as deviant. "Single parent family has become a euphemism for *problem family*, with single parent families taking the blame for many social problems" (Schmitz, p.431). Single-Parent families exceed the accepted boundaries of the community, threatening *traditional* family styles (Kamerman & Kahn, 1988). Labels applied to Single-Parent families include *broken, deviant, abnormal,* and *unstable* (Schorr & Moen, 1984). "Placing families in a deviant category is but one of the artificial dichotomies that have negative consequences for mother-headed families" (Kissman, 1995, p.151).

Knowledge, knowledge seeking and understanding are circular paths. Practitioners working with Single-Parent families are informed by knowledge based on negative assumptions. When negative assumptions are the basis of investigation, negative findings result (Tuzlak & Hillock, 1986). This research is then used to educate practitioners, understand problems and focus solutions which limits practice options. Practitioners are limited by the lack of solid, unbiased information on female-headed, Single-Parent households. There are studies which indicate Single Parenthood, particularly divorce, leaves children at risk of school difficulties and behavior problems (Kinard & Reinherz, 1986; Mueller & Cooper, 1986; Peterson & Zill, 1986), some of which are based on negative expectations and short term consequences of change (Garfinkel & McLanahan, 1986). The reliability of many of these studies is low; relying heavily on teacher reports which in turn, are heavily influenced by the assumption of pathology (Atwood & Genovese, 1993).

A growing body of research indicates that children in Single-Parent families are not necessarily negatively affected and may even thrive (Atwood & Genovese, 1993). A number of studies indicate divorce is a poor indicator of emotional difficulty, delinquency, achievement and long-term, detrimental results (Bernard & Nesbitt, 1981; Hanson & Sporakowski, 1986; Kinard & Reinherz, 1986; Tuzlak & Hillock, 1986). Vosler, Green, and Kolevzon (1987) found family system functioning more important than family structure in predicting outcomes for children. While Single Parenthood can be one possible risk factor for children (McLanahan & Sandefur, 1994), it can also lead to the development of strengths and an increased sense of responsibility (Kurdek & Siesky, 1980).

Identifying and Responding to the Need

Children do not suffer economic or psychological deprivation in cultures where one-parent families are not considered pathological or inferior. The functioning of the female-headed, Single-Parent family is a consequence of the economic resources, supportive social networks and societal attitudes (Bilge & Kaufman, 1983). For many women, Single Parenthood is a choice (Miller, 1992; Chant, 1989). Chant found women in many parts of the world choose to live in women-headed families because of the strength it provides. Even in studying poor, Single Mothers, Nesto (1994) found divorce and separation resulted in growth and positive change in spite of financial problems. Hanson and Sporakowski's (1986) study of Single-Parent families found general good physical and mental health among the participants. Social support is a major factor in assisting the health of Single-Parent families. There are, however, several hurdles female-headed households face, including high levels of poverty and an unequal burden of household chores.

Financial Hurdles

Because the economic problems facing female-headed households are rooted in the social arrangements impacting all women, they cannot be dealt with in isolation (Schorr & Moen, 1984). Only 8% of male-headed, Single-Parent households live in poverty. At the same time, more than half of all female-headed, Single-Parent households live in poverty (Kissman, 1995). While economic expansion helped lift families headed by men out of poverty, the poverty affecting female-headed, Single-Parent families requires a different approach (Pearce, 1989). The interaction of discrimination between race and gender leaves Single Mothers with inadequate financial, political and social support (McChesney, 1989; Pearce). In the United States, Single Mothers are responsible "for both the support and care of their children…without the assistance of either the fathers of their children or the state" (McChesney, p. 1).

Dual Role

The United States is caught in a conflict between women's policy and children's policy. Women's policy is developing as if women have no family responsibilities, while children's policy has developed as if children all had a mother at home taking care of them (Miller, 1987). By 1986, however, the number of mothers participating in the labor force had risen to an all-time high of 65.3% (McFate, 1995) — increasing the dual role burden for all mothers. Single Mothers are hard hit by the conflict, with a higher percentage of them now working full time. Two fifths (41%) of female heads of households with children worked full time as compared to only 27% of women in two-parent household who work full time (Ellwood, 1988).

17

A philosophy of dual or separate spheres has developed, which serves to legitimize the inequality of women and men. Women are responsible for, and have been relegated to, the private domain which encompasses the home; while men have rightful access to the public domain which encompasses the work world. As long as women have been willing to maintain the private sphere, they have been permitted to work. However, once in the work force women find the environment modeled on the patterns of men, with no supports for those who must maintain the dual role of family and work (Miller, 1987; Sands & Nuccio, 1989). In Western Europe, as opposed to the United States, the universal benefit system offered to families with children recognizes the need to integrate these two spheres (Miller).

The dual role of the mother in Single-Parent families as the nurturer and provider is a major contributor to stress and poverty (Ellwood, 1988; McLanahan, Wedemeyer, & Adelberg, 1981). Fine, Schwebel and Myers (1985) found that the 24-hour-a-day commitment to both parenting and working was a major stressor. Although women are expected to retain the primary role in child rearing, Single Mothers are simultaneously criticized for not working. While a number of studies indicate Single Mothers who work experience less role strain, greater life satisfaction and less stress (Jackson, 1992; McAdoo, 1985), adequate supports are necessary. As Kissman (1995) points out "when wage labor and child rearing are artificially separated as two distinct areas for social policies and programs, comprehensive services that could enable women to perform both roles are overlooked" (p. 151).

Social Support

A few studies have looked at the relationship between the adjustment of Single Mothers and their social support networks. These initial studies indicate that the types of support Single Mothers need may (a) differ from those of mothers in two-parent households, (b) change over time, and (c) be mediated by the woman's perception. Leslie and Grady (1985) document the changing nature of support networks during the first year after divorce. While a support network is important to a woman's adjustment to divorce, the exact relationship is complex (Leslie & Grady; McLanahan et al., 1981). Support networks are found to be vital in the viability (the ability of the family to support and nurture child[ren]) of never-married mothers as well (Jarrett, 1994). For these mothers, extended family networks provide support and decrease isolation.

McLanahan et al. (1981) found the role orientation of the mother was a significant variable in the kind of support needed. Leslie and Grady (1985) found a woman's satisfaction with her support system was a significant variable. A study of social support for single and married women in Sweden determined Single Mothers receive more assistance and emotional support than married women.

Composition of the support network also differs. Friends comprise the primary support network for single women while relatives, neighbors and colleagues provide the primary support for married women. In this study, Single Mothers with the most support worked full time and had fewer children (Tietjen, 1985).

Research on the importance of social supports for Single-Parent families is insufficient. Studies need to be undertaken which examine the difference in the kind and quality of social networks for Single-Parent families functioning at various levels. Adaptive Single-Parent families must be compared to nonadaptive families to determine significant differences. Preliminary studies have identified some variables that show promise for further study (Leslie & Grady, 1985; McLanahan et al., 1981; Tietjen, 1985). Looking at the role parents play in supporting each other in well functioning two-parent families, it can be hypothesized that external support for the Single Parent is important to the emotional well-being of both parent and child(ren).

Single Mothers' views of themselves and the world, which are influenced by their support networks, are significant factors for their emotional equilibrium. In studying support networks, McLanahan et al. (1981) found the role the mother perceived for herself determined the kinds of support needs she had found. Most of the women studied wanted to maintain their predivorce role. Some, however, wanted to establish new identities. Fine et al. (1985) studied the world view of African-American and European-American female-headed, Single-Parent households. The study found world view was a significant variable in adjustment. These findings have direct significance for practitioners.

Different Yet Similar/Similar Yet Different

Race. Based on their own analysis of national data as well as a review of available research, McKenry and Fine (1993) present information on both similarities and differences by race. While there is some evidence of potential differences in adjustment for African-American and European-American Single Mothers, there appear to be few differences in parenting style and behavior. Some studies indicate African-American mothers may adjust better to divorce by exhibiting less stigmatization. There's evidence of lower levels of anxiety and depression and higher levels of self-esteem and *inner directedness* in African-American Single Mothers.

While a number of studies note a difference in parenting style by race and ethnicity, when economic status is controlled for with African-American, European-American and Chicano parents, few differences are found in parenting style (McKenry & Fine, 1993). In their own analysis of data on 573 African-American and European-American female-headed, Single-Parent families, McKenry and Fine found more similarities than differences in parenting when controlling for income and time since divorce. There were no racial differences in the involvement of parents with their children or parenting behavior. African-American mothers, however, tended to have higher expectations and saw themselves as having more control. A study of African-American and European-American Single-Mother families by Jacobsen and Bigner (1991), did not find any major differences except in parental satisfaction – with African-American Single Mothers expressing more satisfaction in their parental role than European-American Single Mothers.

Never-Married Mothers. Although many of the growing number of never-married Single Parents are low income (some young and vulnerable) others are older, more established women and men *choosing* parenthood. *Single Parents by choice* are a growing and diverse subgroup in the early stages of study. The degree of variability in this family type is often not taken into account in large statistical studies. Miller (1992) studied a diverse range of families where Single Parenthood was a choice. These families vary in life style, configuration and beginnings. An increasing number of women without partners are choosing parenthood through birth or adoption. Davies and Rains (1995) studied Single Mothers ages 28 to 36 classified as *single by choice*. The study revealed that the women did not choose the pregnancy but, instead, chose to become parents once they became pregnant. The investigators therefore concluded that "single motherhood by default" (p. 550) may be a more accurate description.

Never-married, low-income mothers also show a great variability in family configuration, age and viability – the ability of the family to support and nurture the child(ren). Jarrett (1994) studied low-income, never-married, African-American mothers; finding great variability in family arrangements and personal coping strategies, non-nuclear family support and action taken by the women to counter the negative impact of poverty-effected family viability. The literature often ignores the significance of extended family in supporting Single-Parent families.

Single Fathers. With the changes in social context, the number of Single-Parent families headed by men are also increasing through divorce (Greif & DeMaris, 1990) as well as choice (Miller, 1992). Intervention with Single-Father families requires as thorough an assessment of context as intervention with Single Mothers. Single-Father families (Greif & DeMaris), just like Single Mother families, are affected by social context, parent self-concept and relationship with former spouse. While as a group, Single-Mother families struggle with financial instability and inadequate social support, Single-Father families struggle with a lack of role models (Greif, 1985).

The Role of the Professional

Although Single-Parent families have been perceived as deficient, they "are not by definition dysfunctional" (Strand, 1995, p. 2159). The Single-Parent family is a family, however, with unique needs many arising from economic challenges and significant social support needs. One of the most negative effects on the Single-Parent family is the negative perception and assumption of deficiency (Strand) of society. The social work practitioner can play an active role in challenging this perception for both the family and society. The practitioner needs to help model success for Single Parents. Popular theory and current media trends frequently paint Single-Parent families, especially those headed by women, as inadequate. Through the establishment of support groups and the sharing of stories and articles, the practitioner can provide a grounding in stories of success (Olson & Haynes, 1993).

Practitioners need to do a holistic assessment, including client role perception and world view, and incorporate these factors into practice. Many of the Single-Parent families are affected by inadequate economic and social support with the added stress of dual roles. A thorough evaluation would include an assessment of multiple variables: role strain, income resources, training and educational needs/ assets, life stage (age and developmental level), transition into and adjustment to Single Parenthood, support available, mother's mental health (depression/ anxiety/isolation), self-care skills, personal time, communication skills/family history, child development knowledge, child discipline attitudes and behavior, sense of personal strength and child statistics (i.e. number, age, gender).

Beyond adequate economic support a number of factors have been identified as important to well-functioning, Single-Parent families. Many of the factors important to successful two-parent families are also vital to healthy Single-Parent families. Strong social support systems and good communication skills help influence healthy outcomes (Strand, 1995). Open communication; consistent, nonpunitive discipline; parental self-care; rituals and traditions and the balance between individual identity and supportive family interdependence (Olson & Haynes, 1993) are vital to the healthy functioning of one-parent as well as two-parent households. In addition, Olson and Haynes found two additional intertwined dimensions in successful Single-Parent families: prioritizing the role of parent and accepting the responsibilities and challenges of the lone parent.

Successful programs range from those that intervene with individuals and families to those which intervene on a community/system level. Families benefit from transition programs, ongoing counseling and support and community advocacy/support. Treatment programs designed to address the crisis of transitions help alleviate the potential for ongoing depression and anxiety while providing families with assistance in setting up healthy communication, discipline, attitudes and techniques and interactional patterns as they transform into their new structure. Self-help, advocacy groups and peer support all have proven successful. Stories of success are very useful in shifting perception.

Greif and DeMaris (1990) point to the impact of various social and family systems. As a group, female-headed, Single-Parent families, due to income liabilities, face the stress resulting from increasing residential mobility, decreased quality in the education system and increasing environmental poverty (McLanahan & Sandefur, 1994). Case management and advocacy designed to help families find supportive and knowledgeable child care and educational programs or shift the views of existing programs are also important. The pathology model has resulted in teachers rating children from Single-Parent families lower than others (Atwood & Genovese, 1993). Positive systems intervention involving a re-education of caregivers is vital in structuring positive child environments.

While successful Single Parents accept and prioritize their family responsibilities, they must also care for their own needs so these needs do not become the responsibility of the children. Gringlas and Weinraub (1995) found children from mother-headed families may be more strongly affected by maternal stress and inadequate parental social support systems than children from two-parent families. Single Parents must nurture themselves through hobbies, diet, exercise and outside support/relationships. Single Parents need to develop the supportive relationships with individuals and/or groups which partnered parents often have with their partners. Professionals can play a role in encouraging and nurturing the development of social support networks. Formal groups can fill this niche for those Single Parents without adequate networks and/or the skills necessary for the development of social support networks.

High Risk Single Parents

Perhaps the group of Single Parents facing the highest risk due to the challenges of raising children with inadequate resources and support is adolescent parents. It is important to remember, however, while adolescent parents are heavily stigmatized, "adolescent mothers are not necessarily deficient in their parenting by virtue of their age" (Barratt, Roach, & Colbert, 1991). They too must be approached individually assessing strengths as well as deficits. Several major factors appear to affect the health and liabilities of adolescent parents. Demographically, age is an important variable. Younger adolescents face more risk of inadequate education and decreased income potential (Barratt et al., Strand, 1995). Understanding the risks helps social workers design programs which encourage and support adolescents remaining in school and gaining job skills. The mother's mental health and the child's temperament appear to affect the parenting relationship (Barratt et al.), further indicating the importance of holistic programs serving adolescents and their children on multiple levels. Contrary to popular assumptions, adolescent mothers living with their parents or extended families, do not necessarily exhibit better parenting skills (Barratt et al.). These mothers may not receive adequate support and, in turn, experience interference with the development of their own skills.

Non-custodial Single Fathers are also a diverse group with adolescents again representing the highest risk as a group due to inadequate financial and social support. Adolescent fathers also face the barriers of low expectation and inadequate role models. A number of programs are emerging geared toward engaging those fathers who are not actively involved with their children. Fagan and Stevenson's (1995) self-help program designed to increase the parenting abilities of low-income, African-American men has shown success with adults and has the potential for success with adolescents.

The Teen Age Pregnancy and Parenting program described by Barth, Claycomb, and Loomis (1988) is a comprehensive service delivery system offering a range of programs designed to engage adolescent fathers in parenting and support activities. The results have been positive for the fathers, mothers and children. Another program, of The National Institute for Responsible Fatherhood and Family Development, has been developed by Charles Ballard. It is a multifaceted program which is highly effective in engaging young, low-income fathers in the development of their own future as well as their child's (Santoli, 1994). In order to participate in the program, the young men must claim their role as parent, be in school and take a job—even if part time. The program helps the men develop a career path while working with them to learn how to parent and develop a respectful relationship with their child's mother.

Strength-Based Practice

Single-Parent families are not inherently deficient and the difficulties, problems and hurdles encountered by Single-Parent families are not a reflection of family dysfunction. Rather, they are the result of interacting within a frequently non-supportive social and economic environment. In spite of the social and economic barriers Single-Parent families encounter, they are frequently resilient in surmounting structural obstacles. They are a diverse group with multiple mechanisms and resources which could be a basis for intervention when families are struggling. While differences in culture, ethnicity and styles of living are often perceived as problems the strength model underlying this book results in a view of these differences being resources from which Single Parents can be supported.

Social work, like many professions, has developed its models of practice with Single-Parent families, particularly female-headed, Single-Parent families, around the perceived deficiencies, weaknesses and flaws of being a Single Parent. The strength perspective, on the other hand, asks not what is wrong with the parent but what interferes with effective, quality interaction with the environment. Strength-based practice with its orientation "toward empowering families to maximize their available emotional and financial resources" can help "them move toward a stronger position in society" (Schmitz, 1995. p. 433). The use of the strength model provides a basis for helping families and communities to grow.

The focus of the strength perspective on the regenerative and resilient capacity of people with environmental and social worker supports (Saleebey, 1992, 1996; Weick, Rapp, Sullivan, & Kisthardt, 1989), leads to intervention models with the potential to help Single Parents develop their strengths and have a positive experience of parenting. The worker acts as a catalyst empowering/enabling clients to examine their inner knowledge of ways to best care for themselves while fulfilling their role as parents. It is an assumption in the strength perspective that the parent does and must control her/his interactions as she/he works to make meaning of life. This places the responsibility for control and meaning on the parent. Existentialist Karl Jaspers philosophized that nothing is so crucial in finding meaning in life as the relationship one has with another (Baird, 1985). A client's self-knowing and the meaning she/he gives the situation must be regarded if social workers are to be helpful.

As noted by Weick and Freeman (1983), the basic principle of the strength perspective is the belief that people can influence their lives and their choices. An individual with whom we are working is affected by multiple environments (social, physical, mental, and spiritual) and the strength perspective offers a framework for supporting this holistic view of people. The quality of the collaborative and egalitarian relationship between the worker and the client is the working ground upon which the client can begin to develop changes and plans in her/his life. Weick and Freeman describe the client/worker relationship as a "microcosm of the healing process" (p. 4). The client/worker relationship itself is a beginning of learning for both the worker and the client. With the social worker's belief that the client has the ability to change, the worker can trust the client to know best what will assist her/his growth. The worker becomes a catalyst for change within the client. If the relationship is based on mutual trust and respect, both can take what is learned and extend this knowledge into other contacts within the environment.

The strength perspective as a model of practice operates with the following assumptions:

1. Despite all the problems one encounters in living, a person within her/his environment has strengths which can be collected together to improve the

quality of one's life. Social workers need to acknowledge and recognize these strengths and listen to how the client wants to use them.

2. Motivation is nurtured by a steady emphasis on strengths as defined by the client.

3. The client and worker discover the strengths together as a team–it is a cooperative discovery effort.

4. In emphasizing strengths as a social worker, our attention is turned from blaming the victim/client to finding methods to help the person to survive.

5. All environments have resources and, in order to help clients, social workers must believe the environment to be a resource.

6. The social worker is focused on helping one get on with one's life, validating and acquiring self-esteem and finding or developing a community in which to be a member (DeJong & Miller, 1995; Saleebey, 1992; 1996; Weick et al., 1989).

Saleebey (1996) writes that the strength perspective lauds two points: the capability of the person to remedy injustice with the help of the environment and the hope that things can change. All of us have the ability to regenerate ourselves. The job of the social worker is to assist the Single Parent in finding that regenerative factor. Rodale (1988) presents three ways that one can regenerate: *good living, good thinking* and *good connections.* These three are found in the strength perspective. We must hear stories of regeneration in order to help others as they walk the path of Single Parenthood. The chapters which follow do just that — they tell a story, many stories of strength, resiliency and regeneration. The role of the practitioner, as highlighted, is to listen to the stories, understand the environment/context and move forward with Single Parents within their community toward strength-based empowerment.

Unity and Diversity

Various approaches for empowering Single Parents, particularly Single Mothers, are reviewed in the chapters that follow. The authors present practice models used with Single-Parent families which are frequently ignored in the literature. The reader will find models which provide a context for working with Single-Parent families from many racial, ethnic, income, and lifestyle groups. The editors and the authors bring both personal and professional expertise with Single-Parent families and the cultures presented. The reader is given resources to help them develop an understanding of the strengths and needs of diverse families. This volume looks at the needs and resources of families of color, interweaves economic vulnerability into practice models, illuminates the context surrounding lesbian and gay families and discusses the needs of Single Fathers. Information on the advocacy and care needs of families with children with disabilities is also provided.

A collective of Indian and non-Indian therapists (Linda Anderson, Julia Putnam, Fransing Sinclair-Daisy and Annette Squetimkin-Anquoe) from the Pacific Northwest provide a context for understanding practice issues within the American-Indian community. The authors – who are knowledgeable about and involved with the American-Indian/Alaskan-Native community – present the strengths, supports and dilemmas of American-Indian/Alaskan-Native Single-Parent families. The rich heritage and community strengths available to American-Indian/Alaskan-Native Single Parents become apparent. They review demographic and economic trends while also informing the reader about basic values, family structures and traditions. The authors present models and techniques designed to help practitioners in a therapeutic setting. Native programs are discussed and presented with exemplars. This chapter presents a collective voice gathered through the active pursuit of review and comment by a multi-tribal set of readers.

Victoria Claravel has worked for many years with the Asian, Southeast-Asian and Pacific-Islander communities of the Pacific Northwest. In the third chapter, she does an amazing job of providing an understanding of the cultural/family context for practitioners working with the Single-Parent family within Asian-American/Pacific-Islander communities. She shares knowledge gained through her experience working with Single-Parent families in very diverse Asian, Southeast-Asian and Pacific-Islander communities. She reviews the significance of the extended family and explores the community strengths which provide the backbone for integrated practice. The impact of birth in the United States versus foreign birth, acculturation, language ability and multi-generation families on service delivery, practice models, and family support are reviewed and case examples are illustrative and informative.

Maria Vidal de Haymes from Loyola University, with her expertise on the Latino communities of the United States, reviews the literature on Latino families with a strong emphasis on Single-Parent households. She familiarizes us with both the demographics and the patterns of change in Latino/a families of the United States. This chapter focuses on: (a) the relationships between family structure and socio-economic conditions; (b) familism, fictive kin and social supports; (c) extra-household ties and patterns of exchange; (d) family process and social roles; (e) diversity in family forms across Latino ethnic groups; (f) labor force attachments of Single Parents; (g) female role transformations; (h) fertility and family planning; (i) service utilization and (j) stresses and adaptive cultural responses and resources. An illustrative case example examines the practice implications of a family-support perspective which draws and builds on individual and cultural strengths.

Because social workers serving female-headed, Single-Parent, African-American families need to understand the struggle to overcome multiple layers of oppression, Janese Prince begins with a thorough review and analysis of the historical intersection between racism and sexism. Within that context, program models are presented which provide a combination of economic and socio-political empowerment for low-income Single Mothers. The interventions are practical, strength based and nonjudgmental – programs designed to maintain a mutual balance between income generation and social support are explored.

Sue Pearlmutter, based on extensive professional and personal experience, outlines and discusses the hurdles faced by families headed by lesbian and gay parents. She provides an understanding of the social and legal context within which lesbian and gay families work to survive and thrive. We see how lesbian and gay families experience the joys and frustrations of all families. We also see the added dimensions which both challenge and enrich the lives of all members of the family in a homophobic and heterosexist culture. The strengths and resources which can support and strengthen families headed by lesbian and gay parents are reviewed and discussed.

In a very easy-to-read manner, Janice Chadha, Marjorie Sable and Wilson Watt present practice models which are currently exhibiting success in the "Bootheel" region of Missouri. As if telling a story, a context is provided which allows us to understand the women of the Bootheel region. A program specifically designed to meet the multiple needs of high-risk, low-income, Single-Parent families in this rural area is then described. The case studies provide a glimpse of the importance of understanding the special needs of low-income, rural, Single-Mother families.

Pauline Jivanjee interweaves a case example through her presentation on the theory and practice issues of strengthening and supporting Single Parents who have children with disabilities. While she reviews the stresses and challenges experienced by the parents; she presents a model of practice which supports, strengthens and empowers families. She points out the resilience and coping capacities for families facing extraordinary challenges. A collaborative model for supporting the empowerment of Single Parents is presented. Family-centered support service helps families successfully navigate complex systems resulting in growth and development.

Geoffrey Greif, a well-recognized expert on lone-father families, presents data on Single-Father families. He reviews the historical and social contexts, then presents practice issues and discusses intervention models. After providing a context by reviewing the literature, he discusses issues such as role models, family adjustment and advocacy. Case studies are included which illustrate different ways fathers gain custody and cope with the demands of child rearing.

Finally, Faye Abram discusses the needs of grandparents struggling to raise their grandchildren within drug-affected family systems. She gives us a sense of the diversity in age and complications faced by these families. Some are still raising their own children while others are at a point in their lives when they thought they would be free to pursue their own needs. The families described all face the stress of drug-related problems among grown children while trying to raise their grandchildren. A holistic model for support and intervention is presented.

Conclusion

Single-Parent families reflect a wealth of diversity in family styles frequently unknown or ignored. They vary by formation, race, ethnicity, economic condition, gender, sexual orientation and actual circumstances. Many face transitional or long-term problems due to poverty based in gender inequality. Others do not. And some, but not all, Single-Parent families experience the transitional or long-term stress precipitated by a change in family pattern. Single-Parent families are not deficient by definition. They can provide a secure, solid framework for the healthy growth and development of all family members. Understanding the strengths available to, and causes of stress faced by Single-Parent families, provides a framework for positive, productive, social work practice.

Social structure is not a static condition and Single Parents are not a transitional group. Continuing to practice based on false assumptions will not lead to the empowerment of Single-Parent families. Data is available but often disregarded or misinterpreted in order to continue labeling Single-Parent families as deviant and problematic. The lack of information on Single-Parent households as a diverse, long-term family option limits social work practitioners. Basing practice on assumptions of blame and stigma results in models of practice which leave families without adequate support and resources. Indicators point to a continued trend of increasing Single-Parent households. Single-Parent families are a viable, long-term alternative affected by gender inequality. (Schmitz, 1995)

Due to the economic and social inequality of women globally, female-headed, Single-Parent families face unique challenges. This is particularly true in the United States where Single Mothers rely on inadequate support from income, fathers and stigmatized income support systems. Changes in family structure in coordination with current economic structures operate to keep women out of a labor market which provides a decent wage. The result has been a rapid rise in poverty among women and children. Inadequate income, with the resulting stress and discrimination, along with the dual-role stress of work and home are primary factors the practitioner needs to understand and address. The stress faced by female-headed, Single-Parent families is related to financial hardship, role functions, self perception and changing support needs (Fine et. al., 1985).

Although this volume focuses primarily on the direct intervention role of social work practitioners, it is important for the profession to develop programs which focus on the income-related policy needs resulting from the position of women in society. The stress placed on Single Mothers due to inadequate income must be addressed through advocacy programs focusing on income-related policy issues addressing gender equity at work. Resources and programs which are vital to providing adequate support for Single-Parent families include: safe housing, child care, education, health care, transportation, and food.

The following chapters reflect some of the rich diversity of Single-Parent families. A picture of both struggle and strength emerges. If human service professionals approach Single-Parent families from a deficit perspective, the dilemmas these families face as they struggle to survive in a judgmental society without adequate support will be aggravated. On the other hand, if those in the human service field work with Single-Parent families from a strength perspective, they will help enrich the life of all members of the family and community.

Bibliography

Abramovitz, M. (1989). *Regulating the lives of women: Social welfare policy from colonial times to the present.* Boston, MA: South End Press.

Atwood, J.D. & Genovese, F. (1993). *Counseling single parents.* Alexandria, VA: American Counseling Association.

Baird, R.M. (1985). Meaning in life: Discovered or created? *Journal of Religion and Health, 24,* 117-24.

Bane, M.J. (1988). Politics and policies of the feminization of poverty. In Weir, M.; Orloff, A. S. & Skocpol, T. (Eds.) *The politics of social policy in the United States* (pp. 381-96). New Jersey: Princeton University Press.

Barratt, M.S.; Roach, M.A. & Colbert, K.K. (1991). Single mothers and their infants: Factors associated with optimal parenting. *Family Relations, 40,* 448-54.

Barth, R.P.; Claycomb, M. & Loomis, A. (1988). Services to adolescent fathers. *Health and Social Work,* 13, 277-87.

Bernard, J.M. & Nesbitt, S. (1981). Divorce: An unreliable predictor of children's emotional predispositions. *Journal of Divorce, 4,* 31-42.

Bilge, B. & Kaufman, G. (1983). Children of divorce and one-parent families: Cross-cultural perspectives. *Family Relations, 32,* 59-71.

Chant, S. (1989). Gender and the urban household. In Chant, S. & Brydon, L. *Women in the Third World: Gender issues in rural and urban areas* (pp. 134-60). New Brunswick, NJ: Rutgers University Press.

Chant, S. & Brydon, L. (1989). *Women in the Third World: Gender issues in rural and urban areas.* New Brunswick, NJ: Rutgers University Press.

Children's Defense Fund. (1992, October). Child poverty hits 25-year high, growing by nearly 1 million children in 1991. *CDF Reports,* pp. 1-3.

Danziger, S. (1988). *Economic growth, poverty, and inequality in an advanced economy.* (Discussion paper no. 862-88). Madison, WI: Institute for Research on Poverty.

Davies, L. & Rains, P. (1995). Single mothers by choice? *Families in Society: The Journal of Contemporary Human Services, 76,* 543-50.

DeJong, P. & Miller, S. D. (1995). How to interview for client strengths. *Social Work, 40* (6), 729-36.

Ehrenreich, B. & Piven, F.F. (1984). The feminization of poverty. *Dissent, 31,* 162-70.

Ellwood, D.T. (1988). *Poor support.* New York: Basic Books, Inc.

Fagan, J. & Stevenson, H. (1995). Men as teachers: A self-help program on parenting for African American Men. *Social Work with Groups, 17* (4), 29-42.

Fine, M.A.; Schwebel, A.L., & Myers, L J. (1985). The effects of world view on adaptation to single parenthood among middle-class adult women. *Journal of Family Issues, 6,* 107-27.

Garfinkel, I. (1987). *Welfare policy in America.* (Discussion paper no. 847-87). Madison, WI: Institute for Research on Poverty.

Garfinkel, I., & McLanahan, S.S. (l986). *Single mothers and their children.* Washington, DC: The Urban Institute Press.

Gribschaw, V.M. (1985). Factors that affect economic mobility among single female heads of households with children (Doctoral dissertation, The Ohio State University, 1985). *Dissertation Abstracts International, 46,*3025B.

Greif, G.L. (1985). *Single fathers,* New York: Lexington Books.

Greif, G.L. & DeMaris, A. (1990). Single fathers with custody. *Families in Society: The Journal of Contemporary Human Services, 17,* 259-66.

Gringlas, M. & Weinraub, M. (1995). The more things change…Single parenting revisited. *Journal of Family Issues, 16* (1), 29-52.

Hansen, J.C. & Lindblad-Goldberg, M. (1987). *Clinical issues in single-parent households.* Rockville, Maryland: Aspen Publishers, Inc.

Hanson, S.M.H. & Sporakowski, M.J. (1986). Single parent families. *Family Relations, 35,* 3-8.

Jackson, A.P. (1992). Well-being among single, black, employed mothers. *Social Service Review, 66,* 399-409.

Jacobsen, R.B. & Bigner, J.J. (1991). African-American versus European-American single parents and the value of children. *Journal of African-American Studies, 21,* 302-12.

Jarrett, R.R. (1994). Living poor: Family life among single parent, African-American women. *Social Problems, 41* (1), 30-49.

Kamerman, S.B. & Kahn, A.J. (1988). *Mothers alone: Strategies for a time of change.* Dover, MA: Auburn House Publishing Company.

Kinard, E.M. & Reinherz, H. (1986). Effects of marital disruption on children's school aptitude and achievement. *Journal of Marriage and the Family, 48,* 285-93.

Kissman, K. (1995). Divisive dichotomies and mother-headed families: The power of naming. *Social Work, 40,* 151-3.

Kurdek, L,A. & Siesky, A.E. (1980). Effects of divorce on children: The relationship between parent and child perspectives. *Journal of Divorce, 4,* 85-99.

Leslie, L.A. & Grady, K. (1985). Changes in mothers' social networks and social support following divorce. *Journal of Marriage and the Family, 47,* 663-73.

McAdoo, H.P. (1985, Fall/Winter). Strategies used by black single mothers against stress. *The Review of the Black Political Economy, 14,* 153-66.

McChesney, K.Y. (1989, April). *Macroeconomic issues in poverty: Implications for child and youth homelessness.* Paper presented at Homeless Children and Youth: Coping with a National Tragedy, Washington, DC.

McFate, K. (1995). Introduction: Western states in the new world order. In K. McFate, R. Lawson, & W. J. Wilson (Eds.), *Poverty, inequality and the future of social policy: Western states in the new world order* (pp. 1-26). New York: Russell Sage Foundation.

McKenry, P.C. & Fine, M.A. (1993). Parenting following divorce: A comparison of African-American and European-American single mothers. *Journal of Comparative Family Studies, 24,* 99-112.

McLanahan, S. & Sandefur, G. (1994). *Growing up with a single parent: What hurts, what helps.* Cambridge, MA: Harvard University Press.

McLanahan, S.S., Wedemeyer, N. V., Adelberg, T. (1981). Network structure, social support, and psychological well-being in the single-parent family. *Journal of Marriage and the Family, 43,* 601-12.

Mihaly, L. (1989, April). *Beyond the numbers: Homeless families with children.* Paper presented at Homeless Children and Youth: Coping with a National Tragedy. Washington, DC.

Miller, D.C. (1987). Children's policy and women's policy: Congruence or conflict? *Social Work, 32,* 289-92.

Miller, N. (1992). *Single parents by choice: A growing trend in family life.* New York: Plenum Press.

Mueller, D.P. & Cooper, P.W. (1986). Children of single parent families: How they fare as young adults. *Family Relations, 35,* 169-76.

Nesto, B. (1994). Low-income single mothers: Myths and realities. *Affilia, 9,* 232-46.

Nichols-Casebolt, A.; Krysik, J. & Hermann-Currie, R. (1994). The povertization of women: A global phenomenon. *Affilia, 9,* 9-29.

Norton, A, & Glick, P. (1986). One-parent families: A social and economic profile. *Family Relations, 35,* 9-17,

Olson, M.R. & Haynes, J.A. (1993). Successful single parents. *Families in Society: The Journal of Contemporary Human Services, 74,* 259-67.

Pearce, D.M. (1989, August). *The feminization of poverty: A second look.* Paper presented at the meeting of the American Sociological Association, San Francisco, CA.

Peterson, J.L. & Zill, N. (1986). Marital disruption, parent-child relationships, and behavior problems in children. *Journal of Marriage and the Family, 48,* 295-307.

Rodale, R. (1988, February). The bounce back factor. *Prevention,* 17-18.

Saleebey, D. (Ed.). (1992). *The strengths perspective in social work practice.* New York: Longman.

Saleebey, D. (1996). The strengths perspective in social work practice: Extensions and cautions. *Social Work, 41* (3), 296-305.

Sands, R.G. & Nuccio, K.E. (1989). Mother-headed single-parent families: A feminist perspective. *Affilia, 4* (3), 25-41.

Santoli, A. (1994, May 29). They turn young men with children into fathers. *Parade Magazine,* 16-17.

Schiller, B.R. (1989). *The economics of poverty and discrimination* (5th ed.). Englewood Cliffs, NJ: Prentice Hall.

Schmitz, C. (1995). Reframing the dialogue on female-headed single-parent families. *Affilia, 10,* 426-41.

Schorr, A.L. & Moen, P. (1984). The single parent and public policy. In P. Voydanoff (Ed.), *Work & Family: Changing roles of men and women* (pp. 288-97). Palo Alto, CA: Mayfield Publishing Company.

Stivens, M. (1985). The fate of women's land rights: Gender, matriliny, and capitalism in Rembau, Negeri Sembilan, Malaysia. In Afshar, H. (Ed.). *Women, work, and ideology in the Third World* (pp. 3-36). London: Tavistock Publications.

Strand, V.C. (1995). *Single parents. In Encyclopedia of social work* (19th ed). (pp. 2157-68). Washington, DC: NASW Press.

Tietjen, A.M. (1985). The social networks and social support of married and single mothers in Sweden. *Journal of Marriage and the Family, 47,* 489-96.

Tuzlak, A. & Hillock, D.W. (1986) Single mothers and their children after divorce: A study of those "who make it". *Conciliation Courts Review, 24,* 79-89.

U.S. Children and Their Families: Current Conditions and Recent Trends, 1989: A Report for the House Select Committee on Children, Youth, and Families, 101st Cong., 1st Sess. (1989).

Vosler, N.R.; Green, R.G. & Kolevzon, M.S. (1987). The structure and competence of family units: Implications for social work practice with families and children. *Journal of Social Science Research, 9* (2-3), 1-17.

Weick, A.N., & Freeman, E. (1983). *Developing a Health Model for Social Work.* Unpublished manuscript, University of Kansas, School of Social Welfare, Lawrence.

Weick, A., Rapp, C., Sullivan, W.P., & Kisthardt, W. (1989). A strengths perspective for social work practice. *Social Work, 34,* 350-54.

Wong, Y.I., Garfinkel, I., & McLanahan, S.M. (1993). Single mother families in eight countries: Economic status and social policy. *Social Service Review, 67* (2), 177-97.

Yudelman, S.W. (1987). *Hopeful openings: A study of five women's development organizations in Latin America and the Caribbean.* West Hartford, CT: Kumarian Press.

American-Indian and Alaskan-Native Single Parents

Linda Anderson, MS, Julia Putnam, MSW, DCSW
Fransing Sinclair-Daisy, Ph.D.
and Annette Squetimkin-Anquoe, M.A.

You know how it is.
People come here and they want to know our secret of life.
They ask many questions but their minds are already made up.
They admire our children but they feel sorry for them.
They look around and they do not see anything except dust.
They come to our dances but they are always wanting to take pictures.
They come into our homes expecting to learn about us in five minutes.
Our homes, which are made of mud and straw, look strange to them.
They are glad they do not live here.
Yet they are not sure whether or not we know something which is the key to all
   understanding.
Our secret of life would take them forever to find out.
Even then, they would not believe it.

THIS CHAPTER INTRODUCES issues and effective techniques for practitioners working with members of the American-Indian/Alaskan-Native community in a therapeutic setting, focusing on the Single-Parent family. The rich heritage and inherent strengths of the American-Indian/Alaskan-Native, Single-Parent families and their communities are illustrated in an effort to guide both the Indian and non-Indian professional through a therapeutic process which both respects and builds upon these strengths.

The information presented can serve as a map to a new world – a guide for continued discovery and self-examination for persons who work with American-Indian/Alaskan-Native, Single-Parent families and individuals. We encourage you to use the list of references accompanying this chapter and attend cultural events open to the public. Talk and, particularly, listen to your American-Indian/Alaskan-Native colleagues. Find a mentor and ask for guidance. Listen attentively to your clients.

We do not presume to speak to all Native beliefs, values, cultures and traditions. We represent both Indian and non-Indian therapists. We attempted to honor the collective voice of the American-Indian and Alaska-Native communities by asking readers from various tribes for their input. Finally, we asked non-Indians who have a dedication to cross-cultural issues to evaluate this material's usefulness to a general readership.

Examination of the literature indicates little information is available about Single-Parent families in the Indian community. We discuss the literature on Single-Parent families. Most of the historical, anecdotal, research and programmatic information presented comes from tribal members and professionals. This chapter provides some demographic data, cultural and historical information, brief descriptions of programmatic efforts in Native communities and a context and framework for being a helper with this population. Helper, in this context is defined as a mental health practitioner, social worker, health care worker or other human service provider.

We define Single Parent as a mother or father deprived of a significant other by death or divorce, as well as one who becomes a parent outside a long-term relationship. Single Parent can also refer to grandparents and others who find themselves the primary caretaker for children.

Marital status of the parent or caretaker has not been a significant factor in an Indian child's acceptance into a tribal community. Traditionally, the entire tribe or village is responsible for the well-being of each member – especially children. Children are viewed as a gift and the responsibility of the larger family and community as well as the biological parents. The notion that matrimonial status itself presumes problems is inaccurate.

In 1992, 55.3% of live births to Indian women were to Single Indian Mothers. That figure was up from 22.4% in 1970, but paralleled the increase in the general population. Whether the mothers were unmarried, widowed or divorced is not known. The U.S. Department of Health and Human Services (1995) limits the term Single Parent to mothers because of their status as birth or legal parent. Nevertheless, the noteworthy fact remains that more children are born to Single Mothers than are born to married mothers.

Many Tribes, Many Traditions: A Historical Perspective

Before examining clinical issues and techniques, it is important the reader gain some perspective about American-Indian/Alaska-Native history, in that this history affects Single Parents, their extended families and communities. Without a knowledge of the historical, cultural, economic, and family context, effective intervention is not possible.

The collective term *Indian*, bestowed by Columbus when he lost his way to India, is a misnomer. The more correct and usually preferred identification is through tribe and family. However, for purposes of this chapter, the terms American Indian/Alaskan Native or sometime simply Indian or Native are used. The term American Indian/Alaskan Native acknowledges lifestyle and political differences between village groups in Alaska and tribal groups in the lower forty-eight states.

American Indian and Alaskan Natives have lived in what is now called the New World for at least 30,000 years. The various tribes themselves believe that they have been on earth since creation. At the time of European contact, approximately 2,000 distinct cultures with varying languages and religion ranged from the Alaska's Aleutian islands to the tip of Argentina (Price, 1981). As of 1990, 505 tribes, villages and corporations were recognized in the United States and Alaska (U.S. Department of Health and Human Services, 1995).

Many people mistakenly believe that Indian people are simply another racial group. In fact, they are a political entity. This North American minority group is unique. Their country was taken from them. They are the only ethnic group in the U.S. who had to gain recognition by the federal government (Kickingbird & Kickingbird, 1977). Indians have a special relationship with the United States in its constitution. Article I of the U.S. Constitution, Section 8, Clause 3 states: "The Congress shall have power…to regulate commerce with foreign nations, among the several States and with the Indian tribes." In fact, a federal law book, *United States Code, Annotated, Title 25*, is dedicated to Indian law.

Today, the descendants of these peoples continue to live in the United States as outsiders, knowing that for more than 500 years their nations fought to survive while observing the destruction of their homeland and way of life. American

Indians and Alaskan Natives have dual citizenship and must prove their blood quantum (percentage of tribal blood relatedness) in order to be considered a member of a recognized tribe by the federal government. Members must register with their tribe in order to share political, educational, health and other privileges and benefits (Kickingbird & Kickingbird, 1977). Indian people can claim only one tribe for benefit purposes, even though they may have mixed tribal heritage. The U.S. government recognizes them as Indian only to the extent of their descent from the declared tribe.

The government policies of both the United States and Canada are an inseparable part of the everyday lives of American-Indian and Alaskan-Native people in both tribal and urban settings. The most intimate and personal aspects of their life (i.e., where to live, how to make a living, choice of religious practice, tribal affiliation, right to keep their children) have been, and continue to be, subject to treaty, court decisions, legislation and executive orders. Government policies have vacillated over the years and have included explicit plans for annihilation, assimilation and self-determination.

Whole tribes were annihilated from small pox and warfare. Napoleon (1991) eloquently relates the traumatic effects to the Yup'ik of Alaska due to disease, removal of children and loss of spiritual beliefs and religious practices.

> Like any victim or witness of evil, whether it be murder, suicide, rape, war or mass death, the Yup'ik survivors were in shock... They were quiet and kept things to themselves. They rarely showed their sorrows, fears, heartbreak, anger, or grief. Unable to relive in their conscious minds the horror they had experienced, they did not talk about it with anyone. The survivors seem to have agreed, without discussing it, that they would not talk about it. It was too painful and the implications were too great... Having silently abandoned their own beliefs, the survivors were reinforced in their decision not to talk about them by the missionaries who told them their old beliefs were evil and from the tuurag, 'the devil.'...The survivors were fatalists. They were not sure about the future or even the next day. (pp. 12-13)

The Genocide occurred during the Indian wars and forced removal to reservations of the nineteenth century. The effects of alcohol and huge loss of life from tuberculosis and other diseases became widespread in the impoverished living conditions of the reservations. The boarding schools and urban relocation of the twentieth century continue to present a bleak perspective even today.

The fabric of Indian families and their ability to teach family and community values have been destroyed or deteriorated over many generations. The erosion began with the forced removal of many children to the boarding schools where they were deprived of their language, religion, food, dress and punished severely for any infractions. Children in residential schools were treated as inmates, humiliated by being deloused and having their hair cut. At the worst, children were killed for infractions; the deaths called an accident or suicide. Many of the government-organized and religiously operated schools sought to eliminate any sign of the "old ways". The children in these schools often suffered from neglect and were abused sexually, physically, and emotionally. The Indian children returned to their homes in young adulthood forever altered.

The long-term effects of this system are incalculable. In 1928, Lewis Meriam (Morrissette, 1994) wrote,

> It is, however, still the fact that the boarding school, either reservation or non-reservation, is the dominant characteristic of the school system maintained by the national government for its Indian wards. The survey staff finds itself obligated to say frankly and unequivocally that the provisions for the care of the Indian children in boarding schools are grossly inadequate. (p. 11)
>
> The Indian Service has not appreciated the fundamental importance of family life and community activities in the social and economic development of a people. The tendency has been rather toward weakening Indian family life and community activities than toward strengthening them. The long continued policy of removing Indian children from their home and placing them for years in boarding school largely disintegrates the family and interferes with developing normal family life. (p. 13)
>
> The legacy of the boarding schools remains an embarrassing and suppressed subject even today. (p. 381)

Boarding schools often attempted to eradicate Indian values and customs and to transform Indian students into more acceptable Euro-American clones. One Indian woman related the following about her boarding school experience,

> At Carlisle, the outing was a cornerstone of Pratt's plan of education. Instead of returning home in the summer, students were placed with white farming families for three months and in some cases for up to three years after graduation. Here they could experience firsthand the responsibilities and amenities of civilized life. (Lomawaina, 1994, p. 5)

Another example illustrates how boarding school administrators attempted to isolate their students from the Indian way of life:

> Emma Sleeth wrote that it was Major Haworth's idea to set apart thirteen sections of land to establish a little colony of Indian boys and girls from the school who might marry one another. Each couple would live on ten acres of land where school personnel could assist them to live 'a civilized life'. (Lomawaina, 1994, p. 14).

Children from the boarding schools were often adopted into non-Indian families, sometimes without the knowledge or permission of their birth families. This deprived them of the opportunity to learn, by example, traditional parenting practices, ceremonies or their role in the community and family. Many

America-Indian and Alaskan-Native people were brought up without knowledge or influence of their heritage and today feel lost and confused as they try to reclaim their heritage. Many Indian people in such situations are embarrassed that their knowledge of their own culture comes from Hollywood stereotypes. Some turn away from their heritage because of stereotypes which associate American-Indian/Alaskan-Indian people with poverty and substance abuse.

The effects of the boarding school and other enforced removals and adoptions of children are evident in the following comments. Bergman (1967) states

> I am often struck by the difference between the children I see in the (boarding) schools and the patients on the pediatric wards. In school, the children often seem abnormally subdued and sometimes even apathetic, but in the hospital, where the main difference is the much greater individual attention and consequent lack of regimentation, the patients are more active, spontaneous and trusting. (p. 11)

Metcalf (1976) compares mothering experiences of people raised in boarding schools and those raised at home.

> One of the most disturbing outcomes of this study emerged from the observations of the children in these families. We were struck by the difference in effect demonstrated by the children. If the results of this study are upheld, then the detrimental effects of reservation boarding schools goes beyond the immediate influence on the pupils enrolled and goes forward into succeeding generations. (p. 543)

Single Parents in the American-Indian/Alaskan-Native community are concerned even today about their children being taken from their care. Between 1958 and 1974 the Child Welfare League of America (CWLA) contracted with the Bureau of Indian Affairs to remove many children from their homes, citing as part of the reason that many were "unwed mothers" (Fanshel, 1972). Ninety percent were placed in non-Indian families in the east (Sorkin, 1978). By their own admission, CWLA (and others before them) noted that the marital status of the parents was not a critical issue to the tribal community. However, the majority culture judged this acceptance as a deficiency rather than a strength of these families and communities.

In response to the astonishing number of Indian children placed in foster care, 35% or 3.6 times the rate of non-Indian (Matheson, 1996), the tribes began a movement to get their children back. In Washington state, a small and determined group of Indian social workers led by Goldie Denny pursued legislation for state foster care proceedings that would require committees of Indian child-welfare workers to review any case involving an Indian child in an effort to place that child with Indian relatives, the closest kin in her or his tribe, a related tribe or an Indian home. A non-Indian home with a commitment to the child's cultural awareness and contacts would be used as a last resort. This group captured the attention and energy of the national Indian community and ultimately the U.S.

Congress. In 1978 the Indian Child Welfare Act (ICWA) was passed, without appropriation. The law is difficult to enforce but nevertheless serves as a legal means for American-Indian/Alaskan-Native people to protect their children from disappearing into non-Indian culture. The law continues to inspire debate. On May 10, 1996, it was attacked by the Republican-led U.S. House of Representatives. An amendment to the law was passed holding that such placement does not apply to child-custody proceedings involving a child whose parents do not maintain affiliation with their tribe. This amendment threatens to undermine the ICWA itself and could represent a giant step backwards.

Matheson (1996), an American-Indian/Alaskan-Native social service provider, raised pertinent issues regarding the ICWA, describing a hearing to remove three American-Indian children from their family home. The hearing was attended by 15 professionals, including child and family therapists and professionals from the legal community and child protection agency. Only two of the professionals were American Indian. When the panel reviewed the data on the psychological testing of the children and attendance at family therapy, the non-Indian professionals recommended that the children be placed with a non-Indian family who was willing to take them. The Indian professionals stated that the children's reluctance to respond in the testing situation and lack of attendance at the family sessions were more likely the result of lack of cultural congruence and sensitivity rather than apathy. Many non-Indian panel members questioned whether the ICWA standard for placement should be ignored in this case in order to "protect the best interests of the children." As Matheson summed up, "The conflicts that permeate this meeting stem from the fact that with the exception of the attorney, the non-Indian participants have virtually no understanding of the ICWA." (p. 233)

When the ICWA is understood and supported, placements do work well for American-Indian/Alaskan-Native children in foster care. One author is currently part of a treatment team for a 12-year-old boy of partial American-Indian heritage whose foster mother is an American-Indian descendant from a different tribe. The therapist and child welfare worker are American Indian. The author, foster mother, therapist and welfare worker are all aware of the ICWA and educate other team members, including school personnel, in-home treatment aides, a massage therapist, foster home licenser and guardian-at-litem, about the intent of the ICWA and the importance of honoring cultural heritage.

In the 1950s, the Bureau of Indian Affairs encouraged a massive migration of Native people from reservations to various urban locations throughout the country. The government promised opportunities for jobs and training, good pay and an easy path to a better life. Indians flocked to the cities hoping to make things better for their families and to help extended family members who stayed at home. For most of them, the reality fell far short of the promise. One more broken "treaty" resulting in poverty, cultural alienation, substance abuse and family violence. One person stated,

> I was placed in the fifth grade, and I immediately noticed that everyone in my class considered me different. When the teacher came to my name during roll call each morning, every single person laughed. Mankiller had not been a strange name back in Adair County, Oklahoma, but it was a very odd name in San Francisco. The other kids also teased me about the way I talked and dressed. It was not that I was so much poorer than the others, but I was definitely from another culture" (Mankiller & Wallis, 1993, p. 73).

Today, 45% of all Indians live in urban areas (Anderson & Kaufman, 1987). As of 1987, 29% of Washington State's Indian population lived in the Seattle urban area. Many Indian people living in rural and urban reservation settings (D'Angelo, 1996) still experience problems associated with relocation. Tribal gambling casinos, developed to provide a primary means of income on the reservation, can also injure the family by creating or reinforcing gambling addiction.

American Indian and Alaskan Natives have faced many challenges to their daily survival since the arrival of non-Indian settlers some 500 years ago. Sue and Sue (1990) noted that by the end of the eighteenth century the American-Indian/Alaskan-Native population was reduced by 90% as a result of contact with Europeans and their descendants.

In the American-Indian and Alaskan-Native community, premature death and other family problems such as violence and substance abuse are related to poverty. Health status is strongly associated with income. Indian people have higher incidences of tuberculosis, cirrhosis, diabetes, fetal alcohol effects and infant mortality.

Differences exist in birth and infant mortality rates, age of death, means of death, disease, standard of living and still negative government influences remain. Leading causes of death include heart disease, injury, cancer, liver disease, suicide, brain disease, diabetes, homicide, pneumonia and artery obstruction, in that order (U.S. Department of Health and Human Services, 1995).

As an illustration of the correlation between health and poverty, in 1979, the average annual income on the reservation was $9,920. More than 45% of the population lived below the poverty line. In 1993, the age-adjusted percent of persons with low family income (less than $14,000 annually) who reported fair or poor health was 5.5 times higher than for persons with an annual income of $50,000 or more.

Infant mortality among the American-Indian and Alaskan-Native population during 1986-8 was 60 times greater than that of the non-Indian population. In

1992, 55.3% of the 39,459 live births recorded that year were to American-Indian and Alaskan-Native mothers. This is only 1% of the number of live births to non-Indian mothers and 6% of African-American births for the same year. Longevity of American Indians/Alaskan Natives until recently was 47 years. Recent information shows an upper range of 67.1 years for men and 75.1 years for women (Moncher, Holden, & Trimble, 1990). The modal age among American Indian and Alaskan Native is 25-34 years. The overall death rate among the U.S. Indian population decreased 1.3% between 1980 and 1992, though the death rate for American-Indian and Alaskan-Native males rose 8% during that period (U.S. Department of Health and Human Services, 1995). The accidental death rate remains startlingly high – three times the national rate for motor vehicle accident-related deaths in 1992, and twice the national average for other accidental deaths. In 1992 the death rate for Indian males 15 to 24 years of age was almost 60% greater than for non-Indians and 50% greater for Indian women of the same ages, compared to non-Indians (U.S. Department of Health and Human Services, 1995). Indian children from one to four years of age die from accident at three times the national rate (Hsu & Williams, 1991). The suicide rate remains three times the national average (LaFromboise, 1988).

Poverty also limits educational opportunities and increases the likelihood of violent death and substance abuse. In 1979, the average educational level for American Indian and Alaskan Natives was 10-12 years (less than a high school diploma). Alcoholism, introduced by non-Indians during the initial period of trading and establishment of reservations, is generally considered one of the most devastating killers in the American-Indian/Alaskan-Native population. This legacy has played a crucial role in the cycle of death, high rate of poverty and unemployment, domestic violence and breakdown of the family. In recent years, it has contributed to increased gambling and a higher than average spread of HIV/AIDS infection (Givan, 1993).

As reported by the 1982 National Center for Human Statistics, alcohol-related mortality for motor vehicle accidents was 63.3% for Indians and 19.3% for the United States population in general. Violent deaths were 43.1% for Indians and 20.8% for the general population. Mortality rates for cirrhosis related to alcoholism was 52.7% for Indians and 12.3% for the general population. Finally, for alcohol-dependence syndrome, the rate was 13.2 % for Indians and 1.3% for the general population. Fifty percent of all Indian youth are more likely to become involved with substances either experimentally or abusively. Indian youth are four times more likely than African-American youth and ten times more likely than all non-Indian youth to be arrested for substance-related offenses (Moncher, Holden, & Trimble, 1990).

Domestic violence is also a serious problem among American Indian/ Alaskan Natives. Violence by one person against another, except in battle, was never considered honorable behavior among Indian people. Relocation, placement on reservations, loss of children to boarding schools, experiences in schools, poverty and alcoholism have torn families apart and contributed to the high rates of family violence.

In conclusion, although these statistics and historical events are discouraging, they should not be used to deny or subvert the strengths of the community and hereby diminish hope for the future. Helping professionals, particularly the non-initiated, non-Indian helpers must be open to understanding and valuing cultural diversity; listening and experiencing with "new" senses. In spite of adversity and oppression, the Indian community maintains a dedication to family, respect for others, spirituality and humor transcend the tragedies of history. The dignity of the people reflects cultural strength and resilience. The dignity and essential values of the people remain.

Cultural Values

Now this is what we believe.
The mother of us all is earth.
The father is the sun.
The grandfather is the Creator
    who bathed us with his mind
    and gave life to all things.
The brother is the beasts and trees.
The sister is that with wings.
We are the Children of the Earth
    and do it no harm in any way.
Nor do we offend the sun
    by not greeting it at dawn.
We praise our grandfather for his creation.
We share the same breath together –
the beasts, the trees, the birds, man.

Individuals working with American-Indian/Alaskan-Native, Single-Parent families need a cultural context for understanding many of the responses and expectations clients may bring with them to therapy. For many American Indian/Alaskan Natives, the family is the centerpiece of their world. Individuals identify with the family, clan, tribe and tribal area. That which is referred to as

From Many Winters by Nancy Wood, p. 18. © Copyright 1974 by Nancy Wood. Illustrations © 1974 by Frank Howell. Used by permission of Bantam Doubleday Dell Books for Young Readers.

"extended family" by many non-Indians is "family" to Indian people. In most tribes, social hierarchy has minimal value. Respect is the highest value. Elders earn the title, not only for their blood ties, but for their obligations and life experience. They are revered for their wisdom and looked to for guidance.

In American-Indian/Alaskan-Native culture, individuals cannot speak for others. Each person's voice is part of the whole and her or his input is unique. It is important to respect this value and its essential connection to family and tribe. Many tribal governing practices still use this principle to guide their decision-making processes.

In the course of time, the unique history and conditions of American Indian/Alaskan Natives have been romanticized. Generosity, spiritual life and belief in a harmonious life are highly valued. Many non-Indian people are particularly interested in the spirituality dimension of Indian life. In reality, the spiritual beliefs and practices of Indians vary greatly among tribal groups. Moreover, various intertribal ceremonial practices have developed in recent decades and become an important catalyst for community support, development and personal healing. American-Indian/Alaskan-Native spiritual philosophy – as it applies to mental health – emphasizes restoration of balance of mental, emotional, physical and spiritual health, for the individual, family, community and beyond.

Provision of Services to Single-Parent Families

Single Parenthood in the American-Indian/Alaskan-Native community is not easily defined. In majority culture, the term "Single Parent" is used to primarily describe a woman or man living alone and who is the primary caretaker for the children. This notion of Single Parent focuses on the isolation of a beleaguered parent with children who is without practical, social and emotional resources.

American Indians and Alaskan Natives, on the other hand, often live in extended family or community circumstances; sharing child care, financial resources, spirituality/religion and ritual. Because family is structured differently in these communities, the American Indian/Alaskan Native may be the Single Parent for a niece, nephew or grandchild; rather than or in addition to their own children. Red Horse and Red Horse (1982) describe ways in which family and community members offer help to Single Parents in their tribal area of the Midwest. "We have single-parent households, but that doesn't correspond to a single-parent family – there are probably ten parents in the family. They just don't live in the same house." (Red Horse & Red Horse, 1982, p. 282).

Single Fathers, both custodial and non-custodial, play a role in the American-Indian/Alaskan-Native community. Indian men historically assumed an important role in teaching children how to provide for their families and in passing on cultural practices. Today, however, Indian men are isolated from their

43

culture, community and family as a result of economic hardship, alcoholism, gambling, which can affect a family for several generations – even following recovery.

Grandparents, particularly grandmothers, hold a special place in American-Indian/Alaskan-Native communities. Grandparents represent parental authority because they are older, wiser and have extensive life experience. Historically, in American-Indian/Alaskan-Native communities both biological parents gathered food and supplies for shelter and heat, leaving their children with grandmothers to care for them. Parenting was viewed as a community responsibility and grandparents were a critical factor. Today, grandparents may become Single Parents of their grandchildren because of the death of parents or other circumstances. Young Single Parents may struggle to earn a living or go away to school. The subsequent set of relationships, obligation and responsibility are as relevant today as always.

Young Indian parents may get help, support and advice from a variety of resources. Generally, they are not expected to make all parenting decisions alone. Young parents do not cease to be children themselves when the baby is born, nor are they necessarily expected to move out and fend for their families (Metcalf, 1978).

Some non-Indian human service workers might consider the decision by Single Parents to leave children with other relatives as abandonment. Historically, child welfare personnel have considered these "relative placements" as part of a temporary destructive pattern of foster placement rather than a family and tribe taking care of its children. "Permanency planning" has been used as a rationale to remove these children from their relative's homes and from their communities in order to create "stability" (Mannes, 1990). In the American-Indian/Alaskan-Native, as in other communities, some parents do neglect their children for various reasons. However, care offered by a relative should not be used as the sole evidence of neglect and lack of family stability. The human service worker should assess this carefully and may gather support for the grandparent, who may be relatively young and working outside the home too.

Finally, American-Indian/Alaskan-Native Single Parents do experience many of the ordinary problems which Single Parents in general face, for example, financial hardships and general discrimination in the workplace. Minimal financial resources affect their ability to obtain housing, transportation, adequate nutrition, clothing and education and is a powerful influence in health-related problems such as depression (Napholz, 1995).

Assessment and Rapport Building

In American-Indian/Alaskan-Native culture, seeking help is viewed as a way to restore balance to the whole person – body, mind, emotions and spirit. Mental health counseling is simply one avenue for maintaining or restoring balance. For example, among many native people, the concept of the medicine wheel depicts the physical, mental, emotional, spiritual and, sometimes, sociocultural aspects of the person, family or community. Given this philosophy, treatment is not only necessary for the Single Parent who is suffering, but for the community as well:

> Mental health services for American Indian/Alaskan Natives have been provided traditionally through family, medicine people or other persons within a tight knit community. Extended family and tribe, therefore, historically have organized as a natural support network to facilitate individual and group well-being." (Red Horse, Gonzales-Santin, Beane & Tolson-Gonzales, 1981, p. 1)

The Single Parent is an essential part of the whole community and the suffering of that individual is everyone's concern (McCloud, 1982). Seeking help reflects upon the family and perhaps the tribe or village. Therefore, mental health services must be provided in the American-Indian/Alaskan-Native community with the perspective that the Single Parent and the family are part of a larger social system.

Assessment procedures emanate from the medical model created by the majority culture, which may not be a fair or effective tool in situations involving native families. Red Horse and Red Horse (1982) point out that the Western model of mental health is generally based on the assumption that a need for services is indicative of a pathological condition. This view may cause non-Indian caregivers to view American-Indian/Alaskan-Native culture and family structure as weak and dying. Differences in values and traditions between non-Indian and American-Indian/Alaskan-Native cultures must be noted during assessment. Professional studies and community-based literature suggest possible assessment methods for American-Indian/Alaskan-Native, Single-Parent families. Hollis's (1972) conceptualization of the person-in-situation views the Single Parent or other family member in the center of a series of concentric circles beginning with family and flowing out into the community and larger culture. Whittaker's (1975) family-systems approach views the individual as a fragment of a family when determining the problem and treatment. Red Horse and colleagues (1981) cite the potential strength and clinical usefulness of Indian family gatherings, through which Single-Parent families obtain support and other needed resources. All of these approaches emphasize relational systems.

For the non-Indian therapist, more inclusive and less deductive assessment techniques are preferable. Thus therapy, as well as assessment, becomes a continual process of gathering and examining material in order to initiate change. Finding alternative methods for American-Indian/Alaskan-Native Single Parents to express themselves in order to collect this information is helpful.

Helpers should attempt to identify the family's primary spokesperson. How do people talk to one another? What role does humor play? Practitioners must recognize that American-Indian/Alaskan-Native community and family systems vary across geographic and tribal groups. Shelledy and Nelson (1981) caution that it is essential to listen to the individual Single Parent and family group to determine how they view themselves and how they reveal themselves to others. Families open up in therapy if they feel trust. American-Indian/Alaskan-Native Single Parents and other family members may not respond well to direct questions or demands and may consider a direct approach rude because they have no way to refuse answering without seeming impolite. They may respond to non-Indians with silence or an indirect response. Sharing stories and making third-person observations is a preferable technique. Gathering personal information takes time. In native culture, silence is more polite than in some other cultures – tolerate it. When American-Indian/Alaskan-Native Single Parents are ready to discuss a topic, they will let the therapist know. Spending time with American-Indian/Alaskan-Native Single Parents in various settings and getting to know family members gradually allows helpers to begin to understand and eventually use family strengths to move toward therapeutic goals.

Another factor which can impede rapport building, information gathering, and the therapeutic process is American-Indian/Alaskan-Natives' experiences with non-Indians throughout the years. Traumatic experiences, grounded in racism and cultural oppression, have led the development of defense mechanisms in American-Indian/Alaskan-Native clients that serve to protect them. Indian families have a history of being misunderstood, misinterpreted and ridiculed (as well as romanticized) by non-Indians for their way of life and cultural practices. Many Indians have developed practices which protect them from intrusions by outsiders.

For example, a Single Mother brought her preadolescent son to an American-Indian urban mental health center following his hospitalization at a local children's facility. The family belongs to a Plains tribe. The young man, who was experiencing an initial psychotic episode described hearing a voice that he identified as his spiritual guide. The non-Indian facility focused on this experience as a primary symptom and evidence of psychosis. The Indian mental health agency, however, asked about the family's religious beliefs and practices and learned that belief in spiritual guides was common. The Indian agency then concentrated on a behavioral pattern change and responses to outside stimuli to determine a diagnosis and treatment that respected the family's culture.

Single Parents in the American-Indian/Alaskan-Native community may emphasize different cultural values within a healthy family. In the dominant society, economic achievement and success are measured by the accumulation of material wealth, political power and financial security. In the American-Indian/Alaskan-Native society, such values are viewed as indicators of hoarding and superficiality. Indians, in general, are impressed by the quality of a person's character as represented by his or her actions demonstrating connection and responsibility to others. This value is important in assessment and treatment planning. More family and community members may be included in the process and a health goal may well be community relatedness rather than independence. Red Horse and colleagues (1981) pointed out that for the Ojibway interpreting family interactions and planning interventions must consider the client's cultural context.

For example; Henderson, Brody, Lane, and Parra (1982) studied blame assigned to children by their mothers for various hypothetical misdeeds. The Mexican and American-Indian mothers were more concerned about maintaining a sense of respect and connectedness with their family, while non-Indians emphasized majority cultural values of independence and individual responsibility.

Cross-Cultural Counseling

Cultural values are the central theme of most counseling interactions. Cultural bias leads to therapeutic failure. In may instances, the majority culture blames the minority culture for such failure. It has long been recognized, cultural biases and agendas have caused cross-cultural relationships in many settings to fail. Studies spanning several years show a generally higher preference among Indian clients for Indian counselors with similar world views and values (Bennet & Bigfoot-Sipes, 1991; Bigfoot-Sipes, Dauphinais, LaFromboise & Bennett, 1992; Johnson & Lashley, 1989; Spang, 1965). If people understand one another and the condition of each other's lives, their behavior will seem perfectly natural and differences can be bridged.

Forming a bond based on mutual understanding and respect is crucial to success in cross-cultural therapy (Anderson, 1985). Mental health service delivery in culturally specific settings has developed during the past 40 years of cross-cultural clinical research. Lonner (1979) and Sundberg (1981) recommend that such service delivery begin with the therapist adopting the client's world view in the therapeutic setting – an emic (from within) cultural perspective. Dawis (1977) supports a similar approach, emphasizing that altruism and client autonomy create an atmosphere supportive of therapy.

Cross-cultural counseling includes five important maxims that are effective in therapeutic work with American-Indian/Native-Alaskan, Single-Parent families:
1. Understand one's own values and assumptions; and recognize that other's may differ.

2. Recognize that no counseling theory is politically or morally neutral.
3. Recognize that external sociopolitical and cultural forces may have influenced and shaped culturally groups.
4. Understand, perhaps even attempt to share, the world view of the client.
5. Take an eclectic approach adaptable to the varying needs of clients (Arredondo-Dowd & Gonsalves, 1980; Sue, 1978; Trimble, Fleming, Beauvais & Jumper-Thurman, 1995).

The clinician needs to gather complete information about the American-Indian/Alaskan-Native Single Parent and the family members and community or context in which the client was raised in order to determine what therapeutic methods to use and to understand client responses during the therapeutic process. A good clinician listens attentively to his or her Single-Parent clients, knowing they are the best source of information in the therapeutic relationship. The act of listening itself is especially important in cross-cultural counseling situation and helps to counter past negative, cross-cultural experiences. Effective listening can increase the therapist's knowledge of and access to resources and community connections sustaining the American-Indian/Alaskan-Native, Single-Parent family. For example, Smith (1982), a Klamath tribal member, states, "When I was a kid, the elder told me respect is two words: look again or look twice." (p. 153). This saying seems apropos to the dual nature of therapist as guide and client as teacher in the cross-cultural counseling relationship.

Cross (1986) and Lazrus (1982) outlined traditional values governing American-Indian child rearing that are likely factors in working with Single Parents.

1. Children were protected from abuse and neglect by the extended community. Community opinion governed parent behavior and parents who did not meet expectations were often chastised or ridiculed into compliance.
2. Specific tribal expectations about human relationships and social action were taught by elders. The stories they shared served as primary teaching tools of customs and cultural expectation, providing the group work responsibility and safety. The oral tradition was the primary method for transmitting values.
3. Family or other designated tribal elders took in children as their own if tragedy separated parents and children. Life was harsh, but the community was prepared.
4. Young children were viewed as being very close to the spirit world, having recently emerged from there. Very young children were given a great deal of freedom and later were provided with strict instruction regarding tribal roles and expectations.

Unfortunately the genocide of Indian peoples and their assimilation into the majority culture have eroded many of these values. A Single Parent from a tribal community today may not have an ideal extended family available to help teach and support these values to children. A possible focus for therapy, in such cases, is developing new links to a community system and to grieve the ones which have been destroyed. Red Horse and Red Horse (1982) suggest it may be good to share personal information about one's own community, family, self and concerns; offering hospitality and creating a caring, informal and respectful atmosphere in which American-Indian/Alaskan-Native Single Parents believe their welfare is important. Setting aside time to be social and to establish comfort between the therapist and Single Parent or family members by sharing some refreshment or discussing community events before moving to the problem at hand is considered polite behavior and helps establish trust. Therapists may need to demonstrate why they have chosen their work as well as abide by cultural standards of hospitality and communication methods to develop support. In a community in which the welfare of all is interconnected, such techniques are only logical and represent a good model for all therapeutic settings.

Trust and consistency are key factors in obtaining personal or sensitive information and, as discussed elsewhere, in continuing the therapeutic relationship. Because of a history of child removals and other harmful acts by outsiders, the therapist, whether Indian or non-Indian must prove that she or he will act on behalf of the family and not on the part of an oppressive system. Evans (1982) states that the therapist also has an important function as advocate for the Single-Parent family in helping members negotiate societal systems. Some Single-Parent families are able to access resources, but others need someone who can move between their world and the mainstream system.

Although credibility is linked closely to consistency, it goes one step further. The saying "talk the talk and walk the walk" sums up the need for clinicians to keep their promises. For persons in the position of authority and power which therapists have traditionally held, actions serve as models for others and the means of establishing their credibility. Through a socialization process the helper gets to know the family. It is important to include a time to be social and establish comfort between the therapist and client(s) by sharing some refreshment or discussing other community events before coming to the problem at hand.

Indian politics can end an otherwise successful relationship if the worker is viewed as siding with an opposing group. Taking a position is probably less likely with non-Indian therapists, who probably would not be involved directly in community politics. However, they should measure their opinions carefully. Clients expect therapists who are members of the Indian community to be aware of political issues, have an opinion, and work well regardless of their opinions.

Because the self is the primary "tool" of the work, it is important to be aware of one's own culture and relationship with family and community. For example, one of the authors, who is non-Indian and grew up in a reservation community, was hired by an urban agency that served the American-Indian and Alaskan-Native population in a city distant from the reservation. The director of the agency was a member of the same tribe the author lived with. Upon introduction, the director did not ask about degrees and qualifications but asked about the author's grandparents and parents and talked briefly about their relationship with her mother before turning the conversation to professional matters.

The location and timing of therapy are also powerful determinants of therapy. Therapy in rural and reservation settings may incorporate more informal sites for the therapist and Single-Parent client than are found in inner-city, office settings. The collaterals involved in treatment are likely to include extended family, traditional medicine people and other community supports. Clarke (1987) points out that endorsement of the provider is an essential component of successful therapy.

A bicultural or even multicultural treatment approach is needed to assess and evaluate treatment services. Many American-Indian/Alaskan-Native Single-Parent family units with which we work are multicultural. Intertribal and interracial marriage makes therapeutic work richer and more complex.

A multicultural network approach was used by an author who worked with an American-Indian, Single Mother and her son for several years – both in an Indian mental health agency and a non-Indian setting. The family is multicultural. Though the mother lives in a city and her family on the reservation, ties to family and tribal traditions are strong. Important to the Single-Parent family's growth has been inclusion of the family's role in society, various spiritual elements and other community resources which incorporate the family's network. The therapist continues to learn from this family and extended family, whose sessions have included the grandmother, father, mother's partner, the son's "big brother" and traditional healers.

Therefore, it is clearly a mistake to assume learning about one tribal culture or one Single-Parent family is sufficient to work with all American-Indian/Alaskan-Native clients. Further, clients do not expect their therapist, whether Indian or non-Indian, to know everything about all tribes. Treatment must consider cultural difference among American-Indian/Native-Alaskan Single Parents and their families. For example, Bergman described a former co-worker, a Navajo, who overheard him urging a reluctant young Navajo man to follow his family's wish and have a Sing (a Navajo healing ceremony). The co-worker asked Bergman, who is Jewish, why he didn't "keep kosher", meaning Bergman seemed to assume Navajo healing was the only treatment approach for this Navajo man. By this, Bergman's co-worker was pointing out to him that a person's ethnic, racial or religious culture does not necessarily provide all the answers for people from that culture, nor do all people of the culture choose to follow all the traditions. Bergman was thus reminded that it is important to listen to the needs of the individual client and balance that with the community and cultural perspective.

American-Indian/Alaskan-Native Single Parents vary as to their expectations of and responses to various therapeutic and communication styles (Burton, 1980; Dauphinais, Dauphinais & Rowen, 1981; LaFromboise, Trimble & Mohart, 1990; Richardson, 1981; Youngman & Sadongei, 1974). Studies do not indicate that any particular style is especially effective in work with Indian clients (Burton, 1980; Dauphinais et al., 1981; LaFromboise et al., 1990; Richardson 1981; Spang 1965). The wisest clinical choice is to match therapeutic style to the Single Parent's communication style.

Dtati (1993) provided a stunning example and compelling suggestions for developing therapeutic intervention using the client's communication style. Dtati used art therapy as a tool to communicate with a 15-year-old Blackfoot woman who lived in a Canadian residential facility for adolescents. She had been removed from her biological family in early childhood and unsuccessfully placed in several foster and one failed adoptive home. This young woman learned to maintain an independent life, free from self-mutilation, and was able to reconnect with her culture and her family.

Two concepts, accommodation and restructuring, are fundamental to all counseling work. These concepts have additional significance in cross-cultural settings. Accommodation allows the clinician to join with the Single-Parent client or family. Morishige (personal communication, May 1996) states,

> The consideration of accepting multiple relationships (in contrast to the traditional therapist's avoidance of dual relationships), therapist being self disclosing in contrast to seeing the "client" via a one-way mirror, refraining from working on what is going on with the "client" via induction of transference reaction and interpretation of resistance are just the tip of the iceberg in the issues that a traditional therapist has to address in working with the "client"....The therapist needs to not just intellectually incorporate the knowledge of the unique elements of the "client" and how to modify their mode of "treatment", but also experientially come to terms with their own vulnerability to their subjectivity when addressing issues such as stereotypes, historical and ongoing racism, oppression of American Indian/Alaskan Natives/Alaskan Natives, non-linear perspectives, spirituality (inseparable synthesis of human beings and nature, in contrast to dualistic "traditional" religious induction).... It would be tempting for the therapist to be armed intellectually with all the knowledge of the unique factors and still not understand the nuances of what it means to be an American Indian/Alaskan Native. Speeding up the river in an intellectual power boat does not allow the

therapist to understand the medium of the river and diverse currents that one encounters by struggling to paddle and maneuver up the river in a canoe.

Therefore, the therapist should evaluate whether her or his perceptions are clouded by cultural perception of problem definition, treatment method or desired outcome. The therapist also might be asked to attend tribal festivities and ceremonies. Doing so shows support for the Single Parent and family.

Restructuring is used to meet therapeutic goals and is the instrument for change. Clarke (1987) suggests that all elements of mental health service delivery must be evaluated and perhaps revised to be culturally specific in order to achieve cultural appropriateness. For example, one author worked with a separated Alaskan-Native mother and her three children. Therapy dealt with the loss of a father figure for the children. Therapy content included socializing with tea and treats, storytelling, humor, games, role play and art work. The family's personal and cultural manner of sharing personal information about feelings and family members was honored in order not to cause embarrassment to anyone. Solutions included using extended family and community supports to help this working mother and her children grieve their loss. The family was eventually able to identify their reluctance to acknowledge the father's alcoholism and the effect it had on the family. They improved their ability to listen to and understand one another's feelings, felt more comfortable communicating feelings to one another and began to enjoy family time together.

Community resources can assist in the treatment process tribal newsletters, therapeutic adjuncts and consultants. Therapy can include a team to help rein-tegrate the Single Parent back into the larger community (Attneave, 1974, 1977; Attneave & Speck, 1974). There are many ways to use elements naturally found in the treatment systems of the Indian community itself. Single-Parent clients, their families, and community members can become "healers" in the treatment process (Attneave, 1974). Elders speak about how each person is a potential healer with the resources to solve her or his problems (Banyaca, 1982). Elders recommend using sleep, meditation and dreams as ways to recover from stress and to access personal knowledge and resources. Traditional ceremonies and rituals serve as aids to successful therapy and reintegration into the community.

Some Single-Parent Indian clients who follow their traditional practices may incorporate ceremonies, herbs and other remedies in their treatment. Specifically, one author recalls working with an elderly man from Alaska who was very depressed. Treatment included having him visit localities in the area to gather herbs to make a tea he knew would help with depression. This approach did prove effective. The client quit his job in an urban setting and returned to his home in Alaska, he felt less isolated and depressed.

In summary, Lane (1982), a Yankton Sioux elder, reminds therapists the most effective therapy is affective, "of the heart" therapy. Each family, client, culture and society has unique definitions of therapy and expectations for treatment goals. These expectations must be ascertained through a gradual information gathering process. It's important to address a person's spiritual life, traditional values, available cultural resources, personal cultural identity, familiarity and comfort in dealing with mainstream society, and role in the extended family and tribal or ethnic community (Clarke 1987). For instance, some non-Indian cultures would emphasize independence as a therapeutic goal, while in the American-Indian/Alaskan-Native community interdependence is more valued. The Indian philosophy is one of the interrelatedness of all things: human, animal, plant, animate and inanimate; seen and unseen. Therefore, mental health services in the American-Indian/Alaskan-Native community must be viewed from the perspective not of just the individual, but the larger system of which the client is a part.

The cultural multiplicity among American Indian/Alaskan Natives and the variation among individuals in the endorsement and expression of traditional customs is a crucial component of assessment and treatment. Ensuring the communication is understood and interpreted similarly by therapist and Single-Parent client is fundamental to the therapeutic process. For instance, some non-Indian Single Parents might emphasize independence as a therapeutic goal, whereas others might emphasize interdependence.

Special Treatment Considerations

Treatment Barriers

Therapy with any client population has potential problems that interfere with or create barriers to treatment. The following information is derived from studies of expectant mothers in the American-Indian/Native-Alaskan community. The issues apply equally to health services with American-Indian/Native-Alaskan Single Parents.

Lia-Hoagberg, Rode, Skovholt, Oberg, Berg, Mullett, and Choe (1990) identified three major treatment barriers. Their study focused on prenatal care but noted similar patterns with earlier studies investigating the use of dental, medical and mental health services. The barrier categories are structural, individual and sociodemographic. Structural barriers include organizational services, availability, cost of services and time to access them. Individual barriers include client knowledge, feelings and attitude about services. Sociodemographic variables that influence specific service use vary with the type of service studied; but can include age, sex, ethnicity, marital status, income level, education and employment status.

The study noted reasons for missing appointments or postponing care, including transportation difficulties, costs, lack of child care, fear of services, "learned helplessness", crisis-driven care seeking, poor treatment experiences or poor relationships with caregivers, and family or personal problems (including lack of energy, illness or depression). These barriers underscore earlier suggestions that treatment be provided in a manner, setting and timing that is culture-friendly in order to develop and maintain the therapeutic relationship.

The concept of cultural alienation or "psychosis" or "walking in two or more cultures" is integral to the discussion of treatment and its barriers. American-

Indian/Native-Alaskan Single Parents may feel they are on the outside looking in and never able to prove their worth as individuals and parents despite their best efforts. This is a discouraging reality for all people in the position of minority and is particularly troublesome for American-Indian/Native-Alaskan people who have become guests in their own land.

Good therapists can help Single Parents discover, rediscover and empower their heritage. Indian clients need to feel secure knowing the helper is asking cultural questions for their benefit. It is important to learn from and support the Single Parents in developing cultural pride. However, the individual must also be seen as a unique person and the clinician must follow the client's lead in sharing or learning about tribal background and challenge stereotypes.

Multiple Relationships

American Indians and Alaskan Natives are involved in multiple relationships in their community. Relatives work together and may seek one another's help formally and informally. However, human service professionals may refer to multiple relationships in the therapeutic setting as a problem of "dual relationship". Ethical dilemmas may be posed by being, for example, someone's therapist and conducting a business or personal relationship with that client or someone closely associated with them. For example, one author was asked to be on the board of directors of a private school. She discovered that a current board member was intimately related to one of her clients. In order to avoid a dual relationship, the therapist quietly declined the board invitation. Maintaining a helper-client relationship ensures that the relationship will not be influenced by the therapist's interactions with the client's intimate or business associates and promotes trust. Maintaining a one-on-one relationship with a client is easier in a large urban community than it is in rural or reservation community.

Practice with Indian Single Parents and their community includes assuming multiple roles and using techniques which may not used in most other therapeutic settings. For example, the extended family may become involved in therapy to reintegrate the individual or family into the community. In a small rural setting or tightly knit urban community, the therapist may see a client and the client's family or friends in places and situations outside the office, including community social gatherings. It is important that the therapist know how to navigate these situations and to assume appropriate roles which are expected for everyone (LaFromboise, Dauphinais & Rowe, 1980). The Single Parent should set the tone for public interactions by deciding whether to acknowledge the therapist and be acknowledged in return. It is best to plan for this type of situation and to agree that therapy roles need to be separated from community roles. Therapists must remember that they are viewed as role models and authority figures in all their activities.

Tribes often attempt to hire tribal members who have been educated as mental health workers, alcoholism counselors, social workers and other health care personnel. These helpers are called upon to provide services to people they or their family have known. The human service worker in such situations must be constantly aware of their personal and professional conduct and must have an outside consultation source, even if by telephone, to discuss these complex interactions.

The prospect of multiple relationships calls for a redefinition and under-standing of what it means to provide services to Single Parents in a community (whether urban, rural or reservation). In an urban setting, the term "community" is used very loosely. In urban environments, interactions and reciprocal obligations may be minimal compared with rural or reservation settings. To urban Indian clients community may mean nothing more than a geographic locality in which they reside, share a grocery or pharmacy and see some people with some frequency – perhaps never knowing them by name.

American-Indian and Alaskan-Native communities may be located on, near, or off the geographic boundaries of a reservation. Some reservations are rural communities and some are near or within the urban setting. American-Indian and Alaskan-Native Single Parents may not live on a reservation but may have formed community networks of their own. These types of communities never-theless maintain strong family relationship as well as customs and obligations. For example, one author was raised in a reservation community. Although she has not lived there for many years, she visits often. She has had the same vehicle for many years and as soon as she nears the reservation, everyone she meets on the road recognizes her truck and waves. If her family did not know in advance she was coming, they would be informed of her visit before her arrival because word travels fast in these settings. In this person's home community, when a tragedy befalls a family, the local store places a can with the family name on it for donations. Community members know when major losses have occurred in fellow community members' lives. In this author's life, the store has changed from a little "mom and pop" operation to a tribally operated trading post in a large supermarket. Still the donation cans are there at the appropriate times. The supportive customs endure.

Thus the human service professional works in the context of a community, which sanctions, as well as assists, with therapeutic interventions, even if only tacitly. If a teenager says that she is pregnant and does not know what to do, the helper likely knows the family, the pressures the young woman is under, who will be affected by decisions and what the consequences may be in the family and community. If the helper is a tribal member from the community, the young woman expects the helper to know these issues and to assist her in sorting them out. In fact, the therapist is likely to know beforehand about the young woman's situation and what she is gong to tell them even before she arrives. The young woman knows she is seeing someone who will listen differently from family. She may want the therapist to be with her when she informs others and to help her locate concrete resources. In other words, the therapist is a knowledgeable community helper; not a disinterested, objective observer.

The advantage of this type of community and therapeutic setting is the client does not have to explain their life. However, the helping professional must maintain a balanced perspective and not presume all information garnered through the community network is accurate.

In reservation settings, people commonly know where everyone lives, as well as everyone's personal habits. Some providers choose to live off the reservation in order to remain more neutral. Seeking help in the therapist's home or outside the office would probably not, in and of itself, be seen as a boundary violation, as it may be perceived in some non-Indian cultures or settings. For example, a White therapist in an Indian agency visited the granddaughter of a Single-Grandmother client who was hospitalized for surgery in her home. The visits led to increased support for the Single Grandmother and established a connection between therapist and family facilitating the process of change.

It should be noted that an Indian community in an urban environment can also have a well-developed informal information systems. In the urban setting where most of the authors reside, Indian community organizations provide services and sponsor cultural gatherings. People know one another across tribes, may be employed, receive services and attend community cultural events in one of these organizations. Even though the urban area has extensive resources and allows for a measure of anonymity, the helping professional may still need to deal with multiple relationship.

Regardless of the setting, helpers must think in terms of multiple roles and must have a community-based, conceptual framework and consultants to ensure that quality, ethical services are provided. Non-Indian professionals are not exempt from these dilemmas. If the non-Indian helper is in the community for a length of time and becomes well known, they are likely, for example, to attend a pow wow (intertribal gathering adapted from Plains tribes traditions, in which feasting, honoring, ceremony and dance are used to celebration) and sit next to, say, a client's former sister-in-law who knows a lot about the clinician.

Programs

Various programs developed by American-Indian or Alaskan-Native communities across the nation provided services such as parenting, foster care, support and reunification, traditional gatherings, substance abuse treatment and shelters from domestic violence. These programs highlight how American-Indian/ Alaskan-Native communities conceptualize service to help their families and the ways in which these services are offered in a cultural context. These services help Single Parents maintain, re-establish or establish their families and improve communication and health connections with extended family and community. Services are provided within a community and cultural context, which makes them more accessible to Single Parents and others in need.

Historically, native programs have tended to rely on annual appropriations from Congress for one- to five-year pilot grants. Programs are expected to be absorbed into the community and funded by other sources at the end of the project term. Funding sources have been eager to support programs for Indian people, but not with long-term financing. Some programs have continued through tribal funding efforts and the stamina of those involved. Unfortunately, many other programs have been terminated as a result of lack of funds.

Urban Indian Child Resource Center (UICRC) – Oakland, California

Originally this project was funded by the National Center for Child Abuse and Neglect to provide services for young, challenged families. The UICRC developed a family-support network. Rather than isolating families with problems, it invited the community to join with the center by seeking out families to (a) become officially licensed as foster placements for Indian children for whom there were no alternative arrangements and (b) be designated as volunteer host families.

The UICRC staff were a combination of family workers, homemakers and administrators working together to enhance the natural family-support system of the community to care for families in need. The center became a place where families could gather for mutual support and an enjoyable time. This child resource program focused on total Indian community involvement. The needs of the center, young parents, and children were advertised to the Indian community. Activities such as potlucks brought groups together on a regular basis. Community aid took various forms, whether to decide about foster care and support services or to assist a family so placement of the children in foster homes would not be necessary. Aid took many forms: companionship, transportation and meals. The program empowered the community itself.

The Center development of a new service model based on antecedents from traditional American-Indian/Alaskan-Native cultures in combination with the realities of contemporary Indian communities themselves. In Metcalf's (1978) words, the Urban Indian Child Resource Center "grew its own" (p. 1).

AhBeNoGee – Minnesota

Originally, UICRC and AhBeNoGee were funded through the same source. Both programs developed in ways unique to their urban circumstances and had important similarities. Indian community ownership of the project was a primary objective. Emphasis was on gathering the community together and providing support systems for those in need rather than trying to replace existing relational networks with non-Indian style agency models. This factor was critical to the integrity and success of the program. AhBeNoGee, for example, focused on feast days related to traditional ceremonies of tribal groups in the area. Red Horse and Red Horse (1982) state, "Members of the National Center of Child Abuse and Neglect who attended the feast thought it was to focus on the Year of the Child. This was not our intention. We wanted to honor the generations. We didn't want to divide the generations." (p. 390)

Native American Rehabilitation Association (NARA) – Portland, Oregon

A stumbling block of any alcohol treatment program is a lack of adequate planning for parents with small children who seek treatment for themselves but are understandably reluctant or unable to leave their children for three weeks to three months while receiving help. The NARA included parenting services in the program planning so young mothers could participate in treatment without being unduly separated from their children at the treatment facility.

This program is a fine example of an inpatient treatment facility in a metropolitan area which recognized a community need and met it. The program included a men's and women's treatment center as well as a general outpatient facility. The main treatment center was maintained for older and single people. The women's program provided outpatient care for mothers, particularly Single Mothers. Once the family program began, other natural developments followed. Stone (1982) states,

> Because of our involvement in this area, we have found ourselves being advocates for children's services. We have assisted women in returning or obtaining custody of their children or in arranging visitation rights. At the very least we are helping to keep families together and that was the original purpose of the facility. (p. 416)

The program has expanded beyond the early developments and recently celebrated its twenty-fifth year of service.

White Buffalo Calf Women's Society – Rosebud Sioux Reservation, South Dakota

This unusual shelter for women and children fleeing domestic violence situations was developed by the women of the community. Unlike its urban and non-Indian counterparts which focus on secrecy of location, this shelter is known in the community. The community is responsible for the protection of persons using its services.

The White Buffalo Calf Women's Society developed this shelter for the women of the Rosebud Sioux reservation. The community began by meeting and discussing their concerns about violence and the effects on families. They talked with funding sources, tribal organizations and the community in general. Their painstaking and careful work resulted in a successful shelter supported by the community. The women's group felt spiritually guided. "For about two years we tried to lease it [the building] and we like to think that the Great Spirit had a hand in getting us what we needed." (Long, 1982, p. 454)

It is clear from the description of the shelter that the primary goal of preserving families and family relationship remained the primary concern in the planning despite initial doubts about the project from people whose experience with intervention had been removal of children from families or interventions which exacerbated family problems. In the end, the community created a resource which was visible and whose programs were designed for the needs and spirit of that community.

> Seek the support of churches and medicine people. The hurts of the body can
> be healed with time, but the hurts of the spirit must be healed by the Great Spirit
> and we, who help in this process must also have His power and guidance.
> (Long, 1982, p. 458)

Ina Makah Family Program, United Indians of All Tribes Foundation – Seattle, Washington

United Indians of All Tribes Foundation is one of several major organizations in Seattle founded and run by American Indian and Alaskan Natives to serve the community. A major concern was the splitting of families in the urban area as a result of pressures and the loss of the sense of community support for these families. Government and private agencies designated to deal with the welfare of children and young parents tended to define family in terms inappropriately narrow for tribal people. Thus a family program, Ina Makah, was developed that incorporates a broad array of services including alcohol and drug counseling, home-based crisis intervention, family counseling, foster-care services and counseling for survivors of sexual abuse or domestic violence situations. Treatment includes traditional forms of healing, anger management, education, art therapy and other culturally relevant services. This program continues to operate successfully.

Closure and Resolution

Surprisingly little information has been presented on issues of closure of the therapeutic relationship and process. Spence (1982) states separation is part of growth. Even as we start therapy, we move toward separation and the next life phase.

The Indian community has long recognized the ritual and sacred aspect of therapy, not strictly in a religious sense, but as a process of healing through restoration. Ritual exemplifies important aspects to consider in providing therapy to American-Indian/Alaskan-Native Single Parents and in concluding work. According to Spence (1982), many American-Indian/Alaskan-Native rituals are based on the sacred number four. Therapy also has four phases: the initial meeting establishing the work to be done and how to do it; doing the work itself; and, finally, closure and resolution.

The ideal therapeutic ending occurs at a point mutually agreed upon by the therapist and American-Indian/Alaskan-Native, Single-Parent client. Closure and resolution is a stage in the therapeutic process which must be planned for. However, in reality closure may occur prematurely for either the therapist or Single Parent for various reasons. An abridged form of the closure process can often be used in unplanned situations.

Closure and resolution includes acknowledging the healing process is a part of the ongoing life journey; likened, in some instances, to the ceremonial home-coming of soldiers from war. For example, some tribes of the Southwest welcomed returning soldiers into the community with feasting and storytelling, hereby acknowledging their ordeal and reintegrating them into society and daily life. Although the therapeutic closure and resolution process may not include a formal ceremony, the components of mourning, acceptance, goal planning and celebration can be incorporated into therapy during the final sessions or afterward. Ideally, the client has experienced personal transformation and continues life in the community with new experiences, resources and internal awareness. It is important that the Single-Parent family has tools and skills to generalize healing experiences to daily life experiences. Helping the Single Parent adjust to problem solving without the therapist can take time and can include developing other support resources such as acknowledgment of extended family or community that may have participated in therapy and can continue as resources.

The end of therapy can be left more open-ended in the Indian community. Single-Parent clients may indeed return periodically as they identify a need (Clarke, 1987). Therefore, it may be more culturally appropriate to plan follow-up and a check-in later to see how the client is doing. A therapeutic goal is to align with clients and gain sanction for treatment by the individual, family and community; thus becoming a part of the community network – that fabric of complex multiple relationships and resources beyond the formal bounds of therapeutic sessions. In this sense, therapy is never complete.

Dtati (1993) described having completed the end of her professional work with a young Blackfoot woman and determined that to completely sever the relationship would be damaging to the client. She developed a mentoring relationship with this client. From this post-therapeutic experience, Dtati discovered both professionally and personally the client had taught her the value of relationship in therapy.

Closure and resolution is part of the therapeutic and life process of the American-Indian/Alaskan-Native, Single-Parent client and family. Ideally, this phase is acknowledged and planned for at the beginning of treatment. Using community resources and remembering the importance of interrelatedness in the Indian community is essential to success at this stage of therapy. Finally, it is important to know that the community may integrate the therapist into the community as a result of the therapeutic process.

Future Research

The subject of Single Parenting has received increasing attention in the past two decades as the divorce rate in the United States has risen and more people are choosing to create alternative family groups. Interestingly enough, the alternative family often seems more like the extended family of cultures such as American-Indian/Alaskan-Native, Asian-Pacific Islander or African-American.

Research into Single Parenting in the American-Indian/Alaskan-Native community should include a nationwide survey focusing on families. Such a project could be developed throughout the Indian Health Service and tribal, village or urban providers. Ideally, surveys should be conducted in a manner that protects respondents' privacy and addresses the following issues: who lives where and with whom; how the community or family share child care; child-rearing values and norms; tribal and geographical influences on families and meaningful ways in which the family and community can cope with financial stress, health problems, and related areas of concern. Baseline data would provide the keys to research projects investigating issues affecting the American-Indian/Alaskan-Native, Single-Parent family.

Who conducts the research and how it is conducted is a critical factor. Research must emphasize strengths and community resources as well as problems and needs. It is essential the research be conducted by individuals in the community itself so it is culturally sensitive and does not pry inappropriately into people's lives and impose standards and judgments from an outsider's perspective.

Unpublished materials and program reports from the many fine, innovative programs in the United States and Canada are good sources of data. These programs describe treatment incorporating American-Indian/Alaskan-Native values, spirituality and cultural practices. However, such reports are few. Although some staff active in these programs have published information about their work, many talented practitioners are so busy doing the work that useful data is not shared with the public.

Research might be incorporated into effective programs to provide quantitative data about treatment effects using specific outcome measures such as increased economic opportunities, connections to and use of community resources, school dropout rates, alcohol or substance use – to suggest a few.

Finally, clinically-oriented research can promote American-Indian/Alaskan-Native communities by highlighting existing strengths and building upon them to solve other community problems. Effective research and resulting therapeutic innovations can be used to influence education and attitudes, which in turn can bolster cultural and community pride.

Summary

The American-Indian/Alaskan-Native community is vast and diverse. The federally-recognized tribes represent over 500 distinctive cultures and political entities. It is essential to acknowledge this unique multiplicity of cultures and voices.

It is essential to know the tribal and family values of American-Indian/ Alaskan Native, Single Parents and put them into the context of the community, setting and individual expression. Critical values to consider include: (a) connection with the earth and all living things; (b) children are a gift, the responsibility of which belongs to the entire community; (c) elders are older, wiser and the teachers for everyone else; and (d) grandparents have an honored place in the community.

Single Parents in the American-Indian/Alaskan-Native community are less likely to be alone without potential resources for housing, food and child care if they remain connected to the community and are emotionally capable of accepting resources. American-Indian/Alaskan-Native communities often combine both strict structure and freedom through which individuals develop their spiritual potential. Each person is free to explore options which are right for her or him. Decisions may be based on consideration of self, family and community as a whole.

Various difficulties particular to the American-Indian/Alaskan-Native community can complicate life and affect Single Parenting. This includes the historic legacy of surviving as a collection of nations living within a larger, multiethnic nation with conflicting values, norms and lifestyles. This factor has affected economics, spiritual and religious practice, livelihood, self-esteem, cultural identity and health among Indian peoples. The birth rate to American-Indian/Alaskan-Native Single Parents is high, but personal income remains one of the lowest in the nation. The rate of accidental and poverty-related deaths remains the highest of any ethnic group in the nation. Violence, alcoholism and suicide remain disproportionately high.

Helping professionals traditionally have used the medical model in treatment, which focuses on the individual to the exclusion of the context in which the American-Indian/Alaskan-Native, Single-Parent client lives. More attention needs to be paid to individuals as part of extended family units. Both environmentally and culturally, the move is to consider interdependence among Indian clients as the cornerstones of health.

Knowing about one tribal culture is not sufficient, nor is it appropriate to assume that all American-Indian/Alaskan-Native clients will know about their culture or embrace it in an equal and like manner. Therapists need to have self-knowledge and remain open to learning from the client in order to define treatment focus from that perspective. It is wise to find or create treatment approaches which decrease barriers of place and treatment access to respect the role of the person within the tribe as well as the responsibility of the helping professional to the community, tribe and individual.

Traditional American-Indian and Alaskan-Native, Single Parents who live according to their tribal and cultural beliefs view wellness as the balance of physical, mental, emotional, social, cultural and spiritual energies affecting the entire system: individual, family, community. The community is best served by efforts supporting interconnectedness and a sharing attitude – one of giving back. Helping techniques which use this approach have more potential for success than other methods.

The course of therapy, the change process and multiple relationships in a small community need to be considered and treated in a manner consistent with tribal values by focusing on the cyclical and ritual aspects of healing and therapy as the primary focus of the therapeutic relationship. The relatedness and relationship of the therapist (helper) and client(s) forms the basis for the work. Issues of confidentiality and assessment must be considered in a manner acceptable and appropriate to the individual and community.

Continuing to learn from each individual and situation, consulting with American-Indian and Alaskan-Native community members, studying traditional stories and attending public community events are excellent way to learn about Indian communities. Use the information presented here as a guide for continued discovery and self-examination.

If this chapter has helped one individual or professional to ask new questions, talk to more people, and view a Single-Parent client's complaints with new compassion then we have achieved our goals. Good luck on your journey. To paraphrase a Navajo perspective, may you discover the beauty which surrounds and guides you in all things.

The authors thank the following people who read and provided insightful commentary to us: Patricia Alexander, Ojibway; Janice H. Anderson; Karl Anquoe, Kiowa/Comanche/Creek; Robert Bergman; Patty Boyd; Jo Ann Chapola; Roger Fernandes, Lower Elwha S'klallam; Anna Latimer, Sechelt; Josephine Marcellay, Colville; Jane Middleton-Moz, Anishanabe; Howard Morishige; J. Higgins-Rosebrook, Cherokee; Sandy Tomlin and Joseph Trimble, Lakota. Our thanks to Bob Charlo, Kalispel, for his photographs, as well as to the Seattle Indian Health Board for the use of their library and Kristan Geissel for technical assistance.

Bibliography

Anderson, L.L. (1985). *Indigenous healing practices in Western Washington: Cultural Traditionalism as it influences current methodology, utilization, perceived effectiveness, and cultural significance.* Masters Thesis, Bellingham, WA: Western Washington University.

Anderson, L. & Kaufman, J. (1987). "Seattle Indian Health Board's Culturally Oriented Mental Health Program". In *Multi-Ethnic Mental Health Services: Six Demonstration Programs in Washington State* (pp. 191-226). Ethnic Mental Health Programs Coalition, Seattle, WA.

Arredondo-Down, P.M. & Gonsalves, J. (1980). Preparing culturally effective counselors. *The Personnel and Guidance Journal, 58,* 657-61.

Attneave, C. (1974). Medicine Men and Psychiatrists in the Indian Health Service. *Psychiatric Annals, Nov.,* Vol. 4, No. 11, 49-55.

Attneave, C.L. (1977). The wasted strength of American Indian/Alaskan Native Families. In S. Unger (Ed.), *The Destruction of American Indian Families,* pp. 29-33. New York, NY: Association on American Indian/Alaskan Native Affairs.

Attneave, C.L. & Speck, R.V. (1974). Social network intervention in time and space. In A. Jacobs & W.W. Spradlin (Eds.) *The Group as the Agent of Change.* (pp. 166-90) Morgantown, WV: Aldine.

Banyaca, T. (1982). Traditional Medicine II. In Putnam, J. (Ed.) *Indian and Alaska Native Mental Health Seminars* (Vol. I, pp. 15-31). Seattle, WA: Seattle Indian Health Board.

Bennett, S., & Bigfoot-Sipes, D. (1991). American Indian/Alaskan Native and White college students' preferences for counselor characteristics. *Journal of Counseling Psychology, 38,* 440-5.

Bergman, R.L. (1967, August 10). *Boarding schools and the psychological problems of Indian children.* Presented to the American Indian/Alaskan Native Task Force of the American Academy of Pediatrics. Summer. Presented in Washington, DC.

Bigfoot-Sipes, D.; Dauphinais, P.; LaFromboise, T. & Bennett, S. (1992). American Indian/Alaskan Native secondary school students' preferences for counselors. *Journal of Multicultural Counseling and Development, 20,* 113-22.

Burton, L. (1980). *Counseling Native American high school and college students.* Paper presented at the Annual Conference on Ethnic and Minority Studies, LaCrosse, WI.

Clarke, J. (1987). Cultural congruence in mental health conceptual issues. In *Multi Ethnic Mental Health Services: Six Demonstration Programs in Washington State.* Ethnic Mental Health Programs Coalition. 18-58.

Cross, T.L. (1986). Drawing on cultural tradition in Indian Child Welfare practice. *Social Casework, 67,* 283-9.

D'Angelo, A. (1996). American Indian/Alaskan Native and Alaska Natives: Defining where they reside. *The IHS Provider, March, 21* (3), 36-42.

Dauphinais, P.; Dauphinais, L. & Rowe, W. (1981). Effects of race and communication style on Indian perception of counselor effectiveness. *Counselor Education and Supervision, 21*(1), 72-80.

Dawis, R.V. (1977). A paradigm and model for the cross cultural study of counseling. *The Personnel and Guidance Journal, 55,* 463-6.

Dtati, H.B. (1993). Issues in art therapy with the culturally displaced American Indian/Alaskan Native youth. *The Arts in Psychotherapy, 20,* 143-51).

Evans, J. (1982). Indian family. In J. Putnam (Ed.) *Indian and Alaska Native mental health seminars (vol 1).* Seattle, WA: Seattle Indian Health Board.

Fanshel, D. (1972). *Far from the Reservation: The transracial adoption of American Indian/Alaskan Native children.* Metuchen, NJ: Scarecrow Press.

Givan, J.M. (1993). *American Indian/Alaskan Native/Alaskan Native women with HIV Infection.* Masters Thesis, School of Nursing, University of Washington.

Henderson, R. & Brody, G. & Lane, T.S. & Parra, E. (1982). Effects of ethnicity and child's age on maternal judgments of children's transgressions against persons and property. *The Journal of Genetic Psychology, 140,* 253-263.

Hollis, F. (1972). *Casework: A Psychosocial Therapy.* New York, NY: Random House.

Hsu, J.S. J. & Williams, S.D. (1991). Injury prevention awareness in an urban native population. *American Journal of Public Health, 81*(11), 1466-8.

Johnson, M. & Lashley, K. (1989). Influence of Native Americans' cultural commitment on preferences for counselor ethnicity and expectations about counseling. *Journal of Multicultural Counseling and Development, 17,* 115-22.

Kickingbird, L. & Kickingbird, K. (1977). *Indians and the U.S. Government Institute for the Development of Indian Law:* Washington, DC: Institute for the Development of Indian Law.

LaFromboise, T. (1988). *Cultural and cognitive considerations in coping of American Indian/Alaskan Native women in higher education.* Unpublished manuscript. Stanford, CA: Stanford Univ. School of Education.

LaFromboise, T.; Dauphinais, P. & Rowe, W. (1980). Indian students' perception of positive helper attributes. *Journal of American Indian Education, 19,* 11-16.

LaFromboise, T.; Trimble, J. & Mohart, G. (1990). Counseling intervention and American Indian/Alaskan Native tradition: An integrative approach. *Counseling Psychologist, 18,* 628-54.

Lane Sr., P. (1982). Healing – A Native Perspective. In Putnam, J. (ed) *Indian and Alaska Native Mental Health Seminars, Vol. I,* pp. 47-82, Seattle, WA: Seattle Indian Health Board.

Lazarus, P.J. (1982). Counseling the Native American child: A question of values. *Elementary School Guidance and Counseling, 17* (2), 83-8.

Lia-Hoagberg, B.; Rode, P.l.; Skovholt, C.J.; Oberg, C.N.; Berg, C.; Mullett, S. & Choi, T. (1990). Barriers and motivators to prenatal care among low income women. *Social Science Medicine, 4,* 487-95.

Lomawaima, K.T. (1994). *They Called It Prairie Light: The Story of Chilocco Indian School.* University of Nebraska Press: NE.

Long, Lois. (1982). Women's Shelter. In Putnam, J. (Ed.) *Indian and Alaska Native Mental Health Seminars, Vol. I.* Seattle, WA: Seattle Indian Health Board.

Lonner, W.J. (1979). Issues in cross cultural psychology. In Marsella, A.; Tharp, R. & Cibrowski, T. (Eds.) *Perspectives in cross-cultural psychology.* pp. 17-44. New York: Academic Press.

Mankiller, W. & Wallis, M. (1993). *Mankiller: A Chief and Her People.* New York, NY: St. Martin's Press.

Mannes, M. (1990). *Family Preservation and Indian Child Welfare.* Albuquerque, NM: American Indian/Alaskan Native Law Center.

Matheson, L. (1996). The politics of the Indian Child Welfare Act. *Social Work, March, 41* (2), 232-5.

McCloud, J. (1982). Traditional Medicine I. In Putnam, J. (Ed.) *Indian and Alaska Native Mental Health Seminars, Vol. I,* 4-14. Seattle, WA: Seattle Indian Health Board.

Metcalf, A. (1978). *A Model for Treatment in a Native American Family Service Center.* Oakland, CA: Urban Indian Child Resource Center

Metcalf, A. (1976). From schoolgirl to mother: The effects of education on Navajo women. *Social Problems, 23* (5), 535-44.

Moncher, M.S.; Holden, G.W. & Trimble, J.E. (1990). Substance abuse among Native-American youth. *Journal of Consulting and Clinical Psychology, 58* (4), 408-15.

Morrisette, P.J. (1994). The holocaust of first nation people: Residual effects on parenting and treatment implications. *Contemporary Family Therapy, 16* (5), 381-97.

Napholz, L. (1995). Mental Health and American Indian/Alaskan Native Women's Multiple Roles. *American Indian/Alaskan Native and Alaska Native Mental Health Research, 6* (2), 57-75.

Napoleon, H. (1991). *Yumyaraq: The way of the human being.* Fairbanks, AK: Alaska Native Knowledge Network, University of Alaska.

Price, J.A. (1981). North American Indian/Alaskan Native Families. In Mindel, C. & Haverstein, R. W. *Ethnic Families in America.* (pp. 248-70). North Holland, NY: Elsevier.

Red Horse, J. & Red Horse, Y. (1982). Counseling in the Indian Family. In Putnam, J. (Ed.) *Indian and Alaska Native Mental Health Seminars* (Vol. I, pp. 377-96). Seattle, WA: Seattle Indian Health Board.

Red Horse, Y.; Gonzales-Santin, E.; Beane, J. & Tolson-Gonzales, P. (1981). *Traditional and Non-traditional community mental health services with American Indian/Alaskan Natives.* Phoenix, AZ: American Indian/Alaskan Native Projects for Community Development, Training and Research School of Social Work, Arizona State University.

Richardson, E.H. (1981). Cultural and historical perspectives in counseling American Indian/Alaskan Natives. *Social Casework, 62,* 67-72.

Shelledy, J. & Nelson, J. (1981). The application of structural family therapy with an American Indian/Alaskan Native Family. In Y. Red Horse, E. Gonzales-Santin, S. Beane, & P. Tolson-Gonzales (Eds.) *Traditional and Non-traditional Community Mental Health Services with American Indian/Alaskan Natives.* Phoenix, AZ: School of Social Work, Arizona State University, 4-29.

Smith, A. (1982). Cultural practice in an alcoholism treatment program. In J. Putnam (Ed.) *Indian and Alaska Native Mental Health Seminars* (Vol. I, pp. 139-56). Seattle, WA: Seattle Indian Health Board.

Sorkin, A. (1978). *The urban American Indian.* Lexington, MA: Lexington Books.

Spang, A. (1965). Counseling the Indian. *Journal of American Indian Education, 5* (1), 10-15.

Spence, J. (1982). Self Awareness and Communication. In J. Putnam (Ed.) *Indian and Alaska Native Mental Health Seminars* (Vol. I, 513-48). Seattle, WA: Seattle Indian Health Board.

Stone, S. (1982). Cultural Program for Alcoholism. Putnam, J. (Ed.) *Indian and Alaska Native Mental Health Seminars* (Vol. 1, pp. 411-32). Seattle, WA: Seattle Indian Health Board.

Sue, D.W. (1978). World views and counseling. *The Personnel and Guidance Journal, 56,* 458-62.

Sue, D.W. & Sue, D. (1990). *Counseling the Culturally Different.* New York, NY: Wiley Press.

Sundberg, N.D. (1981). Research and research hypotheses about effectiveness in intercultural counseling. In P. Pedersen, J. Draguns, W. Lonner, & J. Trimble (Eds.) *Counseling Across Cultures.* (pp. 304-42). The University of Hawaii Press for the East-West Center: Hawaii.

Trimble, J.E.; Fleming, C.M.; Beavais, F. & Jumper-Thurman, P. (1995). Essential cultural and social strategies for counseling Native American Indians. In P. Pedersen, J. Draguns, W. Lonner & J. Trimble (Eds.), *Counseling across cultures (4th ed.)* (pp. 177-209). Thousand Oaks, CA: Sage.

U.S. Department of Health and Human Services. (1995). Health United States 1994. DHHS Pub. No. (PHS) 95-1232. U.S. Govt. Printing Office. Hyattsville, MD. May 1995.

Whittaker, C. (1975, March 15). *Family Therapy,* Paper presented at the Conference on Family Therapy, Spokane, WA.

Youngman, G. & Sadongei, M. (1974). Counseling the American Indian/Alaskan Native child. *Elementary School Guidance and Counseling, 8,* 273-277.

Counseling Asian-Pacific American Single-Parent Families

Viqui E. Claravall, MSW, ACSW

T HE SINGLE-PARENT FAMILY is not a new phenomenon in the Asian-Pacific culture, despite the fact that little has been written on the subject. In the literature which has examined this phenomenon, less attention has been focused on the positive characteristics of Asian-Pacific American, Single-Parent families than on family dysfunction or pathology. Although some stress – related to socioeconomic status, child-rearing responsibilities, and lack of support – can be involved in maintaining a Single-Parent family, Single Parenting itself is not found to cause problems in either the development of children or family functioning.

Reportedly more than 10% of Chinese-American, Japanese-American, Korean-American, Filipino-American and Vietnamese families in the United States are headed by Single Mothers (Slaughter-Defoe, Nakagawa, Takanishi, & Johnson, 1990). Variety in family structure among Asian-Pacific American families needs to be explored. With the rise of industrialization, socioeconomic and technological forces have precipitated change in Asian-Pacific family structure. Divorce, work pattern and immigration affect family configuration. Work patterns sometimes require a father to live partly in Asia, where his business is located, and partly in the United States, where the family resides. In addition, some family members may not have immigrated to the United States.

This chapter applies an ecosystemic approach within a conceptual framework for therapy with Asian-Pacific American, Single-Parent families. Discussion focuses on understanding traditional Asian-Pacific family structure, acculturation, biculturalism, help seeking behavior and practice guidelines and treatment approaches.

Traditional Asian-Pacific Family Structure

To grasp a conceptual framework for understanding Asian-Pacific American, Single-Parent families, it is important to understand traditional Asian-Pacific American family structure. This is not to suggest all Asian-Pacific American families follow a traditional structure, nor does it suggest such a structure should serve as a model of how Asian-Pacific American families should function. Rather, such an examination helps us to understand the value differences among Asian Americans and the various types of Asian-Pacific American families along a continuum based on rate of acculturation into American society – traditional, through transitional and bicultural, to westernized.

Asian-Pacific Americans comprise many diverse groups: Chinese, Japanese, Koreans, Filipinos, Samoans, Guamanians, Hawaiians and other Pacific Islanders. Other groups include recent immigrants and refugees from Vietnam, Thailand, Cambodia, Laos and Indonesia; immigrants from India, Pakistan and Ceylon; and children of mixed marriages in which one parent is Asian. Obvious language, historical, social, cultural and economic differences exist. Generational status (new immigrants versus third and fourth generation) should not be overlooked, as well as a group's rate of acculturation into American society. Although Asian-Pacific Americans share some values and norms, the basic foundation of their respective cultures differs and important cultural distinctions influenced by religions – Confucian and Buddhist as well as Judeo-Christian traditions – are evident.

Culture and Family Traditions

The concept of family in the traditional Asian framework is not time-limited as it is in the western concept of the nuclear family. The Asian concept of family extends both backward and forward; the individual is seen as the product of all the generations of his or her family from the beginning of time. Within this context, personal actions reflect not only on the individual and nuclear and extended families but also on all the preceding and future generations of the family. This concept is reinforced by rituals and customs such as ancestor worship and family record books which trace families over many centuries (Shon & Ja, 1982). One must obey the wishes of parents long since passed, perceiving one's existence and identity as inseparably linked to historical past.

The Asian-Pacific family system does not stress the individuals independence and autonomy; rather, the individual is superseded by the family. In contrast with the Anglo-American concept of the individual as the fundamental unit, the family is the fundamental unit for the Asian-Pacific culture. All individual needs and desires are subordinated to family health and security needs. Each family exists within a larger clan, and each clan is tied to a community and, ultimately, the larger society.

The organizing principle of this notion of family is *filial piety* – a concept that any clinician working with Asian-Pacific clients needs to understand. Broadly defined, it means honor, reverence, obedience, loyalty and love owed to those who are hierarchically above the individual (Chao, 1992). For example, this means honoring or obeying the wishes of ancestors or parents who have long since passed, to ones family lineage. In this context, systems of authority, reciprocity, duty and interdependence arise. *Filial piety* is at the root of all Asian-Pacific values such as shame, honor, respect and loss of face. It establishes the parameters for the hierarchical structure of family, community and society: the guidelines for specific family relationships, patterns of communication and negotiations with the outside world – harmonious existence in society. The goal of harmony in interpersonal relationships is accomplished through tact, delicacy and politeness of children toward parents, adult children toward parents, younger siblings toward older siblings, students toward teacher, employees toward supervisors, patients toward doctors and clients toward providers (sometimes at the cost of honesty and forthrightness). Such values are contrary to Anglo-American conception of egalitarianism and individualism.

The Asian-Pacific system is "duty based" whereas the Anglo-American system is "rights based". In the traditional Asian-Pacific framework, the family adheres to strong family ties perpetuated by hierarchical roles established for all members and imposed by a patriarchal or equally authoritative matriarchal system. Rules of behavior and conduct are formalized. Most Asian-Pacific languages include honorific titles connoting position, status and authority within a family. Siblings assume a strong pecking order within a family. For example, younger siblings show respect for older siblings by addressing them with titles as "older brother" or "second older sister" rather than by the sibling's name. Older siblings are expected to serve as role models for younger siblings (Huang, 1981). The individual's adherence and response to this code of conduct reflects on the family and kinship network to which he or she belongs.

The "clan" is responsible for maintaining the status of the family name or lineage. Relationships among husband, wife and in-laws are strictly prescribed, as are relationships between children and parents. To enter therapy and talk about or complain about other family members or even one's teacher or supervisor puts the person perilously close to violating *filial piety*. From this perspective, it is easy to understand why social, health or mental health services are underutilized among Asian-Pacific Americans; which resonates with the cultural stereotype of Asian-Pacific Americans as the "model minority". In fact, this stereotype is a disservice to Asian-Pacific Americans and may be one of the reasons legislatures tend not to fund specialized services to this group.

Family Roles

Traditional ethics emphasize roles within the family and behaviors associated with each role. Affective ties for children are not focused solely on parents but are spread over a range of adult figures. Obligations, responsibilities and privileges of each role are clearly delineated according to a vertical, hierarchical role structure in which the father is the undisputed head. His authority is unchallenged and he is the recipient of total respect and loyalty from all family members. In return, he assumes complete responsibility for the family's social status and economic well-being.

Marital Relationship

In traditional Asian-Pacific families, the dominant relationship is more likely an inter-generational dyad than a husband-wife dyad. A woman is usually dominated by the authority of her father, husband, son and mother-in law. Mothers are generally discouraged from taking on work outside the family (Shon & Ja, 1982). The husband assumes the instrumental role as provider, protector and decision maker. The wife assumes the expressive role of homemaker. It is considered a sign of maturity not to express affection overtly, especially not in front of children and elders. Traditionally, wives are publicly subordinate to their husbands but privately are not so demure. When things go wrong in a marriage, mediators and confidants within the extended family may intervene. Whereas divorce is not a common practice, emotional divorce is not uncommon. In such cases, the mother is likely to transfer her love to the children. The father will compensate by working compulsively and spending his leisure time with other men.

Parent-Child Relationship

The relationship between parents and children is considered more important than the marital relationship. The traditional role of the father is to provide discipline and control. The primary role of the mother is to serve the father and raise the children. She is responsible for the emotional nurturance and well-being of the family. The children feel emotionally closer to their mother than to their father. She is accorded respect from her children, although she is less removed and distant than the father. She will often intercede with the father on behalf of the children. Traditionally, children are expected to care for their parents in old age and maintain connections with them. A daughter does not move out until she is married. A son is expected to live in the parental household with his bride as long as he needs to. Asian-Pacific parents may never experience the "empty-nest".

Sibling Relationship and Gender Roles

Bonding among siblings is very strong in traditional Asian-Pacific families. Siblings play important roles for one another throughout life. Cooperation, sharing, and even sacrifice, for other siblings are stressed. However, quarrels and fights among siblings are common.

Gender and birth position are associated with duties and privileges. In most traditional Asian-Pacific cultures, particularly those dominated by Confucianistic principles, family lineage is passed through the male. Females are absorbed into the families of their husbands. Male offspring are valued more than female and the role expectations of each gender are quite distinct. The first-born son, the most valued child, receives preferential treatment as well as more familial responsibilities. He is expected to be the role model for his siblings as well as to have authority over them. Younger siblings are expected to follow the guidance of the oldest son not only while they are children, but throughout their adult lives.

The prescriptive roles for daughters are less rewarding. The oldest daughter is seen primarily as the caretaker of the household and the nurturant parent for the younger siblings in the absence of the mother. Females often do not take on a position of authority until they assume the role of mother-in-law. With the recent loosening of traditional attitudes towards women throughout Asia and the Pacific Islands, roles vacated by the oldest son are more frequently being filled by a daughter. The youngest daughter is frequently the most acculturated if her family has immigrated to the United States. Generally, her primary sources of emotional support are her oldest brother, grandparents and friends (Lee, 1982).

Rigid family roles were predominant in imperial, feudal China. As China has modernized, these roles have altered radically. Similarly, among acculturated Chinese families in the United States such rigidly defined roles have been altered dramatically. For example, females are not entirely relegated to subservient roles. Fathers are often the figurative heads of families, especially when dealing with the public, although the mother may in fact be the driving force in the family and the decision maker behind the scenes. First sons continue to be highly valued, but the differences between the sexes with regard to duties and privileges are not so glaring. Family authority in the Philippines, which differs from that in other Asian cultures, is bilateral; parents share equally in decisions and responsibilities.

The extended family, rather than the nuclear family, is the primary family unit in Asia and the Pacific Islands. This includes aunts, uncles, cousins, grandparents and great grandparents. Although the process of migration disrupted these family relationships, many Asian-Pacific Americans have attempted

73

to reconstruct this kinship network. For some, the extended family is clearly identified as an important source of social, and sometimes financial, support. For some highly westernized families, however, the extended family may be experienced as a burden and a restriction to autonomy.

Patterns of Communication

Asian-Pacific cultures view open and free communication of thoughts and feelings differently from westerners. Congruent with a rigid system of role relationships, rules of communication are governed by the attributes of the parties involved which includes age, gender, education, occupation, social status, family background, marital status and parenthood. These specific characteristics influence behavior such as who initiates conversation and who will be most accommodating. Within families, gender and age usually govern the degree of open expression allowed, the initiator of conversation, the structure of the language used and the topics to be addressed.

Communication within the traditional family is unidirectional, flowing from parent to child and often indirect. Confrontation is eschewed. A large communication gap often exists between the father and the youngest child (Lee, 1982). Independent behavior or expression of emotions which might disrupt familial harmony are discouraged (Sue 1989) and suppression of *undesirable* thoughts or emotions is highly valued. These rules of communication contrast markedly with American values of expression and the tendency to "speak your mind" or "let it all hang out" (Shon & Ja, 1982).

Obligation, Shame, and "Face"

In contrast with the western concept of contractual obligation and reciprocity, the unspoken and obligatory reciprocity in interactions is of paramount importance in Asian-Pacific cultures and continues to be evident among Asian-Pacific Americans in United States. Obligations are determined by one's role (e.g., the obligation of the child to the parent or *filial piety*) or incurred through acts of kindness or helpfulness. Behavior is frequently dictated by the individual's sense of obligation or desire to avoid obligation. Obligation is seen not only as indebtedness but also as an opportunity to display affection and heartfelt gratitude.

Shame and loss of face similarly guide behavior and serve as powerful motivating forces to conform to societal or familial expectations (Shon & Ja, 1982). Even truthfulness and honesty in the abstract are secondary to "saving face" for oneself and others. Because emphasis is placed on maintaining familial honor, bringing shame on one's family is avoided at all costs. Loss of face involves exposure of one's action as well as withdrawal of support and the suspension of obligatory relationship. Withdrawal of support may shake the individual's basic trust. Therefore, the well-being of the family is placed above individual desires and is held as a virtue. For example, it is not unusual to hear about immigrant Asian-Pacific Americans whose parents determined their major in college. Because the value of interdependence is so important, the fear of losing face can be a powerful motivating force for conforming to family and societal expectations. Given that interdependence is the foundation of Asian-Pacific culture, everything an individual does is viewed as a reflection on the family as a whole.

Acculturation as a Stressor

The process of acculturation is stressful for many Asian-Pacific immigrants and refugees. Refugee status involves involuntary separations, disenfranchisement and exposure to trauma both in the home country and in the search for sanctuary, which have an effects on the family system. Moreover, still grieving the losses associated with migration, family members must adapt to their new culture by finding a new job, locating housing, dealing with the culture shock in a multiracial racist society and frequently needing to learn a new language. The family unit itself may need to be reconstructed, and each family member may experience cultural separation issues, including loss of supportive coping mechanisms such as friends, peers and familiar recreational or vocational opportunities.

Psychologically, the family attempts to incorporate features of its new environment into familiar, controllable patterns; allowing for confidence and security. New patterns of social and intrafamilial interaction emerge. Lack of extended family and changes in family composition create a new internal family organization; which in some instances might include a Single Mother – widow, separated, or divorced.

Environmental concerns and cultural and value differences between Asian-Pacific Americans and mainstream Americans can also be stressful for families. While trying to recover from internal and external stresses, family members experience the additional stress of acculturation. Family members generally experience acculturation at different rates, which leads to transitional and inter-generational conflicts. For example, in a Single-Parent Vietnamese family, the grandparents may stay at home with grandchildren while the daughter learns the new language, values and culture. The adolescent granddaughter/son may speak better English and thus become the "cultural broker" or intermediary between their parents/grandparents and American society, which serves to weaken the authority of the parents and aggravates intergenerational conflicts (Lee, 1982).

Yamamoto (1978) described the acculturation issues for three generations of Japanese-Americans. Instead of fulfilling cultural expectations around care and protection of their families, an increasing number of the *issei* (the first-generation family members) live separately from their adult offspring and thus feel excluded. *Nisei* (the second-generation family members) tend to achieve high educational and occupational levels. *Sansei* (the third-generation) are generally more Americanized and therefore face the issues and problems faced by most young Americans.

McGoldrick (1982) presented an excellent insight regarding developmental changes which take place as a result of migration and its effects on different stages of the family life cycle. The family with a young-adult, Single Mother and young children may be strengthened by having each other but may also be vulnerable to a reversal in the parent-child hierarchy. Families who migrate when their children are adolescent may have difficulty dealing with the Americanization of the children and the fact they have little time together as a unit before the children move out on their own. In addition, parents may experience severe stress in not being able to fulfill their obligations to their parents as they become ill or dependent or die in their country of origin. Thus, the family must struggle with multiple transitions as well as generational conflict.

Families in Transition

Generally, in the immigration process, the Asian-Pacific family undergoes inter-related levels of cultural transitions. Repeated contact with new cultural values during a prolonged period changes the family's outlook on issues such as economic security, education, gender roles, child rearing and philosophy of life. The values, norms and role behaviors learned in the home country become a source of stress when the family comes into contact with the new culture. For example, many Southeast Asian families have faced stressful changes induced by forced migration as the result of war, which in many cases has resulted in families facing abrupt adjustment to urbanization and modernization. For Single-Parent families who migrate, the transition from an extended family to a nuclear unit introduces another dimension as they move from settings with a stability of values and ideas based on traditions, generational continuity and authority to the American society, where the family is based on the centrality of the marital dyad and the cultural codes and norms of the Western industrial world.

Adaptive cultural transition is linked to the environmental context in which the acculturation process occurs. Shon and Ja (1982) identified two interrelated levels of adaptive cultural transition: (a) material transition; whereby economic security, education and language present barriers the family must overcome and (b) cognitive, structural and affective transition; in which the family psychologically attempts to incorporate various features of their new environment and culture (making it familiar, controllable and supportive; which allows for increased confidence and security). Adaptation to the new culture is exacerbated by the interplay between clinging to versus rejecting of values and cultural norms of the context of origin and the new context.

The Single-Parent Family

Various factors account for the precipitous rise in Single-Parent, Asian-Pacific families, including the family's pre-immigration background and their rate of acculturation. Of those Single-Parent families who come to the United States as refugees or immigrants, many parents are mothers who are widowed or custodial female relatives. Acculturation may breakdown the traditional family structure and undermine patriarchal authority leading to the increase in Single Parenthood stemming from separation, divorce or unmarried teenaged mothers. The most dramatic increase of Single-Parent families among Asian-Pacific cultures has occurred among persons with little education, low socioeconomic status and lower status occupations.

The Single-Parent family struggles to blend two contradictory sets of rules: adherence to traditional methods of problem solving, such as reliance on hierarchical authority, extended family network and male domination conflicts with western values and sometimes current circumstance. This can precipitate nonproductive, unsupportive family relationships.

For Asian-Pacific, Single-Parent families, this conflict plays itself out across the generations and, thus, has serious implications for family functioning and therapy. One of the means for immigrant families to establish economic security is by having all adult members, including extended family members, live together and find employment upon arrival in the United States. Single-Parent mothers, who may not have worked in their country of origin, are forced to seek working-class jobs upon arrival in the United States. Without basic English-language skills, these women are often restricted to working in restaurants, garment sweatshops or janitorial positions. These women have little potential for vocational mobility or advancement and are often trapped working jobs that pay below minimum wage and have few or no benefits. In terms of long-term security, their most precious asset is their children's ability to do well in school and move into professional careers.

Overcoming Loss

The Asian-Pacific, Single-Parent family in the United States lacks the nurturance and support of an extended family network which may have supported the family in Asia through loss of a spouse due to separation, divorce or death. A new culture compounds the loss of the extended family network and mutual interdependence. Cognitive reactions to such loss include shock, tension, stress, grief, somatization, anger, depression, acceptance and mobilization of family resources and energy (Shon & Ja, 1982). The severity and duration of cognitive and emotional upheaval resulting from the loss of a spouse and father depends on the factors surrounding the loss – that is, whether the loss resulted from separation, death due to war, illness or infidelity; the degree of social disapproval experienced and the children's reaction to the situation. Lingering attachment to a spouse can inhibit the adjustment to singlehood and the new culture.

Restructuring the Household

Traditionally, interdependence, authority, reciprocity, and duty rooted in *filial piety* help maintain the integrity of the extended family. Even when families have internal hostilities, children's emotional bonds with their aunts, uncles, cousins and grandparents are not necessarily severed. Emotional support from the extended family, as well as shared task of parenting, can ease the psychosocial adjustment for Single Parents and their children. The extent of support of the extended family depends on each generation's rate of acculturation – family members strong adherence to *filial piety* is likely to facilitate psychosocial adjustment among the family members after the loss of a parent.

Among new Single-Parent families, parents, children, relatives and friends take on new roles. Women may lack experience at managing finances, driving and performing other traditionally male roles. For Single Mothers entering the work force, child care may become a problem for the first time. Single Fathers may be ill-prepared for household and child-rearing tasks. Children assume increased responsibility. In addition to cleaning and cooking, older children, as occurs in traditional families, may babysit younger siblings. After divorce or death of a parent, a child may take a more parental role by becoming a helper and confidant to the parent. Children, even those under ten years, may be responsible for their own care for long periods of time (DeVaney, 1988).

The parenting task, particularly at a time when the Single Parent is financially and emotionally stressed, may demand more energy than the Single Parent has available. The Single Parent, as a result of traditional gender roles in parenting, may be inconsistent in the use of parenting styles: nurturing one moment and stern and authoritarian the next. Relations between the child and parent may weaken and the child may engage in behaviors unacceptable to the parent. As a result of the acculturation process and role shift, the child may rebel and act out for having to miss out on important aspects of childhood in their new environment.

Sociocultural Issues in Assessment and Treatment

The assessment approach presented here is supported by an ecological framework. It focuses on interconnected systems – family, institutions, culture and community – which interact dynamically with the individual. Ecological transitions occur when an individual's position in these systems is altered by a change in role or setting. The transitions are a joint function of individual and environmental circumstance (Bronfenbrenner, 1979). This ecological perspective is especially relevant for analyzing the impact of poverty, immigration, discrimination and social isolation on the psychosocial development and adjustment of Asian-Pacific children and families. Mutual accommodation between the individual and the environment affects growth and change.

Asian-Pacific Families

Two issues are key to understanding Asian-Pacific families in general. First, many are immigrants experiencing the disruption which takes place in one's ecological field (materially and cognitively) as one relocates. Second, a large majority of immigrant families are poor. Poverty establishes parameters around one's life and conditions one's world view and value orientation, governing ones interactions. Among families in poverty the dynamics of discrimination based on race, ethnicity, politics, values and culture are underestimated and underaddressed in clinical settings (Inclan, 1990).

Culturally Relevant Knowledge, Attitudes, Techniques

To work successfully with Asian-Pacific, Single-Parent families, clinicians must have an accepting attitude and solid knowledge base of the culture. This must be grounded in culturally specific techniques and skills which can be used across the phases of treatment: joining, problem identification and problem-solving. It is important to have a general awareness and sensitivity to the following characteristics (Ho, 1990):

1. Historically, Asian-Pacific Americans have been dominated by racism and poverty.
2. Asian-Pacific cultures have been affected by the dominant external system causing value conflict for Asian-Pacific groups.
3. Bi-culturalism creates tensions and conflicts within individuals and families.
4. Racism and colonialism have resulted in the assignment of minority status with historical and contemporary forms of prejudice and discrimination.
5. Discrimination is often based on skin color, which leads many ethnic minority individuals to try to "pass" as White. Asians from mixed heritage may feel compelled to define themselves as White. This issue is complicated further when other family members identify with their Asian-Pacific heritage.

6. Language problems arise when Asian clients do not comprehend English well. An Asian client in therapy may need to use his or her native language to describe intimate, personal issues. When forced to use English to express these feelings, counseling can be ineffective.

7. Social acceptance is often difficult to achieve. Asians who achieve material goals may still be frequently reminded of the oppression that plagues Asian-Pacific persons.

8. Asian-Pacific families consider family and extended family members their primary source of support. They may fear and distrust therapists and helpers.

Multisystems Model

Using a multisystem model of family therapy within an ecological framework allows many levels of intervention. In working with Asian-Pacific, Single-Parent families, a therapist might work with an individual within the family, a subsystem (such as mother and children, or mother and extended family members) members of natural support network (e.g., community elders, church family) or various outside agencies such as schools, clinics and housing departments. This approach is empowering for both therapist and families because it widens the lens and enables them to look for problems and solutions at different levels of the ecosystem. This is important for Asian-Pacific families in particular because agencies have a tremendous power to intervene in their lives, especially in the lives of Single-Parent families.

Most families bring concrete problems to the therapist first. Addressing concrete issues early in the treatment process builds trust and credibility for the therapist. Offering concrete help facilitates the joining process, and empowers both the therapist and the family. The multisystem model provides the therapist with a conceptual road map of the family ecological niche and empowers the family to change its internal structure as well as its interaction with outside agencies which frequently intrude in their lives (Boyd-Franklin, 1990).

Asian-Pacific, Single-Parent families can be helped by professionals who assess and appreciate these families within a cultural context. The helping professional must use criteria that recognize the unique challenges facing the family. The therapist must be aware of, and view the family through the lens of, cultural strength – extended kinship networks, spirituality and religious orientation, survival skills and attitudes toward education and work.

Cultural Specific Techniques and Skills

Forming a therapeutic relationship with an Asian-Pacific family has aspects of cultural joining, forming a "cultural relationship" (Ho,1990). The engagement phase focuses on validating and affirming the family's cultural roots. The therapist must identify and respect the family's way of forming trusting relationships, especially help-seeking relationships. Two factors are essential to successful engagement with the Asian-Pacific families: the therapist's credibility and the development of a working relationship based on an active exchange.

Sue and Zane (1987), proposed therapists enter therapeutic situations with an "ascribed" credibility based on characteristic such as age, gender, marital status, ethnicity and position in the agency. To sustain the Asian-Pacific client in the treatment relationship, the therapist must attain a high "achieved" credibility, which arises out of effective therapeutic skills and culturally appropriate intervention. Although one can delineate the traits which contribute to ascribed credibility, it is not always possible to predict the direction of influence. For example, many agencies assume that an Asian-Pacific client would prefer an Asian-Pacific therapist. In some instances, this assumption is correct. One Vietnamese Single Mother, however, was deeply offended when assigned a Chinese therapist. This client harbored much hatred toward the Chinese as her husband died as a result of antagonism between these two ethnic groups in Vietnam. Thus for the client, the assignment of a Chinese therapist reflected the agency's insensitivity to her and confirmed her beliefs that they neither understood nor could help her.

Matching client and therapist ethnicity does not guarantee credibility for the therapist. Some Asian-Pacific clients are hesitant to interact with a therapist of their own ethnicity because of fear confidentiality in the community will be breached or are reluctant to confront painful reminders of the past. However, other Asian-Pacific clients find comfort in a shared culture and history with the therapist. Moreover, language obstacles are minimized.

The combination of a White therapist with an Asian-Pacific client has advantages and disadvantages. If the Asian-Pacific client ascribes higher status to the White therapist, she or he may be more cooperative with the treatment plan, believing that the therapist possesses the power or expertise to obtain the desired resources or to resolve the problem. On the other hand, a Vietnamese refugee might have ambivalent feelings toward a White therapist because of the role the White power structure played in escalating the war in Vietnam; abandoning the country, then begrudgingly providing assistance to refugees.

Active exchange of information is the second critical component of the helping relationship with Asian-Pacific clients. For many Asian-Pacific Americans, the efficacy of "talking" is not readily apparent. Rather, many Asian-Pacific clients expect some form of advice, advocacy, immediate symptom relief or change in the problematic situation. If none of these results occur the client may terminate the relationship prematurely. Most clients are familiar with the physician/patient relationship; which entails a brief encounter, a series of questions from the doctor, concrete answers from the patient and some symptom relief. Asian-Pacific clients frequently generalize from this relationship to their relationship with a mental health worker. When their expectations are not met, they become disillusioned with the process. To establish a working alliance with Asian-Pacific clients, therapists need to engage them in an active exchange whereby clients perceive giving and receiving on the part of both parties. Such reciprocal exchanges help clients realize tangible gains. Clients need to be willing to meet with the helper, self-disclose, remain receptive and offer some payment for services. Therapists must demonstrate a willingness to meet with and listen to the client, share personal credentials or qualifications, empathize with the clients' emotional pain or frustration and acknowledge the client's explanations for the problem. On a concrete, practical level; therapists should provide specific information about social services, resources and social support groups in the community (Huand & Ying, 1989).

Construing the working relationship as an active, reciprocal exchange helps counter the notion of the client as debtor. Most Asian-Pacific cultures discourage obligation and debt. The fear of being indebted to someone may drive Asian-Pacific clients away from a helping relationship. The active exchange promotes a sense of "partnership" in the helping process and transforms the client from a passive to an active participant who is attempting to regain control over her or his life situation.

In the intervention with Asian-Pacific, Single-Parent families, it is critically important to allow them to tell their story. Asian-Pacific youth, for example, rarely have the opportunity to express their thoughts and feelings, as family rules implicitly advocate "Don't talk about it". Community and cultural pressures to keep secrets and not incur shame similarly inhibit disclosure about family problems or stresses caused by the absence of a parent, relocation and emigration. For Southeast Asian, Single-Parent families, ventilation of their remarkable and horrifying stories of death and separation may be cathartic and essential to building trust (Huang, 1989).

A Case Example

A close friend advised May, a Filipino immigrant, to seek services at a family and youth services center. Her husband, half Filipino and half White, had divorced her less than two years earlier after 11 years of marriage. May had custody of their two children, 13 and 11 years of age. May's primary concern was her 13-year-old son's rebellious behavior, poor school performance, and truancy. She was extremely distraught and tearful as she related her dilemma. She had high hopes for her children but felt unappreciated for all her sacrifices as the sole earner, working two jobs. May had developed strong reliance on her daughter, who seemed more mature and responsible than her son. The son was often envious of his sister and resented her for her alliance with May.

I arranged a family session in their home. Upon arrival, I was offered tea and cookies as refreshment. I politely allowed myself to be talked into it, which was the proper etiquette.

May introduced me to her children. In the next twenty to thirty minutes, the identified client was not mentioned. Instead, we engaged in ritualistic small talk, which allowed the family to get a sense of me and vice versa. The daughter asked to be excused because she was aware the reason for my visit was to address the mother-son problem. The son told his mother that he had to call his friend. May excused him but asked him to stay around so I could talk to him later.

During this initial joining phase, I realized that my ascribed credibility was appreciated but somewhat suspect. Because I have lived in the United States a long time, May felt I might not understand her situation. However, she believed I would be able to relate to her children. My native language proficiency was helpful to her. Because I don't have children of my own, my marital and parental status were suspect. My apparent age indicated I was old enough to have experience working with various clients.

Achieving credibility was critical in work with this family. I wished to demonstrate that I understood May's conflict with her son and her dilemma in trying to be a nurturing mother and a bread winner. I reflected on May's strong loyalty to tradition in child-rearing values and practices and mentioned her deep caring and efforts to be everything for her children. These reflections appeared to be helpful. May gradually opened up about her problems and her emotional reactions to them. May seemed willing to self-disclose as long as I did not do anything to reduce my credibility.

At the end of the first session, I wanted to provide May with gifts of normalization and hope. I stated that in the United States value conflicts with children as they grow up are common especially with adolescents. I told her I understood she was suffering from guilt over her failure to be a perfect mother. I conveyed to her that my mother and I went through the same experience and reassured her in therapy we would generate new ideas to resolve her problems.

During the next session, I asked May to name someone who might act as intermediary with her son. She mentioned her older brother who had immigrated to the United States at a young age. She described her brother as being quite understanding and supportive, particularly after her husband left her. She had not asked him for help because she did not want to burden him. She said he was very busy with his small business. We discussed how he might be helpful to her and to her children.

After calling her brother, who lived fifty miles away, May reported he wanted to visit them. He apparently realized May's isolation and stress and offered to help. He came for dinner and May said she overheard a discussion between her brother and her son in which her son complained about his mother being so strict, saying she didn't listen to him and treated him unfairly.

In a joint session with May and her brother, May's brother said he told his nephew May looked unhappy and stressed, that she was working too hard and that she needed more appreciation and respect for her efforts to care for everyone. May's brother continued to maintain contact with her and her children via telephone, occasional visits and invitations to his home which both children liked very much. I continued to work with May. We discussed her acculturation process, her feelings about the divorce, the impact of the divorce on her family role and new ways she might cope with stress. I also acted as her advocate with the school counselor. She agreed to attend a parenting support group which consisted of mostly immigrant women.

Cultural Strengths-Based Tools

Culturally sensitive therapists, Asian American and non-Asians, need to understand the cultural and environmental factors which strengthen and empower Asian-Pacific families. Therapists not only need strong clinical skills (knowledge of therapeutic techniques as well as the ability to listen carefully, empathize, communicate clearly and establish rapport), but they must also be adept at using and understanding Asian-Pacific communication styles. The culturally competent therapist is familiar with Asian-Pacific traditional values, help-seeking practices and variations in family structure. Finally, the therapist needs to understand family and community resources. The following cultural strengths-based techniques should be applied:

1. The therapist should join with the family by allowing the interactions to be guided by the rules regulating the transactional process specific to Asian-Pacific, Single-Parent families. Given that social interactions are governed by hierarchical roles, the therapist should support the existing power structure by acknowledging and addressing the decision maker and head of the household first. In the traditional family, the children are the mother's primary responsibility reflecting on her self esteem; they are her resource for the future. Issues around perceived dependence of children and overprotection of the mother may be raised by therapists who are unfamiliar with traditional dynamics in Asian families and do not understand that mutual inter-dependence is stressed and expected. Individuation does occur and is at times promoted but it is tinged with knowledge of relationships and obligations between the individual and family members (Shon & Ja, 1982).

2. Demonstrating a personal interest is consistent with the family's orientation of reciprocity and mutual exchange. For instance, family members may ask for professional help because of the difficulties they encounter with one particular member. It would still be important to acknowledge the "identified patient" (Ho, 1990). Gathering information about their problem definition is useful because it helps Asian-Pacific families see the relevance of therapy and aids them in feeling understood. This inquiry into the family's cultural perspective and background can help the family shift the focus of therapy away from the problem, allowing the family an opportunity to educate the therapist in the context of active exchange.

3. Because cultural norms emphasize the importance of the parent-child dyad over the marital dyad, focusing on the parent-child relationship, a problem-solving approach in the initial sessions can be helpful. Therapy should not dwell on the parent's family of origin or multigenerational issues before trust has been established. Dealing with such issues may be too threatening, time consuming and antithetical to current needs.

4. Involving significant extended family members is particularly useful in work with Asian-Pacific, Single-Parent families. In many instances, families have problems regarding boundary confusion whereby family members work at cross purposes; or are cut off or isolated from one another. Focusing on cultural strengths and functional Asian-Pacific extended families can empower a family to sort out boundary and role confusions. Because it is not culturally syntonic for Asian-Pacific Americans to be isolated, the therapist can work with a Single-Parent mother and her children to help them to connect with a "non-blood" family support network within their community. This may involve bringing others into sessions.

5. The ecosystem approach enables the therapist to identify unique systems and cultural frameworks and empowers the Asian-Pacific, Single-Parent families to access community resources and agencies, including schools, housing, child welfare agencies, etc. The multisystems model, empowers the therapist to work in multiple contexts and with multidisciplinary teams involving the indigenous helpers.

Conclusion

Despite the limitations of the literature, it is clear that Asian-Pacific Americans, compared to Euro-Americans display different approaches to coping and help-seeking. It is also clear traditional Eastern and Pacific service orientations reflect a holistic system of logic, diverging from the Western tradition. Understanding the rudimentary norms and values governing Asian-Pacific cultures is a pre-requisite to working in these communities. The formulation of culturally appropriate assessment and intervention strategies begins with the examination of the Eastern world view and its operationalization as individuals and families acculturate to Western norms. Because of the diversity in Asian-Pacific American populations, it is important to examine the vast differences in culture and perspective, in terms of child rearing, family development, oppression, trauma, reaction to stress and coping styles.

Asian-Pacific American, Single-Parent families bring a unique set of cultural, linguistic, acculturation, environmental and economic circumstances into the clinical setting. The multisystems model of assessment presented allows for interplay between the Single-Parent family and the treatment system. Practical, cultural-specific techniques and skills should be combined with cultural strength-based methods. Remaining sensitive to the concerns of Asian-Pacific Single-Parent families and acknowledging their strength and endurance as they go through growth and change allows the therapist to support the family as well as each of its members.

Bibliography

Bronfenbrenner, U. (1979). *The ecology of human development: Experiments by nature and design.* Cambridge, MA, Harvard University Press.

Boyd-Franklin, N. (1990, September/October). A multisystems approach empowers African-American families, therapy. *Family Therapy News, 21* (5). p. 8.

Chao, C.M. (1992). The inner heart: Therapy with Southeast Asian Families. In L.A. Vargas, & J.D. Koss-Chioino (Eds.), *Working with culture: Psychotherepeutic interventions with ethnic minority and adolescents.* San Francisco, CA: Jossey-Bass.

DeVaney, S.B. (1988). "Single-parents". In N.A. Vacc, J. Wittmer, & S. DeVaney (Eds.), *Experiencing and counseling multicultural and diverse populations. (2nd ed.)* (pp. 89-105) Muncie, IN: Accelerated Development Inc.

Ho, M.K. (1990, September/October). To work successfully with ethnic minorities – culturally relevant knowledge, attitudes, techniques needed. *Family Therapy News, 21* (5). pp. 5 & 10.

Huang, L.J. (1981). The Chinese American family. In C. Mindel, & R. Habenstein (Eds.), *Ethnic families in America: Patterns and variations (2nd ed.)* (pp. 115-41). New York: Elsevier.

Huang, L.N. (1989). Southeast Asian refugee children and adolescents. In T.G. Jewelle, N.H. Larke, & Associates (Eds.), *Children of color: Psychological interventions with minority youth* (pp. 30-66). San Francisco, CA: Jossey-Bass.

Huang, L.N., & Ying, Y-W. (1989). Chinese American children and adolescents. In T.G. Jewelle, N.H. Larke, & Associates (Eds.), *Children of color: Psychological interventions with minority youth* (pp. 278-321). San Francisco, CA: Jossey-Bass.

Inclan, J. (1990, September/October). In successfully treating ethnic minorities – facilitating environment also vital in treatment. *Family Therapy News, 21* (5), p. 5.

Lee, E.A. (1982). Social systems approach to assessment and treatment for Chinese-American families. In M. McGoldrick, J.K. Pearce, & J. Giordano (Eds.), *Ethnicity and family therapy* (pp. 527-51). New York: Guilford Press.

McGoldrick, M. (1982). Ethnicity and family therapy: An overview. In M. McGoldrick, J.K. Pearce, & J. Giordano (Eds.), *Ethnicity and Family Therapy* (pp. 3-30). New York: Guilford Press.

Shon, S., & Ja, D. (1982). Asian families. In M. McGoldrick, J.K. Pearce, & J. Giordano (Eds.), *Ethnicity and family therapy* (pp. 208-28). New York: Guilford Press.

Slaughter-Defoe, D., Nakagawa, K., Takanishi, R., & Johnson, D. (1990). Toward cultural/ecological perspectives on schooling and achievement in African and Asian American children. *Child Development, 61*, 363-383.

Sue, D.W. (1989). Ethnic identity: The impact of two cultures on the psychological development of Asians in America. In D. Atkinson, G. Morton, & D.W. Sue (Eds.), *Counseling American minorities: A cross-cultural perspective* (pp. 103-115). Dubuque, IA: W.C. Brown.

Sue, S., and Zane, N. (1987). The role of culture and cultural techniques in psychotherapy: A critique and reformulation. *American Psychologist, 42* (1), 37-45.

Yamamoto, J. (1978). Therapy for Asian-Americans. *Journal of the National Medical Association, 70* (4), 267-270.

Latino/a Single-Parent Families: Implications for Social Work Practice

Maria Vidal de Haymes, Ph.D., MSW

SOCIAL WORKERS WILL be increasingly called upon to work with Latino/a families as the Latino/a population in the United States continues to grow. A substantial proportion of Latino/a families are headed by a single adult; a group the social work literature has largely ignored. This chapter reviews the minimal research concerning Latino/a Single-Parent families and discusses their economic and social well-being, stresses, strengths and social supports. Implications for social work practice from a strengths perspective are addressed and a case example is presented.

Background

The Latino/a population in the United States has grown at a phenomenal rate over the past two decades. In fact, it is predicted Latino/as will become the largest ethnic minority group in the America shortly after the turn of the century. In 1990, one out every ten persons counted in the census were Latino/a. The Bureau of the Census projects by the year 2050, one of every five United States residents may be Latino/a (U.S. Bureau of the Census, 1993). The most current estimate of the number of Latino/as living in the United States mainland is 22.8 million (U.S. Bureau of the Census, 1994).

The growing presence of Latino/as in America has been paralleled by an increase in the social science scholarship focused on Latino/a families. While there has been a notable increase in literature in this area, there has been an equally notable silence regarding particular Latino/a family forms. The majority of the research and writing has focuses on two-parent-headed or extended-family households; little has been written about Single-Parent, Latino/a families.

Single-Parent Latino/a Families

In 1993, the majority (69.1%) of Latino/a families were headed by married couples. However, nearly a third of all Latino/a households were headed by a single adult in that same year – 7.7% by men and 23% by women. Among Latino/as, the rate of marital disruption and the formation of Single-Parent households varies by ethnic background. Puerto Ricans are more likely to form single-female-headed families than are Mexican or Cuban women; 40.5%, 19.4% and 18.2% respectively (U.S. Bureau of the Census, 1994).

Experts disagree about the rate at which Single-Parent, Latino/a households are forming and the circumstances which lead to their formation. In a review of social science literature published during the 1980s, Vega (1991) identified increasing rates of marital disruption among Latino/a families as a major trend. Contrary to the long-held assumption Latino/a families enjoy greater marital stability than non-Latino, White families; Bean and Tienda (1987) analyzed 1980 census data and found negligible differences in the rate of marital disruption between Mexicans, Cubans and non-Latino Whites, but much higher rates for Puerto Ricans. This pattern has persisted through the 1980s and early 1990s. In 1993 the divorce rate for non-Latinos was 8.5%. The rate was 6.1%, 9.6% and 8.0% for Mexicans, Puerto Ricans and Cubans respectively (U.S. Bureau of the Census, 1994). Bean and Tienda (1987) argue when separation is included in counts of marital disruption the difference between Mexican Americans and Whites disappeared.

The number of Latino/a families headed by a Single Parent increased by 3% between 1983 to 1993. The greatest growth occurred among the households headed by single men. No significant changes occurred in the proportion of Latina householders with no husband present during the same period (U.S. Bureau of the Census, 1994).

Several authors have explored ethnic differences in divorce rates among Latino/as. Frisbie (1986) found marital stability is enhanced by greater educational attainment among Puerto Ricans. An inverse relationship between marital stability and educational attainment was found among Mexican Americans and Cubans. Bird and Canino (1982) identified greater rates of marital disruption among Puerto Ricans living in the United States mainland in comparison to Puerto Ricans who have stayed on the island. Muschkin and Meyers (1989) noted an overrepresentation of Single-Parent families among recent migrants from Puerto Rico to the United States mainland.

Other researchers have sought to understand the circumstances leading to separation or divorce. Parra, Arkowitz, Hannah and Vasquez (1995) found that

Mexican and Chicana women rated problems with relatives and infidelity as the main marital problem leading to divorce, whereas the non-Latina White women most frequently indicated alcoholism as the reason for marital problems. Mexican and Chicana women cited conflicts with the mother-in-law, who plays a powerful and central figure in family life, as a key problem leading to divorce.

Both early and more contemporary investigations of Latina families have noted a relationship between harsh life circumstances, such as poverty and immigrant status, and increases in marital disruption and female-headed households (Griswold del Castillo, 1984; Carasquillo, 1994 and Lewis, 1968). Carrasquillo (1994) suggests the poorest Puerto Ricans on the mainland tend toward female-headed households because of the inability of some men to provide financially for their families and the structure of the welfare system, which he argues is more accessible to women and children when the husband/father is not present. In the 1960s Oscar Lewis alerted readers to the harsh and degrading living conditions of poor Mexicans and Puerto Ricans and the consequences of these conditions with respect to family life. These families, he argued, were marked by rising rates of separation, divorce, desertion, out-of-wedlock births and female-headed households. He attributed these phenomena to structural factors in the larger society, which he viewed as "both an adaptation and a reaction of the poor to their marginal position in a class-stratified, highly individuated, capitalistic society" (Lewis, 1968).

Although the increasing rate of marital disruption has certainly contributed to an increase in female-headed households, it is not the sole, and possibly not the primary contributing factor. The process by which a family becomes female-headed varies, and differences are evident by race and ethnicity. Non-Hispanic White women are more likely to head a household as a result of divorce or the death of a spouse, whereas Latinas are more likely to find themselves in this position as a result of separation or remaining single. Among Latinas fifteen years of age or older, 32.8% had never married, 4.0% had widowed, and 6.8% had divorced. In contrast, 23% of non-Latina Whites remained single, 7.2% were widowed and 8.5% were divorced (U.S. Bureau of the Census, 1994).

While Vega and others have emphasized the recent growth of female-headed households among Latinos, Griswold del Castillo (1984) noted that in earlier periods more Latino households headed by single women as a result of harsh socioeconomic conditions. For example, in the second half of the nineteenth century, nearly 40% of Mexican-descent families in Los Angeles, San Antonio and Santa Fe were female-headed. The difficulties of frontier life, argues Griswold de Castillo, left Mexican families vulnerable to disruption and reformulation.

Social and Economic Well-Being of Single Latino/a Headed Families

As the data previously presented indicates; single, Latina-headed households are quite common and present a significant and viable family form. Many of the same issues, tasks, strains and supports are shared by all families, regardless of the pattern they take. However, single-female-headed households may differ from two-parent households in a number of important respects, including economic insecurity, limited employment and earning capacity, insufficient public benefits and social supports.

Poverty and Economic Insecurity

Although Latino/as comprise only approximately 9% of the total population, more than one in every six persons living in poverty in the United States in 1993 were of Hispanic origin. Latino/as are nearly three times more likely to be poor than are non-Hispanic Whites. In 1992, 29.3% of Latino/as were living in poverty, whereas 9.6% of Whites were poor (U.S. Bureau of the Census, 1994).

In 1978, Pearce coined the phrase the "feminization of poverty", which describes the process increasing rates of female-headed households and the corresponding drop in socioeconomic status for these women and children. Although Pearce's observation focused primarily on non-Latina White women, the same pattern, albeit more pronounced, applies to Latinas and their families. Single-Latina-headed families are more vulnerable to poverty than other Latino/a families. In 1993, 48.8% of single-Latina-headed households fell below the poverty threshold (U.S. Bureau of the Census, 1994).

Increasing rates of poverty and economic insecurity are evident among all families in the post-industrial United States-era, characterized by diminished wages, increased unemployment and rising female participation in the labor force. This is the first period of American history in which the rate of downward mobility exceeded the rate of upward mobility (Eitzen & Baca Zinn, 1995). These general trends exacerbate the vulnerability of families in general. A working father living in the home does not ensure economic viability for a family, nor does the addition of a working mother to the household. For example, the percentage of full-time, year-round workers with low earnings (less than $11,570 in 1989 dollars) has increased from 12% in 1979 to 18% in 1989, and minimum-wage earnings for a full-time, year-round worker fell below the annual poverty line for a family of three (Lavelle, 1995).

Families with children are even more vulnerable to these trends. Segal (1991) described the increased impoverishment of families with children, regardless of the number of adults present in the home, as the "juvenilization of poverty".

The poverty rate for any household with children is three times that of one which is childless (Segal, 1991). A growing percentage of children living in poverty can be attributed to economic decline of young families with children, most of which have two parents in the home and one or two workers. In 1993, 27% of all workers earned less than the amount needed to keep a family of four above the poverty line. In that same year, nearly half of all African-American and Latino/a children were poor – 46 and 41%, respectively. Poverty rates doubled among young White families with children – those headed by married couples and high school graduates alike. The poverty rates for families headed by college graduates also more than doubled since 1973 (Sklar, 1995).

The figures were particularly devastating for Latino/a families with children headed by Single Parents. In 1991, 60.1% of families with children under the age of 18 headed by Latinas with no husband present were poor. In that same year, 29.4% of Latino Single Father families with children younger than 18 were poor and 23.5% of Latino two-parent families with children were poor (U.S. Bureau of the Census, 1994).

Employment and Earning Capacity

Garfinkel and McLanahan (1986) contend for female headed families, the mother's earning capacity is the most important factor in determining her family's economic status. Unfortunately, Single Mothers earn on average roughly one third as much as married fathers. They attribute this difference in earnings to lower wages and fewer work hours among mothers in the paid labor force. Latina Single Mothers share the experience of inequality in pay, opportunity and job security with other women. However, their experience is exacerbated by racism.

In the last decade, the number of Latinas participating in the paid labor force has increased significantly. In 1993, 51.9% of Latinas sixteen years of age or older were working – up from 47.3% in 1983 (U.S. Bureau of the Census, 1994). Unfortunately, the unemployment rate of Latinas increased during the last half of this period. The unemployment rate of Latinas dropped approximately nine percentage points between 1983 and 1989, but increased between 1989 and 1993. A similar pattern was observed for Latino men. The unemployment rate for Latino/as was 11.9% in 1993, 12.4% for men and 11.1% for women. The overall 11.9% unemployment rate for Latino/as was nearly double that of the 6.2% rate of non-Latino Whites (U.S. Bureau of the Census, 1994).

Working Latino/as tend to be concentrated in lower paying, less skilled occupations. Like non-Latina White women, Latinas are most likely to be found in technical, sales and administrative-support occupational groups (40.9 and 43.9% respectively). However, working Latinas (24.6%) are more concentrated in service occupations than White women (16%), whereas White women (30.9%) are twice as likely to be employed in managerial and professional specialty occupations than Latinas (15.4%). A similar divergence in occupational categories along ethnic lines is found among White and Latino males. For example, according to the U.S. Bureau of the Census (1994), employed Latino males were most concentrated in operator, fabricator and laborer occupations (28.4%), whereas non-Hispanic White males were likely to be in managerial and professional specialty occupations (29.2%).

The actual earnings for employed Latino/as also varied based on gender and ethnicity. The average yearly earnings for employed Latinas in 1993 was $13,587 and the average for non-Latina White women was $17,141. Furthermore, nearly half of employed Latinas (46%) and more than one third (37%) of non-Latina women make less than $10,000 annually. In 1993, the average annual earnings for employed Latino men was $18,488, which is higher than that of Latina and White women but significantly lower than the $29,826 average annual earnings of White men (U.S. Bureau of the Census, 1994).

Child Support

In a Single-Parent household, child support from the non-custodial parent can be an important source of income. In their analysis of national data on child support awards, Garfinkel and McLanahan (1986) found only 58% of Single Mothers with children younger than twenty-one years of age had a child-support award. Of those with child support awards; only 50% received full payment, 26% received partial payment and 24% received no payment at all. Garfinkel and McLanahan (1986) found child support payments accounted for about 10% of the income of White female-headed families with children and 3.5% of African-American, Single-Mother families. Furthermore, they argued award amounts are generally low and their value usually declines in the course of time; in that the award amounts are rarely indexed to the cost of living. Although published child support data for Latina families was not available, no great difference in the general pattern of low rates of award, modest rates of payment and small award amounts with diminishing value should be expected.

Public Benefits

Means-tested, public-assistance programs provide support to a substantial proportion of Latino/a families. Slightly more than one-third (35.2%) of all persons living in Latino/a-headed households received benefits from some type of income-tested assistance program in 1991: Aid to Families with Dependent Children (AFDC), food stamps, Medicaid, General Assistance (GA), Supplemental

Security Income (SSI), subsidized housing and means-tested veterans compensation pensions. Benefits from cash assistance programs such AFDC, GA, SSI and means-tested veterans compensation benefits were received by 18.7% of Latino/a households in 1991 (U.S. Bureau of the Census, 1993). Twenty percent of Latino/a households received food stamps, 30% received Medicaid and 7% lived in subsidized housing in 1991 (U.S. Bureau of the Census, 1993).

Not surprisingly, Latina Single-Parent families are more likely than their two-parent counterparts to receive AFDC. In the 1990, census 8% of married-couple Latino families and 36% of single, Latina-headed families reported AFDC receipt (U.S. Bureau of the Census, 1991). Unfortunately, the average AFDC payment is quite low – $4,400 a year ($367 a month), which is nearly $9,000 less than the federal poverty line for family of three (Abramovitz & Newdom, 1994). Thus AFDC does not spare its recipients from the effects of poverty. In fact, income-support programs lifted less than 5% of Single-Mother families out of poverty during the previous decade (Abramovitz & Newdom, 1994).

Familism: Economic and Social Supports

A dominant theme in the social-science research literature on Latino families is "familism". This concept is used to distinguish Latino from non-Latino households. In general, familism is defined as a strong familistic orientation in which the collective family needs and aspirations are given greater importance than those of individual family members. Familism is described as "emphasizing interdependence over independence, affiliation over confrontation, and cooperation over competition" (Atkinson, Morten & Sue, 1993). Beliefs and behaviors associated with familism include high levels of interaction, cohesion, loyalty, responsibility, support and caregiving shared among family members in elaborate networks which may include extended and fictive kin. Familism and its expression through extended and fictive kin relationships are a source of economic, social and emotional support for Latino/as. It is especially important for Latino/a Single-Parent families.

Extended Families

Latino/as are more likely to live in extended-family households than non-Latinos. One of the most significant areas of research regarding Latino familism has been the role and function of extended family and fictive kin supportive networks. Several researchers have indicated Single-Parent Latino/a families are often embedded in an extended family household (Angel & Tienda, 1982; Pelto, Roman & Nelson, 1982; Perez, 1986; Wagner & Schaffer, 1980). The extended-family households provide important economic benefits by allowing families to pool their resources.

Elaborate exchanges of assistance across generations and households also occur among Latino/a extended family members and informal helpers. Several researchers have found complex, often binational, intercommunity, extra-household linkages and patterns of exchange among Latino/a family networks (Alvarez, 1987; Bird & Canino, 1982; Massey et al., 1987; Muschkin & Myers, 1989; Pelto et al., 1982 and Portes & Bach, 1985). Such networks facilitate the process of immigration and accommodation by providing both social and economic support. Chavez (1985, 1988) also found a strong presence of extended family households among both documented and undocumented Mexican immigrants. Portes and Bach (1985) found that 50% of Mexican Americans live with extended family members during their first three years of post-immigration residence.

Perez (1994) found there was a significantly greater likelihood of grandparents residing with their grandchildren in Single-Parent-headed immigrant households than in such households with two parents. He found this to be especially true of households headed by Single Fathers. Father-only-headed immigrant households also had the greatest proportion of aunts and uncles living with them. Perez suggests these types of arrangements facilitate child rearing.

In their analysis of the social networks and coping strategies of female-headed families, Wagner and Shaffer (1980) uncovered a pattern of "resource specialization" in the kinship networks of Chicana Single Mothers:

> Parents are turned to in circumstances of dire necessity such as illness, when the woman might move in with the parents, or more commonly the mother might live with her temporarily, take care of the children, and fix the meals. Parents are also most often relied on for borrowing money...Siblings tend to be utilized for those problems that are best met through people of one's own generation. Those women with cars, for example, turn to brothers as often as to a commercial garage for repairs...significant siblings were turned to for advice (usually a sister) more often than parents... (Wagner and Shaffer, 1980, p. 82).

Schaffer and Wagner (1996) and Parra and colleagues (1995) found similar patterns of reliance on family for support in their studies of coping strategies and social support networks among Latina Single Parents. Parra and co-workers (1995) observed significantly higher levels of distress-associated divorce among Mexican-American women compared to Anglo and Mexican women residing in Mexico. The Mexican-American women demonstrated greater effort to cope with their distress and to use family as resource and support during the period of the divorce than the other two groups.

Schaffer and Wagner (1996) found Mexican-American, Single Mothers had larger social-support networks than did Anglo Single Mothers. The social-support networks of Single Latina-Mothers had a higher proportion of relatives and a smaller, more cohesive network of friends. However, they cautioned they uncovered within-group variation in social-support networks when socioeconomic status and level of acculturation were considered.

It is important to note although many researchers support the extended-family household thesis with respect to Latino/a families, the work of others suggest a different reality. Griswold del Castillo (1984) argued the extended family patterns which characterized Mexican-American households diminished in the second half of the nineteenth century. Hogan and others (1993) found that Mexican Americans were no more likely to participate in intergenerational exchanges of support than Whites and the "effective kin networks that provided support to multi-generational families in the past decade appear to be of little relevance today" (p. 1454).

Fictive Kin

Fictive kin, a concept associated with Latino familism, refers to individuals who are not related by blood or marriage, yet play important family-like roles in Latino/a households. One such relationship which is frequently discussed in the literature is that of *compadrazgo*. This concept refers to two sets of relationships: (a) *Padrinos* and *ahijados* or godparents and godchildren, and (b) parents and godparents who become *compadres* or co-parents. The compadrazgo system of godparents enlarges the family circle by making connections between families, that carry special "religious, social, and economic responsibilities and relationships" (Baca Zinn, 1994, p. 73). Compadres participate in family life in many ways, such as providing discipline and guidance for children and emotional, social and financial support as needed.

Latino/a Families from a Strengths Perspective

Despite the fact nearly a quarter of all Latino families are headed by single women, the social-science literature provides little information on mother-only, Latina families. In the past two decades, the literature has presented extensive material on White and African-American Single-Parent families. Unfortunately, much of their literature takes a social-problem perspective. From Moynahan's Report (1965) and Lewis's (1968) "culture of poverty" thesis of the 1960s to Wilson's (1987) contemporary urban underclass discussion; mother-only families have more often than not been cited as evidence of personal and cultural pathology, weakened social norms and increased social isolation and decay. Unfortunately, this perspective has, and continues to have, an effect on social welfare policies and social work practice.

From colonial America's Poor Laws to the contemporary welfare state, the development of American public policy and social programs has reflected a preoccupation with the two-parent, male-headed, nuclear household. Abramovitz

(1988) has described this process as the enforcement of a "family ethic" through social welfare programs such as social security, unemployment insurance and AFDC; whose rules and regulations "benefit those who live in traditional family structures while penalizing alternative family forms where poor women and women of color tend to predominate" (p. 2). In fact, the rapidly changing structure and form of families is the center of the current public policy discussions.

Recent social welfare policy initiatives attempt to restore the "family ethic" in poor and minority communities. The Personal Responsibility and Work Opportunity Act, born of House of Republicans' Contract With America (1994) and signed into law by President Clinton in 1996, attempts to restore the "family ethic" in poor and minority communities by: (a) permitting states to impose a family cap which would deny an increase in cash benefits for any additional child born into families already receiving welfare; (b) requiring unmarried parents under age 18 to live with an adult and stay in school to receive benefits; (c) cuttings funding for low-income programs by approximately $55 billion over the next six years; (d) replacing AFDC with a block grant called Temporary Assistance for Needy Families (TANF), thereby removing assurances poor families meeting the state eligibility requirements will receive cash assistance; (e) instituting a five-year lifetime time limit on cash assistance; (f) requiring recipients to work after two years and participate in community service after two months; (g) denying SSI and Food stamps for most legal immigrants and (h) denying Medicaid coverage for most legal immigrants entering the country for five years (NASW, 1996).

These changes are not entirely new. Several states have enacted aspects of the various proposals through the federal waiver process. For example, Wisconsin and New Jersey have experimented with "wedfare" or "bridefare" programs which offer similar bonuses to women who marry and "benefit caps" which eliminate additional increases in grants for children born to mothers who are already enrolled in AFDC (Thomas, 1995).

The underlying assumptions of such policies are particular family structures are more desirable (i.e., nuclear, married, two-parent families with one or more adult workers) in both social and economic terms and that family structure can be shaped through public welfare policies. Unfortunately, such policy orientations and popular and academic discussions often mistake family structure for family functioning. The literature and demographic characteristics suggest Single-Parent families occur commonly among Latino/as, and do not represent pathology or evidence of weakened social norms or family structure. Rather, Latino/a Single-Parent families represent a viable family form which is often part of a larger family network providing needed economic, social, and emotional support. The strengths of Latino/a Single-Parent families presented in the literature include: role flexibility, an enhanced use of kinship relationships, wider social-support networks and significant resource roles played by fictive kin.

This is not to say Latino/a Single-Parent families do not face difficulties. Economic insecurity, limited employment opportunities and minimal earnings capacity, lack of child support and meager public benefits suggest some of the challenges these families face. The corresponding challenge to social workers is to shift the professional and policy debate regarding Single-Parent families from one which pathologies such families to one which recognizes strengths and lends support (Schmitz, 1995).

Implications for Practice

Social workers who provide direct services to Latino/a Single-Parent families should be aware of the demographic, family composition, social and economic well-being and cultural characteristics of these families. Although all social work interactions should aim to empower clients by emphasizing their strengths, empowerment is even more critical with populations marginalized or penalized by social policies and institutional practices. A strengths perspective allows social workers to recognize and engage the "strengths and resources of people and their environments, rather than their problems and pathologies, and should be the central focus of the helping process in social work" (Chapin, 1995, p. 507). The following case study illustrates social work interventions that put family strengths, resources, resilience and cultural practices to work.

The Colon Family

In the spring of 1996, Ms Colon, a 39-year-old Puerto Rican Single Mother of two, requested assistance for her 15-year-old son, Alberto. She initiated contact with the mental health program of a large Latino community-based social service agency with the hope of regaining control of her son and improving his school attendance and performance. Information gathered during the intake interview revealed, from her perspective, Alberto had always been open, well behaved, respectful and honest with her. During the past six months his behavior had changed. She stated he had become defiant, combative, withdrawn and had begun to lie and use disrespectful language. She denied having any difficulty with her 13-year-old daughter, Angela, but indicated the family had experienced a tremendous change and difficulty in the past year as a result significant changes in her health. The case was assigned to Ms Morales, a program social worker.

In first session, Ms Colon provided some background information regarding her present situation. She indicated that during the summer of 1995 she was seen at her health maintenance organization (HMO) for blood in her urine, fever, vomiting, loss of appetite, pain in her lower back and joints and swelling of her face and legs. Although she had experienced some episodes of joint pain and rashes in the past, she had not sought medical attention nor did she connect those previous episodes with her current symptoms. Initially she attributed her body aches, fever and loss of appetite to the flu, but when she began experiencing severe lower-back pain and blood in her urine, she became alarmed and sought medical attention. Upon initial examination, the physician became concerned and hospitalized her. During her stay, a complete medical history was taken and diagnostic tests were performed.

The test results and medical history indicated a diagnosis of systemic lupus erythematosus, an incurable inflammatory disease of connective tissue characterized by remissions and relapses. The prognosis for persons with lupus is variable; in many ways, the symptoms can be controlled or relieved for many years. Unfortunately, Ms Colon's prognosis was not promising due to the severity of the connective tissue inflammation and seriously impaired kidney functioning. Ms Colon was prescribed anti-inflammatory and immunosuppressive drugs to address the symptoms connected with lupus, a renal diet and dialysis for the associated kidney failure and tricyclics to treat her depression. She reported compliance with the drug, diet and dialysis regimen.

Ms Colon's illness resulted in many missed days of work and finally the need to leave her job after she had exhausted all of her sick days. The loss of work meant a substantial loss in family income, which subsequently forced the family to give up their apartment and move to another neighborhood with more affordable housing. Ms Colon found that she could no longer continue to send her children to the Catholic school they had been attending and was now on the brink of loosing her health care coverage. She had continued her health care policy after leaving work but was having difficulty paying the premiums and was falling behind with other bills.

In addition to loosing her job, apartment and familiar neighborhood, Ms Colon also lost Roy, her partner of five years. Ms Colon reported that she had encouraged Roy to leave her because he was fifteen years younger and she felt that "it was unfair to ask such a young man to sacrifice his youth nursing a sick woman." Roy's leaving was a tremendous emotional loss to both Ms Colon and the children as well as a significant financial loss as he had been sharing the rent payments.

In the initial session with Ms Colon, Ms Morales quickly understood although she was seeking support for her son she was in need of support herself. She was struggling under the weight of many emotional, social, material and physical losses. She was terrified the illness would cause her to lose her son. Given the urgency of her situation, Ms Morales asked her to return the next day with both of her children.

During the first family interview, Alberto complained that he "wasn't getting anything out of school and that it was just a waste of time." With further prodding he indicated he did not feel challenged by school because he felt that it was "too basic" and "boring". He also indicated he had not made many friends and would rather spend time with the few who had accepted him. Unfortunately, these students skipped classes and Alberto found himself increasingly cutting classes to "hang" with them. He seemed to understand that his behavior caused his mother great concern, but did not indicate any plans to change his behavior.

Angela was reluctant to complain about the changed circumstances of her family. She expressed a desire to care for her mother and anger towards her brother for acting so irresponsibly and causing her mother extra worries. In later interviews she verbalized her longing for her old school and friendships and the extra-curricular activities she had given up because she felt she should be home with her mother immediately after school.

The family faced overwhelming difficulties. Ms Morales queried the family regarding the social support they had available to deal with their present crises. The children indicated they had friends from their former school and neighborhood with whom they spoke occasionally by phone but noted that the telephone conversations were becoming less frequent with time. Ms Colon stated Roy had been her primary support and, although he currently called her approximately twice a month, she did not want to talk with him about her problems or ask for help. She thought it would be too painful for her to see him or share confidences with him since the nature of their relationship had changed. She noted that her relationship with her parents and siblings, all living in Puerto Rico, had been strained since her divorce and the initiation of her relationship with Roy. Her parents were very fond of her former husband, Stan, and were proud she had married into such a "good" family. They never understand why she left him and were violently opposed to her relationship with Roy, who was a marginally employed 19-year-old high school drop-out when they began their relationship. When they began living together, her family cut off all communication with her. However, they called the children on holidays and their birthdays.

Following their divorce, Stan remained in frequent contact for a year, often bringing gifts and money for the children. However, the next year he left the state because of a promotion, and his contact and gifts became less frequent. Ms Colon had not heard from him for more than a year and was no longer certain of his whereabouts. While Ms Colon had been granted a small child-support award at the time of her divorce, she never sought to collect it because she felt "embarrassed to ask for money" and "guilty" that she had left him. Furthermore, although she could not afford many luxuries, she had always been able to provide for her children's material needs when she worked. Stan had never made a single child-support payment.

The initial reason for seeking help, as expressed by Ms Colon, was to "regain control of her son". However, by the second session, new goals were articulated and agreed to by all participants:

- develop a social support system in their family and community to help them deal with the ongoing challenges of Ms Colon's illness
- enhance the communication and relationship between Ms Colon, Angela and Alberto
- improve Alberto's school attendance and performance
- find constructive ways for the family members to express their grief regarding their recent losses and anxiety about the future
- seek financial assistance for the family

The Colon family's engagement with the social worker lasted approximately five months. During this time, significant gains were made toward the realization of the stated goals. Because the Colon family had functioned well previously, Ms Morales and the family determined their current difficulties were largely situational and related to Ms Colon's recent illness. Ms Morales's work with the family consisted primarily of helping the family to identify and engage their strengths, activate existing social supports and establishing links to new resources.

For example, Ms Morales immediately referred the family to the emergency-services department within her own agency. Ms Colon was informed about available assistance and received help applying for disability benefits, medical benefits, a housing subsidy, AFDC and other relevant programs. The emergency worker also initiated efforts to locate her previous husband in order to seek child support.

Alberto's padrino, David, was contacted and made aware of the family's difficulties. David was considered a family member and compadre of Ms Colon. Although David had been very present in the life of the family for many years, he had not visited the family regularly after he entered graduate school a year-and-a-half ago. The pressures associated with school in addition to his continued full-time employment, left him with little time and energy to devote to his friends and family. Upon learning of the Colon's current situation he immediately became involved. He began to drop by the Colon's home several times a week and took an active interest in Alberto's academic difficulties. He began to bring Alberto to campus with him to use the library, attend athletic games and even to sit in on a class. David even attended school conferences with Ms Colon and pushed Alberto on attendance and study habits. Within several weeks Alberto attendance and performance were markedly improved.

With Ms Colon's permission, Ms Morales and David contacted the children's former school to request tuition assistance to allow the children to return. Given the changed economic circumstances of the family, the principal was able to grant the children a scholarship. Ms Colon volunteered in the library when she was feeling well, which allowed her to return the school's favor and keep on top of her children's schooling. Alberto and Angela quickly resumed extra-curricular activities and friendships with classmates. Return to their former school made a great difference in the lives of the children, giving them a sense of continuity and stability. Alberto's defiant behavior diminished and Angela resumed her after-school activities.

Ms Colon was encouraged to reestablish contact with her parents, a particularly difficult task for her. With support, she was able to do so. Within days, her parents came from Puerto Rico to visit. Mr. Colon returned to Puerto Rico after a week because of work, but his wife stayed on for several months to assist her daughter. Ms Colon's illness had created an opportunity for the family to overcome years of silence and distance.

At Ms Morales recommendation, Ms Colon began to participate in a local lupus support group. She met new friends with whom she could exchange advice, comfort, information, sustenance and hope. The group helped her to begin addressing difficult issues such as planning for the care of her children should she become unable to do so, making treatment decisions and coping with the possibility of increased disability. These interventions, in addition to others, along with continued family counseling, greatly enhanced the communication among family members, the quality of their relationship and their life circumstances. This helped the family gather additional emotional, relational and material strengths and supports.

Conclusion

The Colon case presents a context for understanding the impact of societal issues on Latina Single-Parent families and the strengths provided by practice within a cultural context. Shifting demographics and economic trends leave Single-Parent Latina families with increased stress and decreasing resources. Social work practice needs to be grounded in an understanding of Latino culture and family relationships. In recognition of Latino familism, the social work interventions with the Colon family focused on reestablishing extended family and fictive kin social supports.

The Colon family case study provides an example of a community-based agency and social worker responsive to the needs of a family in crisis incorporating a culturally competent strengths perspective. Both the intake worker and Ms Morales moved quickly to establish a relationship with the family, realizing

Ms Colon had reached such a level of crisis she was ready to be engaged immediately in work on her situation. With the initial interview, Ms Morales began to engage Ms Colon through her concern for her children and her physical health issues. By acknowledging and addressing the issues that Ms Colon was willing to present initially, the worker demonstrated her responsiveness and sensitivity to the client's discomfort in asking for assistance for herself.

Ms Morales secured assistance for Ms Colon in a way which acknowledged her ability to care for her children and allowed her to save face when approaching her family and her former husband for support. Communication and ties with her family and fictive kin were quickly reengaged in a manner that avoided the client's feelings of shame and allowed those who cared for her and her children the opportunity to demonstrate their concern. Sessions with Ms Morales and a lupus support group further widened Ms Colon's support network.

Finally, like other Latina Single-Parent families, many of the Colon's difficulties stemmed from their economic insecurity, insufficient public benefits and limited social supports. In the past, Ms Colon had successfully managed to provide for her children, but her illness left her unable to work. While mobilizing the Colon's natural support network of extended family, fictive kin and parish school, Ms Morales also initiated case management services to seek out additional economic and social resources. In addition to seeking public benefits, Ms Morales helped Ms Colon to seek child support payments from her ex-husband.

Bibliography

Abramovitz, M. & Newdom, F. (1994). Fighting back! Challenging AFDC myths with the facts. *BCR Reports, 6*(1), 1, 4.

Abramovitz, M. (1988). *Regulating the lives of women: Social welfare policy from colonial times to the present.* Boston, MA: South End Press.

Alvarez, R. (1987). *Families: Migration and adaptation in Baja and Alta California from 1800 to 1975.* Berkeley: University of California Press.

Angel, R. & Tienda, M. (1982). Determinants of Extended Household Structure: Cultural Patterns or Economic Model? *American Journal of Sociology 87,* 1360-1383.

Atkinson, D.R.; Morten, G., & Derrald Wing S. (1993). *Counseling American minorities: A cross-cultural perspective.* Dubuque, IA: Brown and Benchmark.

Baca Zinn, M. (1994). Adaptation and continuity in Mexican-origin families. In R.L. Taylor (Ed.) *Minority families in the United States: A multicultural perspective.* Englewood Cliffs, New Jersey, NJ: Prentice Hall.

Bean, F. & Tienda, M. (1987). *The Hispanic population of the United States.* New York: Russell Sage Foundation.

Bird, H. & Canino, G. (1982). The Puerto Rican family: Cultural factors and family intervention strategies. *Journal of the American Academy of Psychoanalysis, 10,* 257-68.

Carasquillo, H. (1994). The Puerto Rican family. In R.L. Taylor (Ed.) *Minority families in the United States: A multicultural perspective.* Englewood Cliffs, New Jersey, NJ: Prentice Hall.

Chapin, R.K. (1995). Social policy development: The strengths perspective. *Social Work 40*(40), 506-14.

Chavez, L. (1988). Settlers and sojourners: The case of Mexicans in the United States. *Human Organization 47*:95-108.

Chavez, L. 1985. Households and migration and labor market participation: The adaptation of Mexicans to life in the United States. *Urban Anthropology 14*, 301-45.

Eitzen, S.D. & Baca Zinn, M. (1995). Structural transformation and systems of inequality. In Andersen, M.L. and Collins, P.H. (Eds.) *Race, class, and gender: An anthology* (pp. 202-6). Belmont, CA: Wadsworth Publishing Company.

Frisbie, W.P. (1986). Variations in patterns of marital instability among Hispanics. *Journal of Marriage and the Family, 48*, 99-106.

Frisbie, W.P.; Opitz, W. & Kelly, W.R. (1985). Marital instability trends among Mexican American as compared to Blacks and Anglos: New evidence. *Social Science Quarterly 66*, 587-601.

Garfinkel, I. & McLanahan, S.S. (1986). *Single mothers and their children: A new American dilemma.* Washington, DC: The Brookings Institute.

Griswold del Castillo, R. (1984). *La Familia: Chicano families in the urban southwest 1848 to the present.* Notre Dame, IN: University of Notre Dame Press.

Hogan, D.P.; Eggebeen, D. & Clogg, C. (1993). The structure of intergenerational exchanges in American families. *American Journal of Sociology, 98*, 1428-58.

Lavelle, R. (1995). *America's new war on poverty: A reader for action.* San Francisco, CA: KQED Books.

Lewis, O. (1968). The culture of poverty. In Moynihan, D.P. (Ed.) *On understanding poverty: perspectives from the social sciences.* New York: Basic Books.

Massey, D., Alarcon, R., Durand, J., & Gonzalez, U. (1987). *Return to Atzlan.* Berkeley, CA: University of California Press.

Moynihan, D. P. (1965). *The negro Family: The case for national action.* Washington, DC: Office for Policy Planning and Research, US Department of Labor.

Muschkin, C. & Myers, G.C. (1989). Migration and household family structure: Puerto Ricans in the United States." *International Migration Review 23*, 495-501.

National Association of Social Workers. (1996). *Personal responsibility and work opportunity Reconciliation Act of 1996 (H.R. 3734) Public Law 104-193 Summary of Provisions.* Washington, DC: National Association of Social Workers.

Parra, E.B., Arkowitz, H., Hannah, M.T., & Vasquez, A.M. (1995). Coping strategies and emotional reactions to separation and divorce in Anglo, Chicana, and Mexicana women. *Journal of Divorce and Remarriage, 23*(1/2), 117-29.

Pearce, D. (1978). The feminization of poverty: Women, work, and welfare. *The Urban and Social Change Review, 11*, 28-36.

Pelto, P., Roman, M., & Nelson, L. (1982). Family structures in an Urban Puerto Rican community. *Urban Anthropology, 11*, 39-58.

Perez, L. (1994). The household structure of second-generation children: An exploratory study of extended family arrangements. *International Migration Review, 28* (4), 736-47.

Perez, L. (1986). Immigrant economic adjustment and family organization: The Cuban success story reexamined. *International Migration Review 20*, 4-20.

Portes, A. & Bach, R.L. (1985). *Latin journey.* Berkeley: University of California Press.

Republican National Committee. 1994. *Contract with America: The bold plan by Rep. Newt Gingrich, Rep. Dick Armey, and the House of Republicans to change the nation.* New York: Times Books.

Schaffer, D.M. & Wagner, R.M. (1996). Mexican American and Anglo single mothers: The influence of ethnicity, generation and socioeconomic status on social support networks. *Hispanic Journal of Behavioral Sciences, 18*, 74-86.

Schmitz, C. (1995). Reframing the dialogue on female headed single-parent families. *Affilia 10*(4), 426-41.

Segal, E. (1991). The Juvenilization of Poverty. *Social Work 36*, 454-7.

Sklar, H. (1995). *Chaos or community: Seeking solutions, not scapegoats for bad economics.* Boston, MA: South End Press.

Thomas, S. L. (1995). Exchanging welfare checks for wedding rings: Welfare reform in New Jersey and Wisconsin. *Affilia 10*(2), 120-37.

U.S. Bureau of the Census (1991). *1990 Census of population: Social and economic Characteristics.* Washington, DC: U.S. Government Printing Office.

U.S. Bureau of the Census (1993). *Hispanic Americans today.* Washington, DC: U.S. Government Printing Office.

U.S. Bureau of the Census (1994). *The Hispanic population in the United States: March 1993.* Washington, DC: U.S. Government Printing Office.

Vega, W.A. (1991). Hispanic families in the 1980's: A decade of research. In A. Booth (Ed.), *Contemporary families: Looking forward, looking back* (297-306). National Council on Family Relations.

Wagner, R. and Schaffer, D. (1980). Social networks and survival strategies: An exploratory study of Mexican-American, Black and Anglo female family heads in San Jose, California. In M. Melvill (Ed.) *Twice a minority, Mexican American women in the United States* (173-90). St. Louis, MO: CV Mosby.

Wilson, W.J. (1987). *The truly disadvantaged: The inner city, the underclass and public policy.* Chicago, IL: University of Chicago Press.

Black Single Mothers and the Politics of Oppression: Efforts to Effect Change

Janese Prince, MSW

The psychology of a people is directly connected to their history and experience. Therefore, to explain yourself you must know your history and your experience.
Dr. Amos Wilson
Third Eye Conference, Dallas, TX 1991

SUCCESSFUL SOCIAL WORK intervention with Black Single Mothers involving effective programs designed to empower Black Single Mothers can occur only in a context of knowledge and understanding. Unfortunately, the inadequacy of our education leaves us sorely lacking in knowledge at the intersection between racism and sexism which come together to disempower and scapegoat Black women.

Education plays a defining role in all societies. It represents more than merely learning to read, write and perform arithmetic. It is vital to the socialization process and in the shaping of the minds of citizens. In studying the socialization process of a group, whether the group is small or as vast as a nation, the structure of the educational system reveals who or what the society values most. In fact, education can be used as a tool to manipulate consciousness, even to educate one into ignorance.

As Malcolm X said, "History is our memory". The ancient Egyptians instructed their citizens to "know thyself". History informs people about who they are and points to their mistakes and accomplishments. History, however, is typically taught from the perspective of a society's dominant group. For instance, the United States comprises numerous racial and ethnic groups, but its history is taught from a White European male perspective. Little attention is focused on the history of American Indians, African Americans, Latinos and Asian Americans. The accomplishments of these persons of color are either trivialized, misconstrued or ignored. Furthermore, women of all groups have been largely overlooked in the teaching of history.

The theologian, James Cone, in a lecture at Saint Louis University in 1994, spoke about the inadequacy of his seminary education in preparing him to educate Black students who, during the civil-rights and Black-power movements, were considered sociopolitical problems. Realizing he had studied the "philosophies of European racists and colonizers", he saw a need to cultivate a Christian theology from a Black experience, focusing on the life and history of Black people. This same failure – the failure to educate students to meet the needs of Black people – is applicable to social work education.

The history of social work focuses on institutions that served White society, such as the early charitable organizations and Jane Addams's Hull House. Little attention was focused on Black Americans, despite their large population and the severity of their problems. Moreover, the organizational skills of blacks such as Nat Turner, Ida B. Wells-Barnett, Father Devine, Malcolm X, Martin Luther King, Jr., Fannie Lou Hamer and others who understood the oppression suffered by blacks were also largely ignored. Their organized efforts designed to meet the psychosocial, economic and political needs of Black people are glossed over if not totally left out of the general social work curriculum.

Overlooking Black Americans in the history of social work suggests they were of little value in America during this period. As a result, the psychological history of the dominant group is used to prepare professionals to work with a group whose psychological history is a mystery to them. Such neglect renders many White social workers ineffective in their work with Black clients and can have detrimental effects.

The superficial teaching of Black history has resulted in social workers focusing on the symptoms rather than the root causes of the problems Black Americans face. These roots reach deep into the very structure of society in the United States institutionalizing racism. The unjust laws and misguided policies driven by racism have had devastating effects on the economic status of Black families, negatively affecting the family.

Divorce, separation and out-of-wedlock births (especially among teens) are seen by some as the primary causes in the rise of female-headed households (Moynihan, 1965; Mulroy 1988). As these poverty-stricken families move onto the welfare roles, the public lashes out, stigmatizing these families by labeling them as one of the nation's primary ills. In fact, low income, Single Mothers have existed in the United States since colonial times. Wars, sickness, desertion and out-of-wedlock births have left many women raising children without a spouse. In the course of time, however, family structure and the public's portrait of the Single Mother have been socially reconstructed in ways weighing heavily on Single Mothers. A social worker can only work effectively with low income, Black Single Mothers when they understand the social and historical context which has been socially and economically constructed to disadvantage both the Black family and Single-Parent families to doubly oppress Black Single Mothers.

This chapter reviews historical events and social policies which have negatively affected the lives of Black Americans – particularly women. It is vital for social workers to understand the history of Black Americans and women. These events come together to increase the vulnerability of growing numbers of low-income, single, Black women raising children. The systemic problems faced by Black families, and the continued attack on the Black family which have given rise to increases in the number of Single Black Mothers living in poverty are discussed. Intervention models which support and mobilize Black Single Mothers to fight political injustice are reviewed. Self-help tools (social, economic and educational) used by Black, Single Mothers are described.

History and Social Policy

Social welfare policy can be traced to England's welfare traditions of the sixteenth and seventeenth centuries. In the early years of the United States, the burden of caring for the poor rested primarily with relatives, friends and religious groups. However, as the country grew and poverty increased, the government became more involved in addressing the needs of the poor. Thus, social welfare policy does not exist in isolation. It is political, rising "out of conflict over the nature of problems confronting society and what if anything should be done about them" (Di Nitto, 1983, p. 8).

England's Elizabethan Statute of Artificers, established in 1562 and the Poor Law of 1601 (which became known as the Elizabethan Poor Laws), served as the guidepost for American public welfare policy (Abramovitz, 1988; Heffernan, 1979) to the year 1935. The government, however, placed the responsibility of caring for less fortunate citizens upon their relatives and friends. The afore-mentioned laws did make some attempt to address the needs of some poor whites who did not have access to the assistance of family and friends.

The poor laws consisted of "outdoor" and "indoor" relief. Indoor relief served "undeserving" poor who were expected to work in exchange for residency in government workhouses or almshouses. Many Single Mothers with children lived in these institutions. The children of these mothers were sometimes forced to work as apprentices (Heffernan, 1979).

Outdoor relief, which refers to aid to poor persons living outside institutions, was given to persons deemed by society to be "deserving" poor. Widows, married women whose husbands were disabled or ill and women with children who were alone for other "acceptable" reasons benefited from this form of aid (Abramovitz, 1988). Outdoor relief allowed its recipients to remain in their homes or some other private residence with no work requirement.

Policies Governing Indentured Servants and Slaves

Indentured servants and slaves were governed by a different, more cruel, set of laws. The laws governing slaves were especially severe and laid the foundation for the institutionalization of racism. During early colonial times, many whites who immigrated to this country were indentured servants. Some voluntarily indentured themselves to pay for their transportation to this country. Others were forcibly indentured to pay off debts. Britain dumped many of its outcasts into this country and exploited them economically. Prior to the American Revolution indentured servants, many of whom were poor White women with children, accounted for more than one third of the country's population (Abramovitz, 1988).

Although indentured servants did maintain a few freedom and rights, their lives were greatly controlled by their masters. For female servants, this included control of production and reproduction. A women could be fined or beaten if she became pregnant and her pregnancy interfered with her ability to work (Abramovitz, 1988).

The first twenty Africans (three women, seventeen men) in North America with status other than free arrived in 1619 as indentured servants. As with White indentured servants, these Africans were under contract to work a given number of years – after which time they would be set free. During this time, free blacks enjoyed many of the same privileges as whites. Black landowners were allowed to vote, hold political office and move about freely – some even owned slaves (Abramovitz, 1988).

In colonial times, cheap labor was a critical concern for the economy of the United States. As the nation grew, more laborers were needed. Problems occurred with White indentured servants who were able to escape and elude capture by blending in with the rest of the population. Therefore plantation owners turned to Africa to satisfy their labor needs by securing massive numbers of laborers whose dark skin led to easy "identification". The Black population in the United States consisting of both free persons and slaves, accounted for 22% of the country's population by 1760 (Axinn & Levin, 1975) and had become a concern to Whites. Unfortunately, a new social policy was put in place which stripped many free blacks of their freedoms, increasing the slave population and removing all human and civil rights.

Slave Codes

Almost every nation has used slave labor; however, the type and extent of slavery experienced in the "new" world would be like none before it. W. E. B. DuBois (1969) estimated more than 60 million Africans were captured and at least 35 million died during the passage experience. Anderson (1994) points to other characteristics of slavery in the Western world:

Black slavery was…racial and economic exploitation, [causing] economic revolutions and entrenched disparities between blacks and whites….
Subsequently, [Black] skin color became a sign of degradation for its wearer and a sign of wealth for its owner….

Enslaved Blacks were…scattered throughout the world as a minority group. Slave holding nations outside the African continent maintained a majority white population or a white power structure that kept the society's racial balance weighted against blacks…. Lastly, black enslavement was the first instance in history that had worldwide collaborative, race-oriented support for slave trading. Prior to the 15th century, slavery was more of a one-to-one phenomenon. Black slavery drew the notice of all religious orders, Christian and non-Christian alike. Yet, religious leaders supported and justified black enslavement. (pp. 68-69)

Whereas slaves initially had been accorded a modicum of rights; the slave codes which remained in place until emancipation stripped them of all civil and human rights, thus placing slaves completely under the control of the slave owner and further limiting the rights of free blacks. By the mid-1700s the inter-actions between whites and blacks, both free and enslaved, were codified (Abramovitz, 1988; Anderson, 1994). Slaves could not move about without written permission from their master. It became illegal to teach a slave to read and write, nor were they allowed to look a White person in the eye while speaking. Free blacks were banned from political office, could not join the militia, could not assemble without a White present among them and in some areas could not walk on the same sidewalk when passing whites. Blacks could not participate in the judicial system by serving on a jury, testifying or being tried by a jury (Abramovitz, 1988). They could not own guns and because drums and horns might be used by blacks to send coded messages, these instruments were banned. Slave owners had the right to brutalize their slaves for any indiscretion. The lack of civil and human rights resulted in slaves experiencing inhumane treatment in every aspect of life.

Family Life, Productive and Reproductive Labor

The structure of society generally dictates how the family is organized. Patriarchal societies, such as that of the United States, place men in the dominant position. This patriarchy, coupled with a dominant Christian ethic which teaches the subordination of women, has resulted in various laws according men the right to "rule over" their wives and children. Laws limited women's ability to own property, denied them the right to vote and, in certain instances, allowed their husband to use physical violence against them.

American society has always expected the White woman to marry, bear children and care for her husband. Laws and social customs punished single persons, especially women. Women who did not marry by a certain age were referred to as "spinsters" and "old maids". Single people and separated couples were fined and taxes were levied against economically self-sufficient men and women for evading their civil duties (Abramovitz, 1988). Consequently, women married young and usually underwent numerous pregnancies. Wives of farmers were especially encouraged to produce children who would work the land.

The absence of effective birth control resulted in most women, married and single, experiencing numerous pregnancies which interfered with their productivity, threatened their health and frequently proved fatal. Before the mid-1800s, the United States had not enacted laws governing abortion; therefore, British common law, which allowed abortions prior to the time of quickening, was used to regulate the practice (Mohr, 1991). Until the nineteenth century, women could terminate a pregnancy during the first few months without community reprisal (Salmon, 1991).

In the mid-1800s a noticeable decline in the birth rate among White, native-born, married women raised the abortion issue as a community concern and brought legislatures into the debate (Mohr, 1991). States began enacting policies outlawing abortion. The Comstock Law of 1873 "reflected a widespread belief that both contraception and abortion were acts of interference with the natural order and with God's intentions" (Kerber & De Hart, 1991, p. 536). Laws restricting and, in some cases, outlawing abortion remained in effect until abortion was legalized with the passage of Roe v. Wade in the early 1970s.

FAMILY AND THE REPRODUCTIVE LIFE OF BLACK WOMEN

Prior to the Civil War, slave masters were *responsible for the welfare of slaves*. This social policy had a major effect on the formation and structure of Black families.

Herbert Gutman's (1976) research on slave and ex-slave family life revealed some slave families survived as two-parent families. The intentional obstruction of two-parent slave families, however, created scores of slave households headed by female slaves. Free, Black, Single Mothers and children were ignored by charitable organizations and government policy. Blacks who were economically able tended to the needs of those who were not.

During slavery the master granted or denied his slaves' wishes to marry. The destruction of the slave family was economically profitable. Having been stripped of all rights; most aspects of slave life, including family life, was controlled by the master. When marriage was allowed, it was usually informal and not recognized by law. Marriages were frequently nullified by the selling of a mate. Children born to slaves were often sold away from their families for profit. In addition to the informal marriage performed by the master, slaves lived in common law marriages and "commuter" marriages occurred in instances in which each spouse was owned by a different master. Visitation (usually by the husband) was sometimes permitted. Because of the frequent selling of slaves, close relatives occasionally became mates. Wesley Burrell, an ex-slave, recounted, "One boy was traded off from his mother when he was young, an' after he was grown, he was sold back to de same master an' married his mother" (Mellon, 1988, p. 297).

The economic worth of a slave rested in the slave's ability to work. Both male and female slaves suffered tremendously under the burden of bondage; for many, death was the result. Similar to White women's role as housekeeper, female slaves assumed most of the responsibilities for the home. However, few clear gender roles were evident among slaves. Black, male slaves were emasculated and Black female slaves were defeminized. Female slaves performed most of the jobs their male counterparts performed. Abramovitz (1988) asserts up to 90% of female and male slaves on large plantations did field work. "Black women hoed, shoveled, plowed, planted, and harvested; they felled trees, split rails, drove and loaded cart" (p. 60). With the rise of industrialization; female slaves worked in mines, built roads, dug canals and performed numerous other jobs deemed, in White society, as men's work.

Black women were not considered weak and fragile as White women. Sojourner-Truth – a Black abolitionist, women's rights advocate and an ex-slave – in her famous "Ain't I A woman?" speech delivered at large women's-rights meeting in Akron, Ohio, in May 1851 dealt with this issue:

> Dat man ober afar say dat womin needs to be helped into carriages, and lifted ober ditches, and to hate de best place everywhar. Nobody eber helps me into carriages, or ober mudpuddles, or bigs me any best place! And a'n't I a woman? Look at me! Look at my arm! (and she bared her right arm to the shoulder, showing her tremendous muscular power). I have ploughed, and planted, and gathered into barns, and no man could head me! And a'n't I a woman? I could work as much and eat as much as a man – when I could get it – and bear de lash as well! And a'n't I a woman? I have borne thirteen children, and seen 'em mos' all sold off to slavery, and when I cried out with my mother's grief, none but Jesus heard me! And a'n't I a woman? (Kerber & De Hart 1991, pp. 229-230).

Work done by slaves in the "big house" was more gender specific but this involved a small percentage of the slave population. Although field slaves viewed house slaves with contempt, believing domestic work accorded a more comfortable lifestyle, many female slaves who worked in the master's house were subjected to sexual and physical abuse:

> Under these conditions, White owners could also rape and sexually assault their female slaves more easily and with impunity…. Minor infractions or failure to accomplish the expected amount of work might result in severe chastisement in both the field or the manor. Masters whipped Black female slaves for burning the waffles or oversleeping. (Abramovitz, 1988, p. 60)

Many slaves were used as beasts of burden and treated as livestock. Just as farmers and ranchers bred livestock, slave owners bred slaves. After the slave trade was outlawed in the United States in the early nineteenth century, the breeding of domestic slaves increased dramatically. The reproductive labor of female slaves was a critical concern to slave owners as a way to meet the demand for free laborers. Slave narratives offer numerous accounts of the reproductive exploitation of female slaves for economic purpose (Mellon, 1988). Female and male slaves were often bred to produce offspring suitable for particular jobs. Strong males were coupled with strong females to produce a more "robust stock" for labor requiring great strength. White men bred with Black slaves to produce slaves who were believed to be better-equipped to work as house servants. These mulatto slaves also sold for a higher price (Abramovitz, 1988).

BLACK WOMEN IN THE RECONSTRUCTION ERA

After the slaves were emancipated, many estranged wives and husbands who had been sold to separate masters during slavery, searched for each other. If a woman or man was able to find his or her spouse, in many instances the spouse had become involved with someone else and started another family. Therefore, the extended family system, which had been effective during slavery, continued. It was a system comprised of multiple generations which could include a grandmother and grandfather, their children and grandchildren. Frequently, these families consisted of several generations of women with children. The extended family system, with its roots in Africa, was critical to the survival of African Americans in the postslavery era.

Emancipation ushered in a period of reconstruction during which ex-slaves were to become full citizens. Laws were passed protecting blacks from physical abuse. Blacks freely traveled through the country, schools for blacks were built and blacks were elected to political office. Blacks purchased land and even established small towns. Because slaves had acquired many practical and useful skills, many ex-slaves became successful business entrepreneurs.

Unfortunately, when people are educated and socialized under the cultural norms, laws and policies of their oppressor, they tend to take on the traits of the oppressor. As in the White society, Black men were granted voting rights, whereas Black women, like White women, were denied the vote. Sexism began to alter the division of labor within the Black community, tipping the more egalitarian relationship between couples which existed during slavery toward paternalism. The following excerpt from *Freedom's Journal*, a Black newspaper, indicates the changing position of Black women.

> Women are not formed for the great cares themselves, but to soften ours. Their tenderness is the proper reward for the dangers we undergo for their preservation. They are confined within the narrow limits of domestic assiduity, and when they stray beyond them, they move out of their proper sphere and consequently without grace. (Sterling, 1984, p. 220 as cited in Abramovitz, 1988, p. 120)

Although some Black women adopted the notion that *a woman's place was in the home,* many rejected it and joined White women in the fight for women's rights. Others, because of racism in these groups and the differences between White and Black women's needs, formed independent equal rights group tailored to their particular needs.

The fact that the South was forced to deal with ex-slaves on a different level – (one of free women and men) meant life in the south would completely change – producing great disdain for blacks and for the federal government which had forced these changes upon the southern states. Jones (1985) states that in the South many Black women whose husbands were able to support them, refused to work in the fields and sometimes withdrew completely from the work force, resulting in a "radical change in the management of [White] households as well as plantations" (p. 58). Although White wives and mothers who stayed home were accepted by White society, Black women who removed themselves from the labor force and became full-time housewives or who refused to perform field work because of the tremendous toll on their bodies were condemned by White society in both the North and South. According to Jones, they were labeled as being lazy and idle. Thus, the gains made by blacks during the period of reconstruction was short lived.

THE POSTRECONSTRUCTION PERIOD AND THE BLACK FAMILY

Violence toward blacks in the South after reconstruction had a negative impact on the Black family just as it did during slavery. Although census information shows that the majority of Black households between 1880 and 1900 consisted of dual-parent families (86.4% and 82.5%, respectively), the short life span of Black males resulted in an increase in the number of widows (Jones, 1985).

Jones (1985) provides insight into the demographic makeup of blacks in the United States from 1880 to 1915. By the end of the nineteenth century, 90% of Black Americans lived in the South, most in the rural South. Long hours of back-breaking work, poverty, lack of education, fear and hostility resulted in many blacks fleeing the South to find a better life in the North.

Segregation laws–Jim Crowism–would soon reign over Black Americans. By the end of the 19th century, southern blacks found themselves living under "neoslavery," having been stripped of most of their civil and human rights. During this time, White hate groups proliferated, using scare tactics and lynching thousands of Black persons in an effort to keep them "in their place". Black women were forced to return to work in the fields and in the homes of ex-slave owners. Their children often worked alongside them. While Jim Crow segregation policies greatly affected blacks living in southern states, northern blacks were also subjected to Jim Crow laws.

The Welfare State

The turn of the century and the progressive movement brought about the Mothers' Pension program — a cash assistance program designed to care for "deserving" widows and their children. Its purpose was to allow "deserving" Single Mothers to stay home and care for their children. The program's objective was to ensure proper child development and to prepare children to participate in the labor pool in the future (Abramovitz, 1988). It also served as a means of keeping women out of the work force and thus preserving more jobs for men. Most of the mothers who qualified for mothers' pension were White widows. Black, Single Mothers were locked out of this benefit program as were many "unfit" whites and persons from other ethnic groups. Not all states adopted the Mothers' Pension program; those that did served only a small percent of the nation's poor Single Mothers. Progressivism, segregation, and White America's lack of concern about the well-being of Black Americans forced Black communities to form organizations to meet the needs of its poor.

The most drastic change in social welfare policies occurred in 1935 with the passage of the Social Security Act. The country had gone through a series of changes, all of which affected women. Industrialization moved many White women into the position of unpaid homemaker and child-care provider. World War I left many of the mothers widowed. Many women who had moved into the work force to support the war effort were removed from well-paying jobs to make room for returning military men. Finally, in 1929 the economy collapsed, resulting in an economic depression which would last for ten years. Unemployment rose from four million in 1930 to twelve million by 1932 (Heffernan, 1979). Twenty-five percent of whites and 50% of blacks were unemployed (Jewell, 1988). Adhering to prevailing attitudes regarding governments limited role in society, the Hoover administration did little to implement federal programs to assist the poor. It wasn't until Franklin Roosevelt took office that the federal government began to address the economic crisis.

An array of Federal work programs were developed to put citizens back to work. Although some White women found employment within these programs, the number of women compared with men who found such employment was grossly insufficient. Gordon (1994) gives two reasons for this disparity: first, the jobs in these work relief programs were considered too strenuous for women and second, female unemployment was not considered a problem. Many women, in fact, were fired from positions so men could fill them.

The Depression fueled racism in the country; a common practice in times of economic hardship. Black men and women were virtually locked out of work relief programs. The director of the Public Works Administration (PWA) issued a mandate that "all PWA contractors should hire at least as many Blacks as their proportion in the 1930 census" (Gordon, 1994, p. 197). However, contractors did not honor this mandate, and the already high Black unemployment rate increased, heightening domestic tension and family decay.

The Social Security Act of 1935 was a massive federal program designed to assist the elderly, disabled, children and other unemployed persons. Under the poor laws, the burden of caring for the poor fell on relatives, friends, the private sector and the state. The Social Security Act attempted to "replace much of the [citizens' economic] loss through tax-financed income transfer programs with presumably well-defined eligibility criteria and benefit schedules" (Haveman, 1985, p. 445). Gordon(1994) discusses the disparities among these programs:

> The law set up two social insurance programs, Old-Age Insurance and Unemployment Compensation, relatively generous and honorable in their terms and restricted in their inclusion. For others, the law provided several public assistance programs, including ADC (Aid to Dependent Children), with stingy and humiliating conditions. The stratification of programs reproduced and deepened already existing social inequalities. Just as labor market forces and cultural changes were allowing women and blacks to move onto the main track of citizenship, Social Security created a new hierarchy of social citizenship in which they were on the bottom again. (pp. 254-255)

Aid to Dependent Children (ADC) was punitive and continued to adhere to the distinction between deserving and nondeserving Single Mothers. Negative stereotypes and racism resulted in policies which restricted most Black mothers from receiving ADC. Though 50% of the Black population was unemployed at the peak of the Depression (compared with 25% of whites), only 15% were deemed eligible to receive public assistance (Jewell, 1988). Thus, ADC from 1935 to the 1950s had little effect on the Black family. During this period, the majority of Black families remained two-parent families.

Legislative changes in the 1950s and 1960s increased the number of families eligible to receive public assistance. This period also saw an increase in both

117

White and Black Single Mothers and children on the welfare rolls. In 1962, ADC became AFDC (Aid to Families with Dependent Children). Under AFDC, the relative with whom a child resided also received a monetary allotment. Although the majority of Single-Mother families receiving AFDC were White, AFDC became associated with Black Single-Mother families. Axinn and Levin (1975) believe this perception developed because the majority of Black families receiving AFDC lived in the inner cities, which gave them greater visibility than their White counterparts residing in small cities and urban areas.

PORTRAIT OF A SINGLE MOTHER

Gordon (1994) provides important facts on the Single Mother "problem" and analyzes its social construction. At the turn of the century, Single Motherhood began to be framed as a social problem. The United States was, at this time, experiencing social and economic unrest as a result of the shift from an agrarian to industrial economy. When a nation's economy is in a state of anomie, society looks for a scapegoat. Recent immigrants "were more ghettoized [than the prior wave of immigrants] and therefore more visible than the nonimmigrant poor who were scattered and more rural" (p. 30). Poor, immigrant Single Mothers were highly visible and thus a perfect scapegoat.

How a problem is defined affects the public's attitude about the problem. Gordon (1994) states at the turn of this century 75% of single women heading households were classified as widows. This term depicted women as being single through no fault of their own. Therefore, their poverty was not generally viewed with contempt. Feminists and social workers aggressively fought to protect White Single Mothers (who were portrayed as victims) from being blamed for their situation. Policy attempted to protect children of Single Mothers by "enforcing paternity and child support…Its goals were to remove the stigma of illegitimacy for the child altogether and to reduce the stigma on unmarried mothers by positioning them as victims rather than sinners" (p. 29). By the 1930s, however, the Single Mother category was subdivided into more descriptive labels: widows, deserted women, unmarried, illegitimate mothers and divorcees. The labels attempted to describe something about the lifestyle of Single Mothers.

During this time, attention focused on gender analysis waned, resulting in a change in language and attitude toward Single Mothers (Gordon). Social problems which had once been the focus of social workers were now ignored or redefined: "What had once been called 'desertion' and blamed exclusively on men was now more and more often labeled neutral 'marital separation' (divorce was still very rare), with an assumption of mutual responsibility for the failure of the marriage" (Gordon, 1994, p. 33). This change in attitude led to Single Mothers being assigned negative labels and being further victimized by society.

While the women's-rights movement of the early- and mid-twentieth century fought to protect the rights of single White women, Black women continued to feel the lash of racism, virtually ignored by the White community. In Black families, two phenomena led to changes in family structure: the increased number of Black Single Mothers who migrated to the North and were not able to live in an established household and the independence some women who had been locked into miserable marriages sought with the help of AFDC (Gordon, 1994).

As the number of Single Mothers and children receiving AFDC increased dramatically in the 1960s; the face of the scapegoat shifted from White to Black. Gordon (1994) attributes the increase in the AFDC rolls to changes in the family structure. Historically, Single Mothers generally lived with relatives or friends. As a result, they were considered a "subfamily" and counted by the Census Bureau as part of the family in which they resided. This made them "less visible and possibly less economically and socially needy than those who head their own household" (p. 18). This was particularly Single Black Mothers living with extended family.

Finally, Gordon (1994) asserts that the term "female-headed household" is problematic because it "is used without a common opposite phrase, we do not normally call a two-parent household either male-headed (or 'double headed'!)" (p. 18). This likely adds to the stigma of Single Motherhood because it is perceived as a break from the "normal" family structure – the nuclear family. However, the nuclear family structure is itself a recent phenomenon, shifting as the country moved from an agrarian to an industrial society from an extended family structure to a nuclear structure.

Decline of the Welfare State

The increase of Black Single Mothers and children on the AFDC rolls led to a study of the condition of the Black family and heightened public attention with regard to this population. Many popular versions such as Moynihan's (1965) labeled the African American family a matriarchy. He concluded the Black community was disintegrating and the primary source for this disintegration was the way in which the Black family is structured. He stated "a fundamental fact of Negro American family life is the often reversed roles of husband and wife" (p. 30). This so-called reversal of roles and power was defined as the primary problem. Moynihan traced the roots of this phenomenon to slavery. In years following Moynihan's report, numerous reports blamed Black Single Mothers and children as a drain on the welfare system. Reports also blame social spending for the increase in Black, female-headed households. Consequently, the welfare system has been under constant attack, with the attack on AFDC the most severe.

Angela Davis (1995) refutes the assertion that this so-called matriarchal Black family is a by-product of slavery or that it ever existed, arguing a matriarchy suggests women possess a measure of power which female slaves in this country never had and of which Black women today have very little. Davis states the American brand of slavery prohibited organized family life and that the notion of a female slave as a matriarch "implies stable kinship structures within which the mother exercises decisive authority" (p. 202). Essentially, Davis asserts, the female slave was owned and controlled by her master, as was the male slave and their children. Therefore, even if she was allowed to have a husband or to keep her children, the female slave had little control over them. Davis believes the emasculation of male slaves, defemininization of female slaves and frequent blurring of gender roles and division of labor resulted in a more equal status between men and women – "the deformed equality of equal oppression" (p. 202), which, in a patriarchal society, could be misconstrued as matriarchal.

Informed and knowledgeable social scientists have dismissed much of the mythology which has grown up around social assistance. Piven and Cloward (1987) refuted the notion social spending led to increased female-headed households by asking a profound question: "If AFDC [Aid to Families with Dependent Children] was responsible for the growth of families with female heads . . . why should that effect have been so much greater for black than for other groups?" (p. 54). They argued the social and systemic elements affected blacks long before the introduction of public aid set the stage for the rise in Black Single-Parent families. Other social scientists support this assertion (Brewer, 1988; Davis, 1995; Franklin, 1992).

The 1980s and early-1990s saw a resurgence in public concern with the welfare system. The increase in low-income, Single-Parent households and the numerous myths about AFDC recipients resulted in the call for a revamping of AFDC. Programs and policies focused on "reducing" the welfare rolls; many through work, child care and housing. Welfare to work programs were ineffective due to inadequate funding and poor design. The types of jobs available to the women who completed the training paid minimum wage and were "unlikely to move people out of poverty" (Gueron & Pauly, 1991, p. 33). Attempts to enforce child support laws were ineffective due, in part, "to the fathers' own poverty" (Pearce, 1978, p. 30). Some housing assistance programs have been beneficial (Popkin, Rosenbaum, & Meaden 1993). The Gautreaux program, arising from a law suit filed against the Chicago Housing Authority, assisted families in moving into suburbs with increased accessibility to employment.

During the 1992 Presidential campaign, Bill Clinton, the Democratic candidate, promised to "change welfare as we know it". Succumbing to many conservative legislators, President Clinton signed the Personal Responsibility and Work

Opportunity Reconciliation Act of 1996 which replaced AFDC with Temporary Assistance to Needy Families (TANF) which repeals the entitlement to benefits and block grants federal program funds. The explicit intention of TANF is to move low-income, Single Parents from the welfare rolls to work. According to Jenks and Edin (1995), the implicit intention of the new welfare law is to control the reproductive ability of poor women signaling that "people should not have children until they are ready to support them" (p. 43). Because poverty will never be eradicated, this attempt would deny some women the right to bear children.

In addition to being punitive, TANF removes the safety net for many low-income families and will likely increase the number of children living in abject poverty. Recipients are restricted to a five year lifetime limit of cash assistance and those who have received assistance for two years must be involved in a work program. Most recipients who will move into the work force will be employed in low-wage jobs and without government assistance will likely be unable to meet the needs of their family. Other insidious tenets of the law are: the ability to set family caps, the denial of benefits to persons convicted of drug-related crimes after receiving benefits, requiring unmarried teen mothers to live with an adult, and unmarried others needing to establish paternity. This new law is the first large step in lessening the responsibility of the State in providing assistance to its poor citizens. While states have leeway in how TANF is implemented, many Black families consisting of a Single Mother and her children face homelessness if states decide to follow the law to the letter.

Program Models

Various misconceptions about Black Americans are a result of a failure to understand Black-American culture. Europeans and White Americans tend to use their own cultural values as a yardstick by which to measure other cultures. As a result, they tend to deem other cultures as inferior – even pathological. Such is the case with the White America's view of the Black culture (Gutman, 1976; Hobles, Goddard, Cavil & George, 1987). This lack of understanding results in the development of programs and services for solving the problems in the Black community on the basis of White America's cultural norms, values and beliefs. Because African-American cultural values are ignored, these programs and services have little or no positive effects and may do more harm than good.

Years of psychological terror have resulted in some Black Single Mothers becoming alienated. Living in constant crisis stemming from economic hardships has resulted in isolation and a sense of hopelessness. While critics view the conditions of these women offering explanations for their behavior and solutions to these problems, the voices of many of these women have been silenced. And because many Black Americans have been "miseducated" (Woodson, 1990) and do not know their history sufficiently, they do not understand how that history shaped their psychology and they become a mystery to themselves.

It's important to understand African-American culture and families in order to assist Black, Single Mothers and their children. Billingsley (1992) contends that African American families can be understood only by examining the African family. He points to several features of the African family which eminently differ from American and European family structures:

- Greater emphasis on the core group than on the conjugal pair
- Primacy of the extended family
- Child-centered societies
- Elders held in high esteem
- Gender role reciprocity
- Balance between individual and family rights
- Emphasis on responsibility to the family over one's personal needs and desires
- Polygamous and polyandrous marriages

Although multiple marriages violate U.S. law and may not benefit African-American families, other features of African culture represent positive values. These values benefit African-American families despite their conflict with European-American cultural values.

Because of recent changes in social welfare policy, particularly the adoption of TANF, it is imperative that Black, Single Mothers find vehicles which speak to their needs and bring about systemic change. The present social welfare policy, if unchanged, will eventually force Black, Single Mothers with children to remain economically dependent on family and friends and hold them captive in hostile marriages. Many women who used AFDC as a temporary means of support while working toward self-sufficiency may, under current law be unable to become self-sufficient.

Prior to the integration movement, Black neighborhoods pulled together to care for children. Although higher education was out of reach for most children, those who showed the most promise were sent to school and supported by working family members and local organizations. Social cohesion was strong in these communities and Single Mothers received social and economic support. Strategies must be developed to restore community for Black, Single Mothers. The programs discussed in the following sections address these needs by offering educational, social, emotional and economic support.

WomanSpirit

WomanSpirit in Saint Louis, Missouri, is a self-help and mutual-help association of low- to moderate-income Black women which organizes, educates and mobilizes its members to participate in the legislative process and to have an impact on policymaking. LaDoris Payne, founder and program director, understands that the policies affecting African-American women are influenced by local, regional, national and global concerns. This grass-roots women's organization has ties to the United Nations. Payne canvasses the country and the world in order to learn about the issues which affect the association and its members. She participates in national and global conferences and brings the information back to members. Members are then able to develop strategies to influence policy.

Members of WomanSpirit receive education and social support through participation in several programs and activities:
- Harriet Tubman Institute, leadership development and training program
- National Congress of Neighborhood Women, a regional training center
- Women's wellness projects
- Empowering Families Program
- Socialization Through the Arts programs, developed in collaboration with Katherine Dunham Children's Workshops
- Enterprising Women, a microenterprise program

As participants in the groups become knowledgeable and are better able to analyze problems and articulate them to others, they in turn become group facilitators.

WomanSpirit examines mainstream and alternative systems of mutual aid in an effort to develop models of mutual aid that will empower Black women and inform reseachers. Roman Catholic nuns who have been in the forefront in developing alternative systems such as hospitals, schools, agencies and complete social service support systems are used as leadership models for group members. Through researching these alternative systems, WomanSpirit hopes to build alternative systems designed to address the needs of low-income, Black women and their families.

For example, North St. Louis, Missouri, the community in which WomenSpirit is located, had no beds or safe places for women victims of domestic violence. Members established a small shelter housed in the Imani Family Center, home of WomenSpirit. Other successes include the microenterprise group, which teaches women how to operate their own business. Women are provided with small start-up loans and offered group support. This has provided the opportunity for women to develop and implement creative business plans.

WomanSpirit has expanded into the Mississippi Delta, where four groups have formed. Payne visits these groups regularly, teaching low-income Black women to stop waiting for someone to save them and to begin saving themselves. The first step in this process, according to Payne, is for Black women to become self-directed.

Women's Support Group

Raheim and Bolden (1995) state self-employment programs can help low-income women become independent of the welfare system. This fundamental belief guides a St. Louis, Missouri women's support group as well. Five women from varying socio-economic levels living on St. Louis' south side came together in 1992 to discuss health-service issues. The women were African American and European American from different religious backgrounds. However, they all shared a background of poverty. Initially, this diverse group of women focused on what could be done to improve health services. As the group began to meet regularly, multiple other issues surfaced: pregnant teenage daughters, tight household budgets, domestic violence and sons involved in gang activities.

Although they had few funds, the members of this group pooled their financial resources to assist members in times of need (e.g., to pay a utility bill). As the group began to grow, women outside the group sought financial help and emotional support from group members. Young, pregnant teens sought support regarding decisions surrounding their pregnancy. Many of these young women felt they could not turn to their mothers, and in some instances the group played the role of mediator in these and similar disputes. Many of the women who received help from the group became members. Eventually, the members organized formally. Its mission was to help any woman in need. Because they occasionally offered assistance to men, their motto became, "Yes, I am my sister's and brother's keeper."

Members' talents were used to provide economic and emotional support to persons in need. In 1993, the organization moved into a building in northwest St. Louis. A second-hand clothing shop was located in the building, one member makes and sells jewelry, another has a donut shop. The group serves as an emergency food pantry and shelter for women. A peer lending service was added with the help of a small grant from the Campaign for Human Development.

The thrust of the organization is consistent with the mission of social work – economic empowerment on a micro level and social justice on the macro level (Raheim & Golden, 1995). The group also added a legislative-advocacy component to attack systemic causes of oppression. A legislative consultant was hired to track legislative activities at the state and federal levels that affect the lives of group members (e.g., welfare reform). The group lobbied the Missouri legislature and initiated voter-education and -registration drives in the inner city. Members also began building coalitions with other advocacy groups to increase their political effectiveness.

The women of the organization educated AFDC recipients on changes in the welfare program. The group seeks to expand women's understanding of oppression beyond the local environment and involves them in legal and political advocacy. Beyond welfare reform, the group has tracked information pertaining to domestic violence. Locally, they have been successful in influencing the passage of an ordinance requiring the hiring of a percentage of city residents when the city contracts services. Because of the large Black population in the city, this ordinance will most likely provide employment opportunities for Black women. In addition, the organization works to achieve a global understanding of issues by inviting international speakers.

Women Inspired to Succeed (WITS)

Much about the way of life of Africans has been misunderstood by outsiders. Western interpretation of African spirituality as well as family structure are among those distortions. The African ontological principal of consubstantiation has been grossly misrepresented. Nobles, Goddard, Cavil, and George (1987) define consubstantiation as "the essence of all things…[being] of the same substance (i.e., spirit, energy)" (p. 23). This concept holds all human beings are of one spirit. Therefore, respect for all people was customary. The underlying value traveled with the Africans from Africa to the United States during the slave trade, remaining a part of the African-American culture for many years. Unfortunately, years of direct and subtle stripping of many African customs has resulted in Black Americans losing many of the principles and traditions traditionally beneficial in sustaining them. WITS is a supportive network for African-American women that attempts to recapture African-American cultural values. Bringing together Black women from all backgrounds, WITS focuses on strengthening culture, family and community development throughout the year. Although the group's intent is to enhance spirituality, it does not promote a particular religion. It uses principles found in Kwanzaa as its guidepost.

The principles and values of Kwanzaa were taken from the "first fruit" celebration, which has roots in many African societies (Karenga, 1988). The event celebrates five values. *Ingathering* not only refers to the gathering of crops, it also celebrates the ingathering of people. In African societies, the ingathering of crops provided the occasion to gather people together in "communion [the] sharing and renewal of peoplehood bonds which strengthen mutual concern and commitment" (Karenga, 1988, p. 17). The second value is *reverence* for the Creator and Creation. The focus here is on appreciation of nature, the universe, the Creator and humankind. *Commemoration of the past* is the third value. Veneration of ancestors and respect for history are central to this aspect of the celebration. The fourth value is *recommitment to cultural ideas*. Finally the *celebration of the good* offers participants the opportunity to celebrate through dance, song, recitals, renewing friendships and other expressions.

Women Inspired to Succeed incorporates the Nguzo Saba (seven principles) of the African American holiday Kwanzaa. Each meeting focuses on two principles, faith and one of the other principles: unity, self-determination, collective work and responsibility, cooperative economics, purpose and creativity.

The group meets three times a year for a one-day retreat (Black Pearls), bringing together Black women of all ages, incomes, religious backgrounds and classes. Each participant is asked to bring a dollar, a canned good and an inexpensive gift. The monetary and food donations are used to support individuals or families in need. A member of the group is often the recipient of the donations. The gifts are presented to each member. Members are not penalized if they cannot afford the contributions; others fill this void by bringing extras.

In many ways the group fills the role of an extended family by providing mentoring and support. Some older women assumed the role of surrogate mother to younger women who are estranged from their own mother. Better educated members provide information to others about continuing education and inspire them to set goals as well as help them plan to achieve those goals.

The women have established a job-networking component. Employed members network with agencies and businesses to compile a job list in an effort to assist low-income women in seeking employment. They also assist unemployed women in resume writing, sharpening interviewing skills and accessing jobs via the Internet. Some of the unemployed women have found employment through this network.

Each new participant is asked to complete a profile. The profile asks about the reading interest of the participant; WITS focuses on African and African-American history; it has established a group which reads books on these topics and writes book reviews in At WITS' End, a newsletter distributed three times a year. Group members are encouraged to read suggested books. The newsletter presents a "Herstory" feature, which looks at the life of women of African descent.

The group focuses on promoting unity among Black women and facilitating individual accomplishments. To this end, suggestions must be based on one of the Nguzo Saba principles. The goal is to build positive values among the women which will have a positive impact on their family lives and inspire them to become involved in community.

Partners in Self-Sufficiency

The Partners in Self-Sufficiency Program is component of the Ecumenical Housing Production Corporation (EHPC) in St. Louis, Missouri. This comprehensive service program is designed to help tenants achieve self-sufficiency. Women are offered mentoring and monitoring as well as opportunities, guidelines, expectations and assistance. The women are empowered personally and professionally. The process helps them "in developing strengths to personally and politically cope more effectively with those systems that are important to them" (Shulman, 1992, p. 18).

To be eligible for the Partners in Self-Sufficiency Program, the women must live in EHPC's scattered-site housing. All of the women in the program are low-income, Black mothers who are single when they enter the group. All of the families live in quality, stable housing in a viable neighborhood. The Partners in Self-Sufficiency Program provides long-term, ongoing support even after the women move or marry. The group becomes a form of extended family, assisting in goal development and offering encouragement, motivation and empathy in times of crisis.

The women in the program are provided with the support, motivation and resources needed to move into adequate employment. Through individual and group contact and services; the program works respectfully, creatively and collaboratively with the women in an effort to provide support, skill development and job training, motivation and education. The program coordinator emphasizes individualized, progressive goal setting to motivate and focus the participants. The participants develop their own educational, personal and work-related goals. The group members and coordinator hold participants accountable while providing financial and emotional support.

Through a combination of activities and components, participants receive encouragement, support, motivation, resources and opportunities. Monthly group meetings serve as a venue for peer support, interpersonal feedback, positive reinforcement, training and education on various topics (including finances, student loans and parenting). Motivation and support are reinforced through regular mail and telephone contact and families are referred for counseling to a collaborating agency when they express an interest and a need.

Financial assistance is available for tuition, training, child care and transportation. Participants also receive assistance in acquiring a GED, remediating defaulted student loans, learning job-readiness skills and developing financial-management skills. Through a combination of support, training and motivation; the women in the program have improved their employment, education and financial position. Several women have managed to buy their own homes by developing a consistent savings program.

The combination of supports and resources helps the women learn to identify achievable goals, develop a realistic time line and monitor their own progress. Participants learn to develop and implement work and education goals while also working on personal and family goals – improved self-esteem, higher expectations, internal motivation and improved family relationships. The combined emphasis on opportunity with high expectations guides the women toward change. As stated by some of the participants, "she [the project director] gave us the oppor-tunity to dare to dream. And upon that…we went out there and took it for whatever it's worth to accept the challenges." "It makes you want to do. And you have no alternative but to do it." "Self-sufficient…financially independent…it's not like we're just getting something for free. We're working for it…. And it's giving us a lot of encouragement to set our goals and to meet our goals."

Conclusion

The psychology of a people is developed through their social experience. To understand the African-American family and the rise of the Black, female-headed household, the issues must be examined from a historical context. The family does not exist in isolation. Therefore, social workers (as well as the rest of society) must begin to understand how social construction has weighed negatively on the Black family. The history of those of African descent in the United States, the intermingling of cultures and social policy development all come together to construct the conditions experienced by Black, Single Mothers, particularly those who have low incomes. Black women experience the impact of their history of slavery, Jim Crow laws, escalating separation and isolation and the entrenchment of racism and sexism.

Years of psychological terror has resulted in some Black Single Mothers becoming alienated. Living in constant crisis stemming from economic hardships results in isolation and a sense on hopelessness. Critics view the conditions of Black, Single Mothers, offering explanations for their behavior and solutions to their problems; the voices of many of these women, however, have been silenced. Because many Black Americans do not know their history, they do not understand how that history shaped their psychological well-being.

The demise of AFDC and the adoption of TANF will most likely aid in the widening gap between the haves and have nots. More Black, Single Mothers and their children will find themselves in need of the services provided by social workers. The effectiveness of social workers in serving this population is directly related to their understanding of the Black family. Workers should involve low income, Black, Single Mothers in programs designed to empower and educate them economically and politically. Black women need access to the resources necessary to develop the skills required to earn a living wage and advance professionally. They also need to develop skills and techniques in policy analysis, political lobbying, planning and program development. These tools will help them better understand the oppressive systems in which they live and help them intelligently wage campaigns to change them.

The history of the Black, Single Mother, facing the intersection of racism and sexism, requires intervention programs grounded in a knowledge of this oppression and focused on empowerment. Group work programs are effective in engaging poor, Black mothers, particularly programs employing a multi-systems approach. The multisystems approach to treatment includes the extended family, health care providers, legislators, schools, employment agencies, job training programs, social service agencies and advocacy groups. Program facilitators can help navigate participants through the web, providing them with pertinent information and helping them interface with the appropriate systems. Involving system representatives as visiting lecturers allows a rapport to develop between agencies and participants reducing perceived system intrusiveness and establishing a comfort level for participants.

Group work has been effective in racially homogeneous groups. It is also an effective model for Black mothers in heterogeneous environments if the worker is comfortable with this clientele and uses a culturally sensitive approach. Humanistic methods are effective tools when working in a heterogeneous environment (Brekke, 1989; William, 1994). These methods encourage participation with hard-to-reach clients because they help the worker relate to the client's view of problems. This may include stories of particular social experiences and how the client was affected by them (Davis, 1989).

While the programs reviewed take into account the victimization of poor, Black women, they also look at the resiliency, resourcefulness and drive of the women and the community. The programs draw on individual strengths using the talents each of the women possesses as an empowerment tool to help elevate these women from feeling worthless and powerless to understanding they can positively affect their situation. Intervention must be grounded in the experience of the group. The focus and purpose of the intervention must be clear to both the worker and the clients. Models of treatment should be structured around client strengths while addressing deficits.

Bibliography

Abramovitz, M. (1988) . *Regulating the lives of women: Social welfare policy from colonial times to the present.* Boston: South End Press.

Anderson, C. (1994). *Black labor, white wealth: The search for power and economic justice.* Edgewood, MD: Duncan & Duncan.

Axinn, J. & Levin, H. (1975). *Social welfare: A history of the American response to need.* New York: Dodd Mead.

Billingsley, A. (1992). *Climbing Jacob's ladder: The enduring legacy of African American families.* New York: Simon and Schuster.

Brewer, R.M. (1988). Black women in poverty: Some comments on female-headed families. *Signs, 13,* 331-39.

Davis, A. (1995). Reflections on the Black women's role in the community of slaves. In Guy, B. & Hall, S. (Eds.) *Words of fire: An anthology of African American feminist thought.* New York: The New Press.

Di Nitto, D.M. (1983). *Social welfare: Politics and public policy.* Englewood Cliffs, NJ: Prentice-Hall.

DuBois, W.E.B. (1969). *The suppression of the African slave trade.* New York: Schocken.

Franklin, D.L. (1992). Feminization of poverty and African-American families: Illusions and realities. *Affilia, 7* (2), p. 142-55.

Gordon, L. (1994). *Pitied but not entitled: Single-mothers and the history of welfare, 1890-1935.* New York: FreePress.

Gueron, J.M. & Pauly, E. (1991). *From welfare to work.* New York: Russell Sage Foundation.

Gutman, H.G. (1976). *The black family in slavery and freedom 1750-1925.* New York: Random House.

Haveman, R.H. (1985). *Does the welfare state increase welfare: Reflections on hidden negatives and observed positives. De-Economist, 133* (4), 445-66.

Heffermen, W.J. (1979). *Introduction to social policy: Power, scarcity, and common human need.* Itasca, IL: F.E. Peacock.

Jenks, C. & Edin, K. (1995). Do poor women have a right to bear children. *The American Prospect, 20,* 43-52.

Jewell, K.S. (1988). *Survival of the Black family: The institutional impact of U.S. social policy.* New York: Praeger.

Jones, J. (1985). *Labor of love, labor of sorrow.* New York: Basic Books.

Karenga, M. (1988). *The African American holiday of Kwanzaa:A celebration of family, community, and culture.* Los Angeles: University of Sankore Press.

Kerber, L.K., & De Hart, J.S. (Eds.) (1991). *Women's America: Refocusing the past.* New York: Oxford University Press.

Mellon, J. (1988). *Bullwhip days: The slaves remember.* New York: Avon Books.

Mohr, J. (1991). Abortion in America. In Kerber, L.K. & De Hart, J.S. (Eds.) *Women's America: Refocusing the past.* New York: Oxford University Press.

Moynihan, D.P. (1965). *The Negro family: The case for national action.* Washington, DC: Office of Policy Planning and Research. U.S. Department of Labor.

Mulroy, E.A. (1988). *Women as Single-parents: Confronting institutional barriers in the courts, the workplace, and housing market.* Dover, MA: Auburn House.

Nobles, W.W.; Goddard, L.L.; Cavil, W.E. & George, P.Y. (1987). *African-American families: Issues, insights, and directions.* Oakland, CA: Black Family Institute.

Pearce, D. (1978). The feminization of poverty: Women, work and welfare. *Urban and Social Change Review, 11,* 28-36.

Piven, F.F., & Cloward, R.A. (1987). The historical sources of the contemporary relief debate. In Block, F.; Cloward, R.A.; Ehrenreich, B. & Piven, F.F. (Eds.) *The mean season: The attack on the welfare state.* (pp. 1-45). New York: Pantheon.

Raheim, S., & Bolden, J. (1995). Economic empowerment of low-income women through self-employment programs. *Affilia, 10* (2), 138-54.

Salmon, M. (1991). *Women and property in South Carolina: The evidence for marriage settlements, 1730-1830.* New York: Oxford University Press.

Shulman, L. (1992). *The skills of helping: Individuals, families, and groups (3rd ed.).* Itasca, IL: F. E. Peacock.

Woodson, C. G. (1990). *The mis-education of the Negro.* Nashville: Winston-Derek Publishers, Inc.

Lesbian and Gay Single-Parent Families

Sue Pearlmutter, Ph.D., MSW

As lesbian and gay parents, we are all under the stress of knowing that some people harbor violently negative feelings about our families. It is an awareness that may remain a mere whisper in the dim recesses of our consciousness or move to the foreground with frightening clarity, but it is an ongoing part of our lives.... Each time we address the issue of our visibility we balance our ideals, our politics, our hopes for support, and our parenting goals against our caution, our need for privacy, and our fatigue.
(Martin, 1993, p. 308-309)

Introduction

LESBIANS AND GAY MEN create families. Sometimes those families include children. Children may come to us as the result of donor insemination, foster parenting or adoption or they may be part of our families as the result of a previous heterosexual marriage. Our families are deliberate and, for the most part, a highly desired part of our lives. They exist in multiple dimensions and contexts – within larger, extended families of origin, in gay and lesbian communities and in society as whole.

In many ways, my children's lives are no different from those of their friends who have been affected by divorce and Single Parenthood. In some ways, however, their lives are very different. Since I came out as a lesbian ten years ago, my children (now very grown) have been part of three other families in addition to their family of origin or first family. They joined a former partner, her children, and me for holidays, visits and summer vacations; they joined their father, his wife and her children for other holidays, visits and vacations; they join my partner and me for family celebrations and visits. My partner co-parented two children

131

(the biological children of a former partner) who are a part of our lives and family rituals.

My life as a lesbian mother has been altered as well. As a feminist and a lesbian, I have questioned mothering and my own traditional views of what mothers do; how we care for our children, and how we view ourselves, our partners and our children. I have struggled to define what an alternative family structure would look like for me and for other lesbians and gay men. Along the way, I have made some wondrous discoveries: alternative family is what occurs as a result of being family to and with each other; my sons can accept, participate in and sometimes even celebrate the life I live. Family is bound together with love and caring, not guilt and obligation.

I have also learned much about the choices gay and lesbian people make regarding their families and children. This chapter is a reflection of that learning and of the many discussions my partner and I have had about mothering. Finally, it recognizes many gay and lesbian parents remain hidden and unable to come into the light.

A Context for Considering Lesbian and Gay Single-Parent Families

Understanding Homophobia and Heterosexism

It is not possible to comprehend the complexity of issues facing lesbian women and gay men in our society without first recognizing the impact of homophobia and heterosexism. Homophobia is:

> the irrational fear and hatred of those who love and sexually desire those of the same sex … [it is] that societal disease that places such negative messages, condemnation, and violence on gay men and lesbians that we have to struggle throughout our lives for self-esteem. (Pharr, 1988, p. 1-2)

Homophobia posits that the behavior of lesbians and gays is deviant, sinful, immoral, and dangerous to the society. Examples of homophobic acts abound. Judges deny child custody solely on the basis of a parent's sexual orientation. School boards deny students the right to form gay and lesbian clubs or groups and attempt to prohibit literature in school libraries which presents gay and lesbian people in a positive light. State laws criminalize consensual relations between adults of the same sex. Youth and adults perpetrate violence which results in injury or death to gay or lesbian persons.

In addition to suffering the direct effects of homophobia, lesbians and gays may internalize the negative attitudes of others and believe they are morally repugnant and damaged as well as damaging to others. Internalized homophobia sometimes results in denial of same-sex attraction and sexual orientation. It can cause the gay or lesbian person to hide his or her identity from family, friends and community. It can result in prejudice against those who are very open and active in lesbian and gay communities or against other minorities. It increases the risk of suicide among gay and lesbian youth (Blumenfeld & Raymond, 1993).

> Heterosexism is a close ally of homophobia. It is the system by which heterosexuality is assumed to be the only acceptable and viable life option. …[H]eterosexism is a form of discrimination. Its subtlety makes it somehow even more insidious because it is harder to define and combat. Heterosexism is discrimination by neglect, omission, and/or distortion, whereas often its more active partner – homophobia – is discrimination by intent and design. (Blumenfeld & Raymond, 1993, p. 244-245).

Heterosexism renders gay and lesbian culture, history and communities invisible. Parents assume their children will grow up and marry a person of the other sex and raise children as a result of that marriage. Students learn about those who contributed to art, music, literature, history and philosophy and presume all were straight. Health care providers seek answers to questions based upon a presumption of heterosexual behavior. If gay and lesbian parents talk about their children, people assume the existence of a partner or former partner of the opposite sex. In each situation, the assumption of heterosexuality blinds people to the lives and experiences of gay and lesbian persons.

Lesbian and gay parents live in at least two cultures. They share a culture with others who are part of a sexual minority group and struggle with oppression which results from being part of that group. Gays and lesbians are taught to believe they have no history or culture. They are hidden. Attempts to acknowledge their numbers are directly or subtly subverted. They are viewed as sexual beings only with no recognition of other aspects of their lives. They do not have the right to define and name themselves. They may live in ghettos–often as a way to escape homophobia. They live with negative stereotypes and images created by the dominant culture while working in and otherwise participating in societal activities. They value family and community, want to care and be cared for by others and have the right to safety and acceptance. Moreover, persons in the lesbian and gay community struggle with the racial attitudes and stereotypes which affect society as a whole.

Gay and Lesbian Families

Background

Gay men and lesbian women have been parents for hundreds of years (perhaps thousands of years, although documentation of gay and lesbian parents in earlier times does not exist). In general, gay and lesbian parents have been hidden, silent and constrained by the social mores, values and laws of society. In the past thirty years, however, lesbians and gay men have begun to emerge and to redefine for themselves the concept of family. Although gay political movements in Europe during the late nineteenth century and in the United States during the early years of the twentieth century occurred, discussions of gay and lesbian parenthood and parenting were absent from those movements (Blumenfeld & Raymond, 1993; Duberman, Vicinus & Chauncey, 1989; Faderman, 1991). In the years following the 1969 Stonewall riots in New York City, in which gay people fought with police who attempted to close a bar – the Stonewall Inn – by harassing customers, and in the wake of the civil rights and feminist movements, gay men and lesbian women have struggled to build a strong sense of community and identity. Lesbian- and gay-headed families are a clear and absolute reality.

To understand these families it is important to question the definition of family which has become traditional in American culture – two married heterosexual adults and their children (preferably, biological offspring). Although today's culture clings to this construct of family, in reality out-of-wedlock pregnancy, divorce or death of a partner create Single-Parent families. Stepfamilies create diverse blendings of adults and children. Reproductive technology permits complex configurations of family, and in-vitro fertilization, sperm donor fathers and surrogate mothers become part of the language defining families. Lesbian and gay families constitute another alternative in a wide array of family structures, families of choice.

A constructive definition of a gay and lesbian family is "a family in which two generations are present and one of the primary caretakers is gay or lesbian" (Ariel & Stearns, 1992, p. 99). These families may result from several different combinations of events. A gay or lesbian might have had children in a heterosexual marriage, before coming out as a lesbian or gay man. Gays or lesbians may adopt a child or children, either individually, or (far less likely) as a couple. A lesbian could be inseminated and raise the child alone, with a co-parent, or as part of a larger support system of friends and a partner (Harrison, 1995). Other family configurations occur when relationships begin and end and new partners join an existing family, perhaps bringing children of their own, or when a heterosexual person who may be a surrogate mother or biological father participates as a co-parent or support to a gay or lesbian family (Ariel & Stearns, 1992; Barret & Robinson, 1990; Benkov, 1994; Bernstein & Stephenson, 1995; Bigner & Bozett, 1990; Bozett, 1987c, 1989; Burke, 1993; Clunis & Green, 1995; Gottlieb, 1995; Hanscombe & Forster, 1981; Martin, 1993; Morgen, 1995; Pies, 1990; Pollack & Vaughn, 1987; Pollack, 1995; Polikoff, 1992; Ricketts & Achtenberg, 1990; Rohrbaugh, 1989; Shogun & Filax, 1995; Weston, 1991).

The Legal System

Gay and lesbian families face significant constraints because family or domestic relations law does not recognize the viability of these families. Gay and lesbian marriages are not socially sanctioned or legally binding. In 1992, lesbians and gay men in Hawaii challenged the state's laws restricting marriage to heterosexual persons. Two state Supreme Court justices concurred that the exclusion of same-sex marriages was discriminatory in May 1993 and ordered a trial to determine whether the discrimination was permissible because it supported a "compelling" state interest (Eskridge, 1996). In December 1996, Kevin Chang, a Hawaii Circuit court judge ruled "the state had failed to show a 'compelling legal interest' in barring same-sex marriage" (Human Rights Campaign, 1997, p. 1). However, this ruling has been stayed pending an appeal to the Hawaii Supreme Court. The court did not rule prior to the 1998 election. Instead voters in Hawaii were asked to approve a referendum which could result in a constitutional amendment to allow the state legislature "to limit marriage to one man and one woman" (St. Pierre, 1998). The Defense of Marriage Act, passed by Congress in 1996, specifically denies federal recognition of gay and lesbian marriages, ensures no states will have to recognize such marriages and precludes the receipt of marital benefits such as a gay or lesbian spouse's Social Security or veterans' benefits. In addition, twenty-six states have passed laws limiting marriage to heterosexual persons and denying recognition of same-sex marriages from other states. Legislation is currently pending in sixteen other states (Human Rights Campaign, 1997; Leach, 1997; St. Pierre, 1998). Thus, gays and lesbians currently cannot enjoy the benefits of legal marriage.

Lesbian and gay partners do not automatically have access to employer-provided family health insurance. Educational, medical and legal officials question the right of lesbians and gays to speak and act on each other's behalf or on behalf of their children. A gay or lesbian person does not automatically have custody or guardianship of children upon the death of a partner. They cannot file joint tax returns (Poverny & Finch, 1988). In addition, two states (New Hampshire and Florida) specifically prohibit gay men or lesbians from adopting children and several prohibit gays and lesbians from becoming foster parents.

Child custody cases, in general, are decided according to the best interests of the child as interpreted by the courts. When lesbian or gay parents and their heterosexual former spouses attempt to resolve child custody issues, however, the heterosexual parent often retains custody, regardless of the best interests of the child or the fitness of the parent. Custody of a minor child or children may be awarded to a lesbian or gay parent at the time of divorce, but the custody award may stipulate the custodial parent not participate in an intimate relationship and not permit the child or children to meet or see the parent's partner.

135

If a lesbian or gay couple chooses to adopt a child, one member of the couple usually enters into the adoption, and the other partner remains a "stranger" according to the law (Benkov, 1994; Martin, 1993; Ricketts & Achtenberg, 1987; Rivera, 1987). Should a lesbian or gay partner to a biological or adoptive parent choose to pursue a second-parent adoption, the judge's decision may be based on his or her prejudices regarding homosexuality, on prejudicial reports by the agency performing the adoption study and, rarely, on the best interests of the child.

Questions regarding the fitness of lesbians and gays to be parents often underlie child custody decisions.

> Courts have sometimes assumed that gay men and lesbians are mentally ill and hence not fit to be parents, that lesbians are less maternal than heterosexual women and hence do not make good mothers, and that lesbians' and gay men's relationships with sexual partners leave little time for ongoing parent-child interactions. (Patterson, 1992, p. 1028)

From the research conducted to date, however, it is clear these fears are not accurate. The American Psychological Association and the American Psychiatric Association removed homosexuality from their lists of psychological disorders in the mid-1970s (Blumenfeld & Raymond, 1993). Lesbians do not differ from heterosexual women with regard to their mental health or their approaches to child rearing (Flaks, Ficher, Masterpasqua & Joseph, 1995; Golombok & Tasker, 1996; Kweskin & Cook, 1982; Lyons, 1983; Miller, Jacobsen, & Bigner, 1981; Pagelow, 1980; Rand, Graham & Rawlings, 1982). Romantic and sexual relationships among lesbians do not detract from their ability to care for their children (Pagelow, 1980). Research on gay fathers indicates no reason to question their fitness to be parents (Bailey, Bobrow, Wolfe & Mikach, 1995; Barret & Robinson, 1990; Bigner & Jacobsen, 1992; Bozett, 1987c, 1989, 1990). Despite the results of research, gay and lesbian families seeking redress for custody, visitation and adoption through the legal system face significant barriers.

Homophobia, heterosexism, the narrow definition of family is the norm in the United States and the ways in which the legal system has denied access to lesbian and gay families collude to assure little social sanction or support for these families (Maggiore, 1992). Nonetheless, the number of lesbian and gay families continues to grow, and literature, support for and discussion of parenting among lesbians and gays has become commonplace.

> Lesbians and gay men have always broken the mold in creative ways. Though we were raised with the same prescriptions as heterosexuals for what a woman should be, what a man should be, and how a life should be lived, long ago we started inventing our own rules. Even under the most severe persecution, our spirits have prevailed. We have learned how to make our differentness our

strength. The creativity of our community, which has allowed us to redefine healthy sexuality, loving relationships, and the bonds of friendship, is now evolving new ways of having, loving, and relating to children. (Martin, 1993, p. 6)

Diversity Among Lesbian and Gay Families

Estimates of the Number of Gay and Lesbian Families

Because lesbian and gay families remain a hidden population, it is extremely difficult to ascertain their numbers accurately. Many fear the loss of custody or visitation; others simply value their privacy and the privacy of their children. Nevertheless, various estimates are available: one to five million lesbian mothers (Gottman, 1990; Patterson, 1992; Pennington, 1987); one to three million gay fathers (Bozett, 1987c; Gottman, 1990; Patterson, 1992); and six to fourteen million children of gay or lesbian parents (Bozett, 1987a; Editors of the Harvard Law Review, 1990; Martin, 1993; Patterson, 1992). Although most of these numbers represent lesbians and gays who became parents in a heterosexual relationship before coming out, it is thought that increasingly lesbians and gays are becoming parents after coming out. It appears also the number of lesbians choosing to become parents is increasing (McCandlish, 1987; Martin, 1993; Pies, 1990). One estimate indicates that five to ten thousand lesbians have borne children (Patterson, 1992). Although little accurate information is available on the number of gay fathers living with their children, it is clear from anecdotal evidence the number of gay men living with their children, adopting or otherwise parenting children is increasing as well (Barret & Robinson, 1990; Bozett, 1989; Martin, 1993).

Discerning the number of Single-Parent lesbian and gay families is more complex. Because the legal system fails to recognize the legitimacy of lesbian and gay partnerships, all lesbian and gay families are assumed to be Single-Parent families, in the same way heterosexual families are Single-Parent families if the partners are not legally married. However, some very real differences exist between lesbian and gay families in which two adults have a committed partnership and those in which a single lesbian or gay man chooses to parent or seek custody of existing children. Single-Parent gay and lesbian families are a minority population within a minority group; although it is impossible to report their numbers accurately, they nevertheless exist. The following three paragraphs present three snapshots of lesbian and gay Single-Parent families. Each family differs from the others, but each shares the purposeful decision to parent.

Susan had wanted to have a child for many years. When she was thirty years old, she met some women in the lesbian community who instructed others about how to proceed with artificial insemination and she began a search for a donor. Marlyn,

137

Susan's daughter was born less than two years later. Several women in the communities in which Susan has lived have assisted her in caring for and parenting Marlyn. Susan made the choice to parent on her own. Although she has dated and had relationships with other women, she has maintained her Single Parenthood.

Larry and his wife had been married for seven years and had two children. He became involved in a relationship with a gay man. After a period of struggling with his identity, Larry came out as a gay man. He and his wife divorced and they maintained joint custody of the children despite much enmity between them. Larry lived alone, was partnered with a man for several years and then dated others. His children stayed with him on weekends, during school vacations and during the summer.

Elaine's mother had been married when Elaine was born, but left her marriage shortly afterward. Elaine remained with her mother and saw her father during Christmas and summer vacations. Her mother's friend Julia was always around for special occasions, holidays and vacations. Elaine understood about the significance of her mother's relationship with Julia, but neither her mother nor Julia openly discussed this relationship with her until Elaine was a teenager.

These three families represent only a few of many possible family constellations. The various constellations are difficult to describe because they are hidden and marginalized. Many gay and lesbian Single Parents, wanting to protect their children from the effects of homophobia, seek and maintain invisibility. Some remain hidden to protect themselves from former partners, family members or others who might attempt to obtain custody of their child(ren). Others may fear loss of employment and family income. Because gay and lesbian Single-Parent families have experienced these negative consequences, invisibility remains as a strategy for family survival.

It should also be stated here gays and lesbians do not unanimously approve of establishing families with children. Many lesbians denounce traditional family structures within a capitalist economic system. Some feel uncomfortable with the presence of any children in space which is set aside for women; others believe male children should not be part of women's community (Bowen, 1991; Lesser, 1991). Many gay men and lesbians want neither the responsibility nor the commitment children require. Some believe societal homophobia and heterosexism remove or severely limit their choices about parenting and they are not willing to subject children to the prejudice and discrimination they have encountered.

Ethnic and Racial Diversity

Lesbians and gays are a very diverse group. Estimates indicate that five million gays and lesbians claim ethnic or racial minority status. Many of these persons are parents. Some are Single Parents. Thus, African-American, Asian, Latino, Native-American and other ethnic minority gay and lesbian parents are both visible and invisible minorities. As visible minorities, they must cope with racism and racial discrimination; as invisible minorities, they can try to remain discrete, silenced and closeted (Morales, 1990). The choices are not really choices at all. As Morales indicates,

> The minority lesbian or gay man must balance a set of often-conflicting challenges and pressures. The multi-minority status makes it difficult for a person to become integrated and assimilated. Within the mainstream society, ethnic minority gays and lesbians experience prejudice and discrimination for their ethnic minority identity, as well as for their sexual orientation. In the gay and lesbian community, the social values mirror those of the mainstream society… [including] negative stereotyping and prejudicial attitudes about ethnic and racial minorities….In the ethnic minority communities the social norms and values concerning homosexuality foster homophobic attitudes and consequently gays and lesbians within minority communities face disapproval and rejection. (p. 220)

Socioeconomic Diversity

Age, education or income differences between lesbian and gay parents and hetero-sexual parents have not been accurately determined. Many gay and lesbian Single Parents appear to be older and have higher incomes and education than their heterosexual counterparts. The choice to parent is often deliberately made by parents who believe they can both emotionally and financially support a child. However, lesbians are often more economically vulnerable than are gay men. Because they are women, their work may be less valued than that of men. They are usually paid less for what they do than their male counterparts. Finally, they are more likely to participate in the secondary labor market for low wages and few benefits.

Theory

Little theory has been advanced regarding gay and lesbian families in general and Single-Parent gay and lesbian families in particular. Existing theory regarding child development and traditional families, however, has been applied to gay and lesbian families. These families share many of the issues traditional hetero-sexual families face, including (a) developmental concerns such as separation and individuation, self-esteem, moral judgment, development of behavior problems, gender and sexual identity and gender role behavior; (b) family adjustment concerns such as the strategies used by adults to involve children in their lives and create family and (c) concerns regarding potential divorce or the loss of a partner. Also important for consideration here are psychosocial theories which indicate the need for the presence of two heterosexual parents to ensure proper individual and social development for children.

Existing theory in each of the areas cited above holds children of heterosexual parents fare better than do children of lesbian and gay parents. However, the research to date clearly demonstrates the development of children of gay and lesbian parents is not compromised when compared to the development of children in heterosexual families (for a review of the literature and details regarding this research, see Patterson [1992]). According to Patterson, "concerns about difficulties in personal development among children of gay and lesbian parents are not sustained by results of existing research" (p. 1033). Results of research on peer and other social relationships also indicate children of gays and lesbians fare well and, in some instances, better than children of heterosexuals. The children of divorced lesbian mothers have more contact with their fathers than children of divorced heterosexual women and lesbian mothers tend to have more frequent contact with their former spouses (Golombok, Spencer & Rutter, 1983). Finally, as Patterson (1992) notes, the research results indicating normal development of children of lesbian and gay parents raise questions about the emphasis on the importance of two heterosexual parents to assure proper development. Thus, existing theory fails to account adequately for both children and adults in gay and lesbian families.

In addition to the problem of weaknesses in theory noted above, no theory addresses specific concerns of Single-Parent lesbian and gay families. We need to examine systems of social support available to these families and the relevance of such support to children and their gay and lesbian parents. Research has not investigated how children cope with their parent's coming out process or their acceptance or rejection by peers and extended family members. We know little about life-cycle stages of these families, the tasks which must be completed for healthy development of all family members or the intergenerational effects of gay and lesbian parenting (Bozett, 1987b). For example, theory pertaining to gay and lesbian Single-Parent families might address the following questions: How do the children of gay and lesbian Single Parents experience adolescence? What kinds of relationships prevail among gay and lesbian grandparents, their children and grandchildren? How do these families deal with teachers, physicians, and others for whom the parent's sexual orientation might be an issue? Current research has examined primarily White middle- and upper-class lesbian and gay families and has not examined lesbian and gay families from other racial, ethnic or socioeconomic backgrounds. According to Patterson (1992), research examining the diversity of lesbian and gay families has barely begun. Finally, the research discussed above is limited by small sample size and lack of multiple methodology. Thus, it is of little use for theory development.

Bozett (1987b) indicated the need for "theory development at both the micro and macro levels, both substantive and formal theory, middle range and grand" (p. 234). He observed several assumptions should be made in developing such theory.

1. Recognition of the gay and lesbian family as a true family form
2. Assertion this family form should be studied
3. Awareness that gay and lesbian families are unique, and current theory, tested with heterosexual families, may not fit

It is also clear any theory developed must be sufficiently broad to include variation in the families of gay men and lesbian women – both those headed by a couple, and those headed by a Single Parent.

Practice Concerns

Lesbian or gay Single-Parent families have experiences similar to those of other Single-Parent families. They seek help for similar kinds of problems and needs: parent-child relationships, children's behavior and/or developmental issues, social and emotional support, physical health, substance abuse, income security. In addition to these, lesbian and gay Single-Parent families face needs unique to the parent's sexual orientation.

The coming out process. For gay and lesbian people, the coming out process reflects the development and articulation of a positive identification with, as well as participation in, the gay and lesbian community. Coming out is not usually an event. Rather it is an unfolding, a series of realizations about oneself and one's relationships with others. Lesbians or gays who choose to parent or seek custody of children may experience difficulties in some part of their coming out process (even if they think they have completed that process).

Several theories have attempted to describe the coming out process. Most of these theories discuss linear stages of coming out which include (a) attempts to conform with the dominant group (heterosexual society), (b) exposure to gay or lesbian life and resulting feelings of dissonance and conflict, (c) beginning of pride in minority status and anger at the dominant group, (d) attempts to form an identity separate from but also part of the group and (e) movement to self-appreciation and identity integration (see Cass, 1979, 1984; Sophie, 1985/86; Sue & Sue, 1990). Other models, such as that articulated by Lee (1992) propose coming out is a series of issues, milestones and experiences including (a) coming out to self, (b) coming out in a relationship, (c) coming out to family and friends and to those in a wider circle and (d) full acceptance and identity integration. Lee identifies specific issues facing lesbians in their identity development process: feelings of difference, dissonance, inner conflicts, dealing with relationships, separatism, family, a stable identity and integration. Other models are concerned with understanding identity development within a social, historical and cultural context (Faderman, 1984). These models recognize the multiple identities people have (e.g., lesbian and mother, gay man and father) and attempt to distinguish and integrate these identities.

No particular model appears to capture best the coming out process for all gay men and lesbians. It is important, however, to consider according to any or all of the models how the lesbian or gay male parent manages the coming out process and to examine the impact of coming out for the family as a whole. The parent's coming out to her or his child(ren) may present difficulties. For instance, the parent may seek help to deal with discomfort and fears about discussing sexual orientation with the child(ren) or members of the family of origin. He or she may want to talk about the impact of disclosure for both parent and child(ren). The coming out process may remain an unspoken issue until raised by the practitioner. For example, a family might seek help to deal with a child's behavior problem, at the root of which is the parent's discomfort with his or her identity.

Effects of homophobia/heterosexism. Gay men and lesbians may experience significant worry, anxiety, and fear because of the societal response to their sexual orientation, which, in turn, may have an impact on the family's well-being. The adult in the family may believe it is essential to hide his or her identity, thus teaching the child(ren) that "keeping the secret" is vital to the family's well being. Struggling to maintain this family secret creates pain and turmoil within the family. Society's assumption of heterosexuality adds to the already stressful situation for these families, for only with great and purposeful effort can they be honest and open about themselves. If the gay or lesbian parent has been out to his or her child(ren), the effects of homophobia may still be felt within the family. Children and adolescents may have varying degrees of comfort with a parent's honesty regarding sexual orientation, dating or relationships.

Levels of comfort are influenced by age, maturity, social situation, and the perceived acceptance or non-acceptance of others. Internalized homophobia also affects these families. Lesbian and gay parents may reproach themselves, feel guilt or shame, and in other ways show self-blame, because they have assumed others' negative response to their sexual orientation.

Because it is impossible to escape the effects of homophobia and heterosexism, it is vitally important practitioners explore these issues with families. Social workers can be especially helpful by providing education about homophobia and heterosexism and assisting clients to access lesbian and gay affirming experiences foster self-awareness, respect for difference and pride in their identity (Grace, 1992). It is also vital social workers and other clinicians examine their own homophobia and the very subtle ways heterosexism affects their thinking, language and actions. Practitioners need to have an understanding of alternative life styles, non-traditional families and diversity within a community.

Decisions about lifestyle. Gay and lesbian families must choose how they will live as families. A Single-Parent gay or lesbian adult may choose to remain single and uncommitted. He or she may participate in a loving relationship with a same-sex partner, but live apart from that person. The parent may become a partner in a relationship in which the family lives together and both partners share in child-rearing. Each of these choices has positive and negative consequences for both the parent and child(ren) and alters family dynamics in both expected and unexpected ways. A parent may experience deep sadness, loneliness, anger, exhilaration or elation about the choice she or he has made. Children may feel sad, guilty, angry or jealous about the parent's behavior or decision. Their feelings may provoke behaviors the parent finds unacceptable. The worker's role here includes several tasks: (a) assist both the adult and child(ren) in the family to explore and understand their feelings; (b) facilitate problem-solving; (c) open communication so both parent and child can discuss feelings, behaviors and reactions and (d) help the family use its own and other resources to obtain support.

Additional concerns, linked with these lifestyle choices, include ways in which Single-Parent lesbian and gay families deal with the loss of a significant relationship or the death of the parent and the resulting grief experienced by family members. When the Single-Parent family has included another adult and that adult leaves or dies, the remaining family members may face a crisis. It may be possible for the child to maintain contact with the former partner, co-parent or friend; but this contact may prove difficult for the custodial parent and for the child. If the co-parent, partner or friend dies, the family's crisis is exacerbated. Should the custodial or biological parent die or be permanently lost to the family, the crisis for the child and other caring adults is acute and grave. Loss of a child is devastating in gay and lesbian Single-Parent families where the choice to parent and create family has been very deliberate.

The grief process for these families resembles that experienced by heterosexual families. However, supports available to other families may not be present for lesbian and gay families. Both children and adults experience such losses with deep and lasting sorrow. Non-biological parents or former partners may receive little support or acknowledgment of their loss and grief. Social workers can provide validation and support to these families as they deal with their grief. They can assist family members to explore both personal and external resources which will ensure additional and long-term support. Clinicians must recognize, however, the unique ways in which these families might require assistance to move through disbelief and denial, to anger, sadness and acceptance (Terry, 1992).

Such help might include finding support groups where members are comfortable with and accepting of gay or lesbian persons so feelings of grief and loss are validated. It might include helping the family to pursue legal and financial arrangements in complex, bureaucratic systems. It might also include assisting several family systems – a family of choice (the actual family unit), a family of origin and members of the larger gay and/or lesbian community – as they attempt to cope with grief.

The parent who has HIV disease or AIDS presents multiple challenges to the practitioner. Infected gay and lesbian parents require consistent medical care. They may need many social and financial supports and families may need emotional and other supports. Once again, social workers must consider their own prejudices and biases regarding these adults. The presence of the disease brings ethical dilemmas – whether and how to inform present and past sexual partners, how to inform children and assuring the parent is using and will continue to use safe sex practices in current relationships. If the adult's health deteriorates, issues for the helping relationship may change as well. Social workers must be prepared to deal with alternative strategies for helping and caring for families affected by HIV, such as locating additional supports in the community for the adult and family members, scheduling home and hospital visits, discussing quality of life issues and assisting the adult in preparations for dying and planning for care of his or her child(ren) (Shuster, 1996).

Families of origin. Many lesbian and gay adults are estranged from their family of origin because of family members' negative responses to the individual's coming out and their articulation of homophobic attitudes. These responses are closely allied with generalized homophobia and heterosexism. For the gay or lesbian parent, loss of extended family support can be devastating and have a negative impact on the family's life and relationships. Family-of-origin members may be completely unaccepting of or uncomfortable with their adult child's sexual orientation. Parents of a lesbian or gay man may believe it is not good, healthy or wise for their daughter or son to parent. Some parents are embarrassed about explaining the presence of a new grandchild when their child clearly is not in a heterosexual marriage. Lesbian and gay parents recognize and feel this discomfort or embarrassment and feel anxiety, pain, guilt, and shame. Most lesbian or gay adults have developed strategies for dealing with lack of support from their family of origin. However, these strategies can become ineffective when the adult becomes a parent and seeks the family's acceptance of her or his own new family. Social workers can assist lesbian and gay parents to develop new strategies for dealing with their family of origin. They can also help both family units to find ways to communicate with each other. It is important practitioners recognize the significance of the family of origin as part of the context for working with lesbian or gay Single-Parent families. Even if no relationship exists between family of origin and family of choice, each nevertheless affects the other. Lesbians and gay men who parent live with the complexities of these dual families. Practitioners must often work with both, or at a minimum, consider those resources, strengths, needs and desires which each family brings (Gunter, 1992; Pies, 1987).

Child custody/legal issues. Legal threats to parental custody held by lesbians or gay men are common. Because domestic relations courts often discriminate against gays and lesbians who are parents, a parent who has long retained custody of her or his children continues to live under the shadow of potential custody-change litigation, despite the best interests of the child. A lesbian or gay man who chooses to adopt must either hide or elect to reveal her or his sexual orientation to the court. If sexual orientation is acknowledged, the parent faces an uncertain result. Many courts have used information about sexual orientation to indicate a "change in circumstances", and grounds for re-opening custody litigation. Thus, the situation of a parent who wins initial custody remains uncertain.

> For gay and lesbian parents, the legal system is
> profoundly inequitable…[and] affects not only the unfortunate parents and children who fall into the snares of that system but also those who never enter a courtroom but whose lives are unduly restricted by the harshness of antiquated legal doctrine. (Rivera, 1987, p. 206)

A gay or lesbian parent may decide a custody battle with a former spouse, partner, family member or social agency is harmful to the child. In this situation, the gay or lesbian parent gives up custody and is left with feelings of self-blame in addition to the anguish brought about by the loss of the child. At the same time, the parent must bear the negative reactions of those who do not understand or were unaware of their decision to relinquish custody.

Social workers can assist parents in their attempts to deal with custody issues. First, practitioners should understand the impact of the legal system and its discriminatory and homophobic practices on gay and lesbian families. They also must recognize these families consider the well-being of their children most important and will take actions to protect their children from hurt and perceived danger. Finally, social workers should realize that gay or lesbian families may make choices about custody which are different from choices they would make if they were heterosexuals. Help which encourages the parent to (a) explore her or his feelings about parenthood, the significance of the custody battle and the child's well-being; (b) examine the consequences of each custody choice and (c) make an informed decision is most often sought and deeply appreciated.

Common Errors and Misconceptions

A worker or client's belief in or acceptance of any of these misconceptions will have a significant impact on the helping process. Practitioners should examine their own attitudes and assist lesbian and gay parents to clarify their beliefs as a part of the work they do together.

Lesbians and gay men can't have children. Clearly this is a fallacy, given the fact that lesbians and gay men can and do have children. Single-Parent lesbian and gay families of choice consist of an adult and child or children from a former (or continuing) heterosexual marriage or other significant relationship. They may also be the result of adoption or foster care. Finally, insemination using sperm of a known or unknown donor or a surrogate mother (and subsequent adoption) may have occurred.

Lesbians and gay men shouldn't have children. This misconception is based both in homophobia and in narrow definitions of family. It assumes lesbians and gay men are interested only in themselves and have no room for children in their lives. Again, lesbians and gay men have demonstrated their caring and regard for children and their willingness to protect both their own and others' children (Bozett, 1987c; Gunter, 1992; Poverny & Finch, 1988; Ricketts & Achtenberg, 1987; Rivera, 1987).

This statement reflects several fears with regard to children growing up with lesbian or gay parents. One fear is children in gay and lesbian families are more likely to be sexually molested by parents or by partners or friends who are also gay or lesbian. However, no evidence supports this fear. In fact, heterosexual males are more likely than gay males to be involved in incidents of child molestation (Finkelhor & Russell, 1984; Groth & Birnbaum, 1978; Jones & MacFarlane, 1980; Sarafino, 1979). Nonetheless, this assertion continues. Another fear is children of gays and lesbians are more likely to be gay or lesbian. Research, however, indicates no basis for this fear (Patterson, 1992). In addition, the statement itself is homophobic in that it is based on the assumption that being gay or lesbian is wrong. Another fear holds children in gay and lesbian families will be harmed by the stigmatization process which surrounds these families within a homophobic and heterosexist society. Although little long-term research has been done with these families, anecdotal evidence suggests this fear is unfounded (Baptiste, 1987; Gottman, 1990; Patterson, 1992). In fact, some evidence suggests children raised in such households demonstrate heightened sensitivity to others, empathy, and awareness of social inequities (Basile, 1974; Riddle, 1978), perhaps because of their family circumstances. Finally, some fear children living in these households (especially those living in gay male-headed households) are at great risk for exposure to HIV disease. However, evidence does not support greater occurrence of HIV disease among children of infected gay men and lesbians in any greater numbers compared with children of infected heterosexual men and women. In addition, lesbians who have not been in heterosexual relationships or used intravenous drugs are among the lowest risk group for contracting HIV disease and AIDS (Berer, 1993).

Children of gay or lesbian parents will not have exposure to opposite sex role models. Many gay and lesbian parents are most creative about developing opportunities for children to have role models (Pies, 1987). Lesbian-headed families often choose gay men or gay male couples to provide alternative experiences for children. Gay male-headed families have women friends who participate in child rearing. Extended family members may also provide these experiences for children. Some lesbian-headed families may decide to raise a child only among women. Although adult males are not present, such families often seek opportunities to expose children to various kinds of people and experiences so there are multiple role models and diverse perspectives from which to learn.

Family and Community Strengths and Resources

Many lesbians and gay men are actively working to assure human rights in gay and lesbian communities. A positive response to homophobia and homophobic acts has been the growth of an active and strong lesbian and gay civil rights movement. Through legal defense funds, human rights organizations, friends, family and other supporters; gays and lesbians have fought to overturn discriminatory laws, alter custody decisions and end the violence that has been directed at their communities.

Gay and lesbian families are resourceful and independent. These adults work diligently to create a strong family and community. For many persons, this is a necessity as a result of estrangement from their family of origin. Others develop a strong family and community as a way to enrich their own and others' lives. Recognizing they must count on themselves rather than on their family of origin, these families of choice readily seek what they need from the environment and develop resources which are not immediately available.

Lesbian and gay parents care deeply about their children. Whether they deliberately choose to become parents or retain custody of children from a previous relationship, lesbian and gay Single-Parent families are committed to the welfare of their children. Parents are very much involved in decisions about education, children's activities and socialization. They also take very seriously their role as nurturers and caregivers. They teach their children about the benefits of diversity and living in a multi-cultural world.

Social support abounds in lesbian and gay communities. Lesbians or gays choosing to parent often seek others in their communities who have chosen to parent. Formal or informal groups provide support for adults interested in exploring parenting options. Some groups continue to meet once families are established. These individuals and groups can provide support and encouragement to those considering parenthood. In addition, lesbian and gay Single Parents may seek out others who have children to ensure the availability of a support network, cooperative child care, and affirming adult friendships.

Practice Principles

Underlying the practitioner's knowledge and understanding of the difficulties lesbian and gay families face and the misconceptions surrounding them are several rules or standards for practice. These principles are generic and apply to work with gay or lesbian parents or their children as well as work with members of families of origin and others in their families of choice.

Examine personal attitudes regarding diversity, homophobia and heterosexism. Few can escape homophobic attitudes in a culture which is permeated with negative stereotypes of gay and lesbian persons. If a practitioner is to work successfully with gay and lesbian families, self-examination is necessary. Practitioners must be accepting of diversity, able to hear the stories and situations of clients without judging them, willing to set aside misconceptions and stereotypes to permit the individuals their full human rights and honest with themselves and clients about their agenda as helping persons. Respect and the ability to celebrate another's sexual orientation and lifestyle are essential. The following questions may help to provoke thinking about personal attitudes:

1. Are you comfortable in the presence of two men who are affectionate with each other?
2. Do you believe that heterosexual couples should have children?
3. If a lesbian couple and their child came to see you, would you ask (or want to ask) "Which of you is the real mother?"
4. Do you believe children growing up in lesbian and gay families are automatically at risk?
5. Do you view people from one perspective (i.e., their sexual orientation) or multiple perspectives (i.e., sexual orientation, racial/ethnic identification, parenthood status, career, physical location)?
6. Would you be comfortable asking lesbians or gay men questions about themselves, or are you more comfortable making judgments based upon the advice of others, material in a book or your own thinking?
7. Are you familiar with gay and lesbian organizations in your community?
8. Would you tell or have you told a young woman who described her strong caring for another young woman that "it's just a phase; you'll get over it"?
9. Do you believe lesbians hate men and gay men hate women?

Social workers who are not able to support the goals and world view of lesbians and gay men should remove themselves and refer clients to other services.

Learn and become comfortable with the terminology and language. The worker's use of appropriate language can help to create an atmosphere conducive to relationship building. Gay men and lesbians prefer "gay man" and "lesbian" to "homosexual" or "gays". Although lesbian and gay persons may use terms such as "queer", "dyke", or "queen" in referring to themselves, it is not appropriate for others to use this terminology. Rather, gay men and lesbians use this language to reclaim parts of their culture and history and to deny the power of these pejorative terms. Practitioners also need to understand who constitutes "family of choice" and who is part of "family of origin" or "first family". Workers should ask clients to describe their relationships and not assume a relationship is based on a heterosexual model. For example, gay male friends or lesbian friends may live together and consider themselves a family of choice. There may be an intimate yet not sexual relationship between partners. On the other hand, gay or lesbian adults may participate in an intimate relationship for many years and maintain separate living spaces.

Understand the importance of social environment and context in the lives of gay and lesbian Single-Parent families. Work with gay and lesbian families is an appropriate venue for applying a person-in-environment focus. Gay and lesbian adults manage their lives within gay and lesbian communities and in the dominant heterosexual culture as well. Within these cultures, they influence and are influenced by the behaviors and attitudes of their family of origin. If they are African-American, Hispanic, or from some other ethnic background, they must operate in an additional culture as well. If they form a family, they must learn the rules of another culture and a more demanding and vigilant environment. Some gay and lesbian friends and members of the family of origin may be accepting and excited about the choice to parent; while others may be doubtful, questioning and uncomfortable with the decision. Each of these environments influences the emotions and behavior of both adults and children. Each can provide strengths, resources, and support and each can present challenges. The social worker must be aware of these environments and their influence so she or he can use the resources and supports and assist the family to overcome its problems.

Recognize the importance of the coming out process and respect the client and family's choices about coming out. Many gay and lesbian parents recognize both the benefits and drawbacks of disclosing their sexual orientation. Practitioners can help clients and families examine their decisions with regard to coming out if they have requested that assistance. Practitioners can assist clients to explore the effects of disclosure of sexual orientation and anticipate the reactions of others, including children, to coming out. Practitioners can provide support, encouragement, validation and information about resources. However, they cannot make decisions about coming out or come out for the client.

Understand the impact of the family of origin and family of choice in the lives of gay and lesbian Single-Parent families. To accomplish this task, it is most important practitioners have a broad view of family constellations and recognize gay and lesbian families are involved in at least two family systems. Each system has consequences for gay and lesbian adults and their children. Each system offers opportunities for intervention and requires the worker use a multidimensional focus in work with individuals and the family.

Become familiar with the community resources available to support gay and lesbian Single-Parent families. Social workers can develop referral networks for legal assistance, health care, spiritual or religious resources and positive role models. They can become familiar with formal and informal parenting groups in the community and investigate discussion, information and on-line support groups on the Internet. Practitioners can seek consultation with gay or lesbian social workers who are familiar and comfortable with the gay and lesbian community and its resources. Social workers can also assure resources in the larger community are appropriate, safe and affirming for gay and lesbian clients and their families.

Use practice models which focus on strengths and resources rather than deficits and disadvantages. Such practice models affirm a person's experiences, identity and orientation. These interventions focus on the discovery and articulation of the strengths gay or lesbian families bring to the helping relationship. These models focus on the environment and culture as they affect and are affected by the person or family. They stress the discovery, development and use of naturally occurring environmental resources to address individual and family goals. In practice, the worker should use an approach which recognizes and addresses the pervasive effects of homophobia and heterosexism upon the adult and child(ren), the helper and the helping relationship. Overall, the models used should be those devoted to helping people discover a personal vision of their ideal world and foster the knowledge, skills and personal power to manifest these desired outcomes.

Teaching and Learning Styles

Work with gay and lesbian Single-Parent families requires the use of core clinical practice skills. The helping process is best accommodated by social workers who adopt the principles cited above and use those core skills such as meeting the client where he or she is, listening actively to both the client's words and actions, providing open and honest feedback and permitting the client to set both the tone and direction of the helping. The teaching of skills (e.g., effective communication, conflict resolution, money management) is enhanced when the practitioner discusses the experiences of the client or family as examples of ways or opportunities for using the specific skills, permits the client to rehearse the skills using her or his own context and encourages the client to be a full partner in determining those skills which will be most helpful.

Clients learn best from practitioners who have examined their own attitudes, who understand and respect diversity and who treat people with honor and regard. Important to the learning process for gay and lesbian Single-Parent families is the discovery and acknowledgment of their hopes and dreams. Also vital for client learning is practitioner awareness and confirmation of the complexity of the issues lesbian and gay Single Parents face in their struggle to create and strengthen their families.

The following case study, discussion of strengths-based practice and suggested interventions builds upon the practice knowledge and principles discussed above. It is only a scenario however; although it can guide practitioners, it cannot provide the richness of the family's story nor fully describe this family's capacity to resolve its own problems.

Case Example

Sarah is a 39-year-old, White lesbian and Single Parent of a 10-year-old girl. Sarah has been self-employed as an accountant and financial planner for the past seven years. Before returning to school to obtain an accounting degree, Sarah had been a jewelry maker. She had traveled extensively throughout the country selling jewelry at art and craft fairs. In 1984, she decided that she wanted to have a child. At the time, she was partnered with a woman (Jerri) who did not share her desire to parent. Sarah was determined however, and after a few months, developed a plan for obtaining a sperm donor. Jerri agreed to help Sarah with her plan and stay through the baby's birth.

Deciding she could not hope to support a child on the money she made from her jewelry business, Sarah had applied and been accepted to the city college. She had decided to obtain a degree in accounting and become certified as a financial planner. She knew she had skills and could do the work to pursue this career. At school, she identified four possible sperm donors. Jerri made initial contacts with the men, so Sarah's identity could be hidden. Sarah planned to raise the child herself and did not want any contact with the biological father, either for herself or for the child. After several months and extensive interviews, Sarah chose a potential father from the group, and Jerri acted as the go-between, obtaining fresh semen from the donor for several days over a period of four months, until Sarah became pregnant.

Sarah sought pre-natal care from a nurse practitioner and began planning for home delivery. She chose a mid-wife whom she liked and trusted, participated in childbirth-education classes, and prepared for her child's birth. She also searched among the women in her community to find others who had decided to parent (or were already parenting) and locate some women who would help care for her new child. Sarah believed these women would offer advice, support and companionship when she was alone with the baby. She discovered many in her community did not support her choice to parent. They were disinterested or opposed to her plans and did not want to help. She was able to find a few who wanted to help and one woman who offered to assist with child care in exchange for living space in Sarah's home.

Corey was born at home, attended by the mid-wife and Jerri. Corey experienced some breathing difficulties, but they seemed to dissipate without intervention and all seemed well. Jerri left shortly after Corey's birth and Chris moved into Sarah's home to help Sarah care for Corey. The arrangement worked well for Sarah and Chris, and Corey seemed to thrive.

During the next three years, Sarah completed her education and Chris provided much of Corey's care. Although Sarah deeply appreciated Chris' participation, she also was uncomfortable about the bond between Chris and Corey. Sarah was short-tempered with Corey and at times very impatient, and used physical discipline. Sarah felt unprepared for Corey's behaviors, outbursts and neediness and experienced a great deal of stress because of assignments and exams. She also felt very alone. Chris spent time with a group of her own friends and members of her extended family were close by. Sarah had only a few friends and little free time. She had also been involved in several short-term intimate relationships. The women with whom she was involved were either not interested in co-parenting Corey or were not interested in a committed relationship.

By Corey's third birthday, friends told Sarah they had observed developmental problems. Corey was speaking very little. She had a very short attention span and often seemed distracted. She did not appear to listen or comprehend what others were saying. Sarah talked about some developmental testing, but was uncomfortable and hesitant and finally decided to delay testing until Corey was older.

At the same time, Sarah decided to move to another city and buy a tax accounting practice. In her new home, Sarah was alone again. However, she soon saw the validity of friends' concerns about Corey. Developmental testing revealed Corey had significant delays of unknown origin. Sarah placed Corey in a developmental pre-school and began working with her at home as well. For several years, Corey attended a special program. Two years ago, she was mainstreamed into some parts of the regular elementary school program. For Sarah, times were difficult. She managed her business and cared for Corey by herself, with few friends or support in the community; costs of Corey's care resulted in little discretionary money. Corey's unpredictable behaviors produced discomfort for both Sarah and other women in the community. Sarah received few invitations to gatherings, and Corey often was not welcome at these events. Sarah continued having short and very intense relationships, but did not find a partner who seemed comfortable with Corey.

Sarah built her practice and a financial planning service with great effort. She managed her finances with skill and saved sufficient money to renovate the apartment above her office where she and Corey have lived. Chris and Jerri have visited several times and provided some respite for Sarah. She recently contacted her mother and attempted to re-establish a long-dormant relationship with family members.

Sarah's parents reacted very strongly when she came out to them. Her father was angry and belligerent. Her mother was sad and self-blaming. During the intervening years, Sarah maintained infrequent contact with her mother, providing minimal information about her life. She told her mother about Corey and sent pictures. Sarah's younger sister visited and her grandmother called several times. Finally, two years ago Sarah's mother came to visit and stayed for two weeks. Contact has been more frequent, but Sarah and her mother have had minimal communication with each other. Sarah's father remains completely uninvolved in attempts to rebuild family connections.

Recently, Sarah recognized she was feeling overwhelmed with work and caring for Corey. All of the strategies she had used to maintain balance seemed now to be ineffective. She felt frustrated with Corey, often lonely for adult company, and, despite her efforts, still isolated from her family and community. She met with one of Corey's teachers to discuss Corey's progress and look at ways she could be more helpful at home. During the discussion, the teacher asked about Corey's father and his presence in her life. Sarah explained that Corey's father was not involved, but she had other friends and supports. The teacher indicated the importance of having positive male role models for Corey. She told Sarah it was unhealthy and unnatural for Corey to grow up surrounded only by women. Sarah knew these comments were homophobic and heterosexist, but she was so overwhelmed she simply left the meeting without commenting. She decided she needed to get some help for herself and Corey.

Strengths Based Practice

Sarah sought assistance from a practitioner who used a strengths perspective (Saleebey, 1992, 1997; Weick & Saleebey, 1995) in her work with clients. The social worker had seen other lesbians and had been recommended to Sarah as a person with whom she could be completely open and comfortable. The practitioner used several sessions to get to know Sarah and to explore her story. She noted and discussed Sarah's strengths and resources. For example, the worker commented Sarah was very courageous to have attempted to rebuild relationships in her first family, it must have taken a great deal of determination to return to school and Sarah's successes in business showed her tenacity and independence. When Sarah and she had developed trust in the relationship, the worker began to explore other aspects of Sarah's life which Sarah did not automatically discuss: her hopes and dreams, her sense of spirituality, ways she spent her leisure time and her knowledge and achievements. This laid the groundwork for a deeper examination of the issues concerning Sarah, with the social worker continuing to emphasize the ways Sarah had coped with very difficult situations in her life.

Once they had fully discussed the parts of her life Sarah wanted to share, she and the worker begin talking about specific goal setting. Sarah told the social worker she wanted to find some new ways of working with Corey, wanted some time for herself, wanted other adult friendships and relationships and wanted to strengthen the tenuous connection she and Corey had built with her family of origin. Together, Sarah and the worker examined these wants; each want became the basis for a plan and a series of steps to reach the goal. They agreed they would work on one goal at a time, recognizing that accomplishing one goal might have an impact on the others. When one goal was accomplished, they began working on the next. Acknowledging the goals were interrelated made it possible to remain flexible in establishing plans, thus reducing Sarah's overall feeling of being overwhelmed.

Sarah chose to begin working on developing some new strategies for working with Corey. First, Sarah and the worker explored the strategies Sarah had already used. They talked about discipline, activities that Sarah and Corey did together, mealtime, bedtime, school attendance and work, vacations and private time for both of them. They also discussed the ways Sarah found support including Corey's pre-school teacher and her own friends.

In each segment of the discussion, the worker asked Sarah what she was experiencing now, what she wanted for the future and how she had solved problems in the past. As they reviewed each of these parts of Sarah and Corey's life together, Sarah began to identify a deep sense of sadness and confusion. Sarah began to talk about feelings of loss and disappointment–Corey would not be the perfect child, she wouldn't accomplish all Sarah had failed to accomplish, she wasn't going to be smart. The worker helped Sarah acknowledge that she felt angry and guilty, a revelation which frightened Sarah but became a breakthrough for her. Sarah realized she had always wondered if Corey's breathing difficulties at birth had led to her developmental problems. She questioned her choice to have a home birth and had wondered if she had failed to find out some important piece of medical information about Corey's biological father. She not only was sad Corey wasn't perfect, she was angry with Corey. She was angry at the women in her community who did not support her or her choice to parent and at her parents who did not accept her life choices. As time went on, she saw these feelings also had an impact on her relationships with her parents and other adults. Throughout this process, the worker focused on supporting Sarah by emphasizing her feelings and reactions were both valid and normal, and she encouraged Sarah to identify the positive choices she had made.

Individual and Family Interventions

The social worker maintained a strengths perspective throughout her work with Sarah. She did not ignore or downplay the problems Sarah wanted to address, but she consciously noted the strategies Sarah had used previously to get through difficult times as well as the talents and skills she already possessed to address problems as they arose. She communicated these to Sarah consistently until Sarah was able to hear she did indeed have strengths and could identify personal and environmental resources which could assist her in accomplishing her goals.

Work on Sarah's feelings of guilt and anger. Together, Sarah and the worker should continue to explore Sarah's coping strategies to develop ways for her to deal with these feelings. If opportunities present themselves (if Sarah raises the issue or one related to it), the worker and Sarah should examine responses to homophobia and heterosexism and explore any internalized homophobia.

Facilitate contacts in the gay and lesbian community. Because it seems clear Sarah wants to broaden her social networks, the worker can assist her to build a resource network in the community through the local Metropolitan Community Church, university gay and lesbian organizations, gay or lesbian bookstores and community centers.

Facilitate contact with developmental specialists. Sarah commented she feels isolated from other mothers and families because of Corey's developmental delays and it would be helpful for her to have contact with other mothers and families who face similar concerns. These contacts can be educational for Sarah and also result in establishing a support group which would help other families.

Family Interventions

Joint work with Sarah and Corey. The worker should offer to refer or identify a second counselor or social worker who can meet with this family. The person should be familiar and comfortable with both lesbian Single Parents and children with developmental disabilities.

Discussions at Corey's school. The practitioner can help Sarah prepare for a visit with Corey's teacher and school counselors or other representatives which will result in a plan for integrating home and school expectations. If Sarah requests additional assistance because of the need to confront the teacher about her earlier comments, the social worker should accompany Sarah on an initial visit and request a meeting with the teacher.

Explore the availability of naturally occurring resources in the community. Together, Sarah and the worker can seek opportunities already in the community for this family to have positive leisure experiences, improve their communication with each other and increase their social skills with each other and with other families.

Bring together members of Sarah's family of origin. As Sarah feels less overwhelmed, she may begin to talk about her desires to reestablish relationships with her first family. If she wants to pursue this goal, the worker should help Sarah develop a plan and explore the consequences of attempting increased contact. The worker should be available to act as a discussion facilitator if the opportunity for a visit occurs.

Group Interventions

Establish a support group for lesbian Single Parents. With the worker's help, Sarah might contact lesbian Single mothers in her community and in surrounding towns to develop a support and social activities group. Some of their meetings might be for parents only and include a formal agenda or a speaker, whereas other meetings might be social and recreational, either with or without children.

Educate school staff and administration about homophobia and heterosexism. When Sarah feels stronger, she may want to discuss the teacher's comments with her. She might suggest teachers and staff participate in training or a workshop about homophobia and heterosexism.

Community Intervention

Explore ways to educate people in the gay and lesbian community about children with special needs. This large task could be of great value. This intervention could help to increase the understanding and acceptance of children by women and men in the community. It would help Sarah to see she was not alone or isolated from the rest of the community and could expand her resource possibilities. It could also create opportunities for support and encouragement for many people where none had previously existed.

Outcomes

Sarah continued to see the social worker for several months and worked to develop new strategies for dealing with Corey and taking care of her own needs. With the worker's help, Sarah examined her feelings of guilt and anger and recognized how those emotions affected her actions with Corey. She tried several alternative approaches for dealing with Corey's behavior and developed a specific plan that works for both of them most of the time. Sarah places Corey in "time out" when her behavior is not acceptable and carefully discusses with Corey the behavior she desires. She no longer raises her voice or uses physical discipline with Corey. As a way of dealing with anger and frustration, Sarah also takes time out to read, listen to music or exercise.

She and the worker met with a developmental specialist and established a family support group. Through the group, Sarah increased her knowledge and understanding of Corey's abilities and now has realistic expectations for Corey's future. Working together, the families developed a resource network including people who agreed to provide respite care.

On the advice of the social worker, Sarah contacted a practitioner who met with both Corey and Sarah to increase their ability to talk and play with each other. They use art projects, jewelry making and other creative endeavors to strengthen their relationship and time with one another. Sarah has expanded her capacity to be with Corey and is far more satisfied in her parenting role.

A gay and lesbian community center opened in the community and Sarah attended several events. Both she and the social worker view this participation as another positive step in Sarah's growth. She met several other lesbian parents at the center and they have formed a lesbian mothers support group. The women participate in activities together and have regular outings with their children.

Sarah accomplished many of her goal plans and continues to work on others. She and her mother have more frequent contact, but they have not yet attempted to resolve the family's relationship. Sarah is firmly committed to remaining a Single Parent. She also wants to have satisfactory adult relationships. She sees the accomplishment of both of these goals as her greatest challenge.

Conclusion

The use of a strengths perspective is especially relevant to work with lesbian or gay Single-Parent families. With this perspective, families can discover their own power and find the resources they need within themselves and within their communities. Recognition of family strengths helps to overcome the effects of societal heterosexism and homophobia, as people begin to see they have the power and knowledge to grow and change their lives. In addition, a focus on strengths is essential to the development, location and use of resources which naturally occur within these families' environments. Finally, discussion of strengths assists lesbian and gay Single Parents to view themselves within a broad expanse of normative human development and to see their families as vital and healthy.

Social work practitioners most suited to work with Single-Parent gay or lesbian families are self-aware. They have examined the ways in which they use stereotypes. They consciously struggle against their own personal biases and can truly accept their clients' lives and orientations. These workers recognize the similarities between their clients and other Single-Parent families and they are also able to see the distinctions which mark these families' lives. They understand the effects of heterosexism and homophobia on their own lives and the lives of their clients. These workers recognize the constraints on gay and lesbian families imposed by the cultural context of idealized heterosexual love and marriage. They are able to fully support adult family members as gay or lesbian persons and as Single Parents. They can also lend support to the children in these families who must cope with societal attitudes about their parent, their Single-Parent family status and their own growth and development. Workers who feel comfortable in these roles should also be adept at understanding and using a strengths perspective in their work. They are able to see the resources within these families and can share their views with family members. They understand and uphold the strengths of family culture, stories, and rituals (Weick & Saleebey, 1995). Last, using a strengths perspective social workers can affirm family members' experiences and celebrate the hopes and resiliency evident in the lives of lesbian or gay Single-Parent families.

Bibliography

Ariel, J. & Stearns, S.M. (1992). Challenges facing gay and lesbian families. In S.H. Dworkin & F.J. Gutierrez (Eds.) *Counseling gay men & lesbians: Journey to the end of the rainbow* (pp. 95-112). Alexandria, VA: American Counseling Association.

Bailey, J.M.; Bobrow, D.; Wolfe, M. & Mikach, S. (1995). Sexual orientation of adult sons of gay fathers. *Developmental Psychology, 31,* 124-9.

Baptiste, D.A., Jr. (1987). The gay and lesbian stepparent family. In Bozett, F.W. (Ed.), *Gay and lesbian parents* (pp. 112-37). Westport, CT: Praeger.

Barret, R.L. & Robinson, B.E. (1990). *Gay fathers.* Lexington, MA: Lexington Books.

Basile, R.A. (1974). Lesbian mothers: I. *Women's Rights Law Reporter, 2:*3-25.

Benkov, L. (1994). *Reinventing the family: The emerging story of lesbian and gay parents.* New York: Crown Publishers, Inc.

Berer, M. (1993). Sexual transmission of HIV. In Berer, M. with Ray, S., *Women and HIV/AIDS* (pp. 116-27). London: Pandora Press.

Bernstein, J. & Stephenson, L. (1995). Dykes, donors & dry ice: Alternative insemination. In K. Arnup (Ed.) *Lesbian parenting: Living with pride and prejudice* (pp. 3-15). Charlottetown, P. E. I.: gynergy books.

Bigner, J.J. & Bozett, F.W. (1990). Parenting by gay fathers. In F.W. Bozett & M.B. Sussman (Eds.) *Homosexuality and family relations* (pp. 155-175). Binghamton, NY: Harrington Park Press.

Bigner, J.J., & Jacobsen, R.B. (1992). Adult responses to child behavior and attitudes toward fathering: gay and nongay fathers. *Journal of Homosexuality, 23*:99-112.

Blumenfeld, W.J. & Raymond, D. (1993). *Looking at gay and lesbian life.* Boston: Beacon Press.

Bowen, A. (1991). Another view of lesbians choosing children. In B. Sang, J. Warshow, & A.J. Smith (Eds.) *Lesbians at midlife: The creative transition* (pp. 99-107). San Francisco: Spinsters Book Company.

Bozett, F.W. (1987a). Children of gay fathers. In F.W. Bozett (Ed.) *Gay and lesbian parents* (pp. 39-57). Westport, CT: Praeger.

Bozett, F.W. (1987b). Gay and lesbian parents: Future perspectives. In F.W. Bozett (Ed.) *Gay and lesbian parents* (pp. 231-6). Westport, CT: Praeger.

Bozett, F.W. (1987c). Gay fathers. In F.W. Bozett (Ed.) *Gay and lesbian parents* (pp. 3-22). Westport, CT: Praeger.

Bozett, F.W. (1989). Gay fathers: A review of the literature. In F.W. Bozett (Ed.) *Homosexuality and the family* (pp. 137-62). Binghamton, NY: Haworth Press.

Burke, P. (1993). *Family values: Two moms and their son.* New York: Random House.

Cass, V. (1979). Homosexual identity formation: A theoretical model. Journal of *Homosexuality, 4*(3): 219-235.

Cass, V. (1984). Homosexual identity formation: Testing a theoretical model. *Journal of Sex Research, 20*(2): 143-167.

Clunis, D.M., & Green, G.D. (1995). *The lesbian parenting book: A guide to creating families and raising children.* Seattle: Seal Press.

Duberman, M.; Vicinus, M. & Chauncey, Jr., G. (Eds.) (1989). *Hidden from history: Reclaiming the gay and lesbian past.* New York: New American Library.

Editors of the Harvard Law Review. (1990). *Sexual orientation and the law.* Cambridge, MA: Harvard University Press.

Eskridge, W.N., Jr. (1996). *The case for same-sex marriage: From sexual liberty to civilized commitment.* New York: The Free Press.

Faderman, L. (1984). The "new gay" lesbians. *Journal of Homosexuality 10*(3/4) 85-95

Faderman, L. (1991). *Odd girls and twilight lovers: a history of lesbian life in twentieth century America.* New York: William Morrow.

Finkelhor, D. & Russell, D. (1984). Women as perpetrators: Review of the evidence. In D. Finkelhor (Ed.), *Child sexual abuse: New theory and research* (pp. 171-187). New York: Free Press.

Flaks, D.K.; Ficher, I.; Masterpasqua, F. & Joseph, G. (1995). Lesbians choosing motherhood: A comparative study of lesbian and heterosexual parents and their children. *Developmental Psychology 31*, 105-114.

Golombok, S.; Spencer, A. & Rutter, M. (1983). Children in lesbian and single-parent households: Psychosexual and psychiatric appraisal. *Journal of Child Psychology and Psychiatry*, 24, 551-572.

Golombok, S., & Tasker, F. (1996). Do parents influence the sexual orientation of their children? Findings from a longitudinal study of lesbian families. *Developmental Psychology, 32*, 3-11.

Gottlieb, A. (1995). Adopting Sami. In Arnup, K. (Ed.), *Lesbian parenting: Living with pride and prejudice* (pp. 46-56). Charlottetown, P. E. I.: gynergy books.

Gottman, J.S. (1990). Children of gay and lesbian parents. In F.W. Bozett & M.B. Sussman (Eds.) *Homosexuality and family relations* (pp. 177-95). New York: Haworth Press.

Grace, J. (1992). Affirming gay and lesbian adulthood. In N.J. Woodman (Ed.), *Lesbian and gay lifestyles: A guide for counseling and education,* (pp.33-47). New York: Irvington Publishers.

Groth, A.N., & Birnbaum, H.J. (1978). Adult sexual orientation and attraction to underage persons. *Archives of Sexual Behavior, 7,* 175-81.

Gunter, P.L. (1992). Social work with non-traditional families. In N.J. Woodman (Ed.) *Lesbian and gay lifestyles: A guide for counseling and education* (pp. 87-109). New York: Irvington Publishers.

Hanscombe, G.E. & Forster, J. (1981). *Rocking the cradle: Lesbian mothers: A challenge in family living.* London: Peter Owen.

Harrison, K. (1995). Fresh or frozen: Lesbian mothers, sperm donors, and limited fathers. In M.A. Fineman & I. Kaplan (Eds.) *Mothers in law: Feminist theory and the legal regulation of motherhood* (pp. 167-204). New York: Columbia University Press.

Human Rights Campaign (1997, March). *Same-sex marriage: Where the issue stands* [online]. Available HTTP: http://www.hrcusa.org/issues/marriage/marria.html.

Jones, B.M., & MacFarlane, K. (Eds.) (1980). *Sexual abuse of children: Selected readings.* Washington, DC: National Center on Child Abuse and Neglect.

Kweskin, S.L. & Cook, A.S. (1982). Heterosexual and homosexual mothers' self-described sex role behavior and ideal sex role behavior in children. *Sex Roles, 8,* 967-75.

Leach, D. (1997, April 4). 18 states ban marriage; 24 more are considering it. *Gay People's Chronicle,* p. 2.

Lee, J.A.B. (1992). Teaching content related to lesbian and gay identity formation. In Woodman, N.J. (Ed.) *Lesbian and gay lifestyles: A guide for counseling and education,* (pp.1-22). New York: Irvington Publishers.

Lesser, R. (1991). Deciding not to become a mother: In B. Sang, J. Warshow, & A. Smith (Eds.) *Lesbians at midlife: The creative tradition* (pp. 84-90). San Francisco: Spinster's Book Company

Lyons, T.A. (1983). Lesbian mothers' custody fears. *Women and Therapy, 2,* 231-40.

McCandlish, B. (1987). Against all odds: Lesbian mother family dynamics. In Bozett, F.W. (Ed.) *Gay and lesbian parents* (pp. 23-38). Westport, CT: Praeger.

Maggiore, D.J. (1992). *Lesbians and child custody: A casebook.* New York: Garland Publishing.

Martin, A. (1993). *The lesbian and gay parenting handbook: Creating and raising our families.* New York: Harper Perennial.

Miller, J.A.; Jacobsen, R.B. & Bigner, J.J. (1981). The child's home environment for lesbian vs. heterosexual mothers: A neglected area of research. *Journal of Homosexuality, 7,* 49-56.

Morales, E.S. (1990). Ethnic minority families and minority gays and lesbians. In Bozett, F.W. & Sussman, M.B. (Eds.) *Homosexuality and family relations* (pp. 217-39). New York: Haworth Press.

Morgen, K.B. (1995). *Getting Simon: Two gay doctors' journey to fatherhood.* New York: Bramble Books.

Pagelow, M.D. (1980). Heterosexual and lesbian single mothers: A comparison of problems, coping and solutions. *Journal of Homosexuality, 5,* 198-204.

Patterson, C.J. (1992). Children of lesbian and gay parents. *Child Development, 63,* 1025-42.

Pennington, S.B. (1987). Children of lesbian mothers. In F.W. Bozett (Ed.) *Gay and lesbian parents* (pp. 58-74). Westport, CT: Praeger.

Pharr, S. (1988). *Homophobia: A weapon of sexism.* Inverness, CA: Chardon Press.

Pies, C. (1987). Considering parenthood: Psychosocial issues for gay men and lesbians choosing alternative fertilization. In F.W. Bozett (Ed.), *Gay and lesbian parents* (pp. 165-74). Westport, CT: Praeger.

Pies, C. (1990). Lesbians and the choice to parent. In F.W. Bozett & M.B. Sussman (Eds.) *Homosexuality and family relations* (pp. 137-54). New York: Haworth Press.

Pollack, J.S. (1995). *Lesbian and gay families: Redefining parenting in America.* New York: Franklin Watts.

Pollack, S. & Vaughn, J. (Eds.) (1987). *Politics of the heart.* Ithica, NY: Firebrand Books.

Polikoff, N.D. (1992). Lesbians choosing children: The personal is political revisited. In D.J. Maggiore (Ed.) *Lesbians and child custody: A casebook* (pp. 3-10). New York: Garland Publishing Company.

Poverny, L.M. & Finch, W.A. (1988). Gay and lesbian domestic partnerships: Expanding the definition of family. *Social Casework, 69,* 116-21.

Rand, C.; Graham, D.L. & Rawlings, E.I. (1982). Psychological health and factors the court seeks to control in lesbian mother custody trials. *Journal of Homosexuality, 8,* 27-39.

Ricketts, W. & Achtenberg, R. (1987). The adoptive and foster gay and lesbian parent. In F.W. Bozett (Ed.) *Gay and lesbian parents* (pp. 89-111). Westport, Ct: Praeger.

Ricketts, W., & Achtenberg, R. (1990). Adoption and foster parenting for lesbians and gay men: Creating new traditions in family. In F.W. Bozett & M.B. Sussman (Eds.) *Homosexuality and family relations* (pp. 83-118). New York: Haworth Press.

Riddle, D.I. (1978). Relating to children: Gays as role models. *Journal of Social Issues, 34*(3), 84-100.

Rivera, R.R. (1987). Legal issues in gay and lesbian parenting. In Bozett, F.W. (Ed.) *Gay and lesbian parents* (pp. 199-227). Westport, CT: Praeger.

Rohrbaugh, J.B. (1989). Choosing children: Psychological issues in lesbian parenting. In E.D. Rothblum & E. Cole (Eds.) *Loving boldly: Issues facing lesbians.* New York: Harrington Park Press.

Saleebey, D. (Ed.) (1992). *The strengths perspective in social work practice.* New York: Longman.

Saleebey, D. (Ed.) (1997). *The strengths perspective in social work practice (2nd edition).* New York: Longman.

Sarafino, E.P. (1979). An estimate of nationwide incidence of sexual offenses against children. *Child Welfare, 58,* 127-134.

Shogun, D. & Filax, G. (1995). Biddy & Libby in minusland: Adventures in reproductive technology. In K. Arnup (Ed.), *Lesbian parenting: Living with pride and prejudice* (pp. 3-15). Charlottetown, P. E. I.: gynergy books.

Shuster, S. (1996). Families coping with HIV disease in gay fathers: dimensions of treatment. In J. Laird & R.J. Green (Eds.) *Lesbians and gays in couples and families: A handbook for therapists.* San Francisco: Jossey-Bass.

Sophie, J. (1985/86). A critical examination of stage theories of lesbian identity development. *Journal of Homosexuality, 12*(2), 39-51.

St. Pierre, T. (1998, Spring). *Countdown in Hawaii.* Available HTTP: http://www.hrc.org/issues/marriage/index.html.

Sue, D.W., & Sue, D. (1990). *Counseling the culturally different: Theory and practice (2nd ed.).* New York: John Wiley and Sons.

Terry, P. (1992). Relationship termination for lesbians and gays. In N.J. Woodman (Ed.) *Lesbian and gay lifestyles: A guide for counseling and education* (pp. 111-122). New York: Irvington Publishers.

Weick, A., & Saleebey, D. (1995). Supporting family strengths: Orienting policy and practice toward the 21st century. *Families in Society, 76,* 141-149.

Weston, K. (1991). *Families we choose.* New York: Columbia University Press.

Health Outreach to Low-Income, Rural Single-Parent Families in the Missouri Bootheel Area

Janice H. Chadha, Ph.D., MSW, Marjorie Sable, Ph.D., MSW and J.Wilson Watt, Ph.D., MSW

THE MISSOURI DELTA area borders the Mississippi River in the far southeast corner of Missouri. Commonly known as the Bootheel, this six-county rural area in Southeast Missouri has the highest concentration of both poor people and rural, African Americans in the state. For generations, families here have lived in poverty. This chapter presents the problems these rural residents face and outlines practice models for rural practice with Single-Parent families. Finally, a successful outreach program targeting Single-Parent families to encourage pre- and post-natal care, well child care and nutrition is presented.

The Strengths Perspective and the Single-Parent Family

Social work has traditionally attempted to provide a balanced view of the client within the environment. However, pathology-based models for understanding human behavior have influenced policy and practice in the United States for many years. The problems of many client groups have often been viewed as indicators of personal weakness and moral failings. Saleebey (1992, 1996) countered this tendency by focusing on the strengths clients can bring to their problems when the physical, social and cultural environment is willing to recognize and work with those strengths. Others (Cowger, 1994; DeJong & Miller, 1995; Weick, Rapp, Sullivan & Kisthardt, 1989) stressed the need for client strengths to be primary focus in every phase of work, from assessment on. The strengths perspective considers the capacities, aspirations and possibilities available to

163

clients and client groups within their current environments. This approach is valuable in work with Single Parents, especially those in economically depressed rural environments where services are few and clients must rely on themselves and their informal social supports rather than formal social service programs. The strengths perspective offers a way to "re-vision" our understanding of the Single-Parent family.

The strengths perspective takes into account the uniqueness of the client system. This focus allows the researcher and the practitioner the freedom to reexamine old misconceptions and to challenge assumptions about the needs and aspirations of Single Parents and their children. Current research (Anthony, Weidemann & Chin, 1990; Bianchi, 1995; Morrison, 1995; Nesto, 1994; Trent & Harlan, 1994) shows Single-Parent families are not monolithic in their behaviors or relationships with their environment. Single Parents are a diverse group: teenage mothers, unmarried older women who choose parenthood, divorced parents and parents who have been widowed. Thus, the client's particular situation must be considered when designing interventions for Single Parents.

Trent and Harlan (1994) pointed to up the need to understand how the environment can function as a strength for the Single Parent. Their study revealed 90% of the teenage mothers in their sample lived with a spouse, a parent or an older relative. Other studies have shown the different ways in which the family system and the larger social environment work for Single Parents in different life situations (Greif, 1995; Jackson, 1993; Kissman, 1992 Thompson & Peebles-Wilkins, 1992). These studies point to the importance of the strengths perspective's emphasis on community membership as well as the need to design interventions using available social resources rather than assuming isolation or disconnection on the part of the Single Parent.

Empowerment of clients within their environments is another essential feature of the strengths perspective. Practice strategies which reinforce the Single Parent's abilities to access and use resources in the community increase the likelihood they will become more self-reliant within that community. This approach overlaps in some ways with the recent work of feminist scholars and practitioners (Kissman, 1991; Sands & Nuccio, 1989). Dealing with issues of empowerment from a feminist perspective clearly falls within the domain of the strengths approach; especially given the predominance of women as heads of Single-Parent households (Donati, 1995). Even for fathers who are heads of Single-Parent households, the feminist perspectives on role behaviors, shared responsibility and recognition of the importance of the work of parenting constitute a strong empowering factor (Greif & Demaris, 1990; Meyer & Garasky, 1993).

The strengths perspective neither denies nor minimizes the body of work documenting the various problems faced by many Single-Parent families, particularly those families located in a depressed social environment. Such issues as economic stress (Lino, 1995; Neubauer & Hormann, 1993; Nichols-Casebolt, 1988), child abuse (Gelles, 1989), school performance (Alessandri, 1992), legal complications (Walters and Abshire, 1995), housing difficulties (Mulroy, 1990; Steinbock, 1995) or family dysfunction (Lindblad-Goldberg, Dukes, & Lasley, 1988; Zastowny & Lewis, 1989) are important factors in the success or failure of any Single-Parent family. The strengths perspective, however, views these issues as a challenge to the individual, family and community to activate their strengths (often in collaboration with professionals) to deal with and resolve such issues. Programs which build on the principles of the strengths perspective and emphasize empowerment, resilience and membership in the community can provide the structure needed for Single-Parent families to succeed in making changes in their lives (DiLeonardi, 1993; Julian, 1995). The model presented here describes a strengths-based program for Single-Parent families in rural, economically depressed areas.

Demographics of the Missouri Delta

The Lower Mississippi Delta Commission designated the Missouri Bootheel and surrounding areas as one of the two most socially and economically deprived areas in the nation. By any indicator of poverty, the citizens of this region are disadvantaged. For example, 31.6% of households report incomes of less than $10,000 annually compared with a rate of 17.7% for all households in Missouri. Median family income, at $16,995 per annum, is dramatically lower that the Missouri median household income of $26,362. Further, median household income has declined by 3.6% during the past decade. More than 25% of the population live below the poverty line compared with 13.6% of all Missourians, a 3% increase in the past decade. The proportion of the population eligible for Aid for Families with Dependent Children (AFDC), Medicaid and food stamps, is more than double the state figure. Although the rural areas in Missouri are predominantly White, the Bootheel has a high proportion of Black residents (16.48% compared with a statewide rate of 10.71%). Three counties (Mississippi, New Madrid and Pemiscot) have minority populations of 20%, 16%, and 26%, respectively (Missouri Department of Health, 1992).

Infant mortality rates are a good indicator of the relative prosperity and the general health of a population. The Bootheel has been cited consistently for its high rates of Black infant mortality (24.6 per 1000 live births, 1979-88). Pemiscot County had a mortality rate of 31.3 per 1000 live births and low-birth-weight rate of 16.2% for Black infants (Department of Health, 1990). Other poor maternal and infant health-status indicators include a 1990 fertility rate which was significantly higher than the state rate for both White and African-American women. The state fertility rate for African-American women in the Bootheel is 3% higher (137.46/1000) than the Black statewide fertility rate (96.67/1000). Table 1 shows family-planning health-status indicators in the Missouri Bootheel. The rates for both Whites and Blacks are significantly higher than the state figures. Over 32% of the births in the Bootheel (79% of Black births and 20% of White births) are to unmarried women.

TABLE 1. FAMILY PLANNING HEALTH STATUS INDICATORS, 1984-88

	All Races	White	Black
Births to women under 20	23.7% H*	20.9% H	34.0% H
Births to women under 18	9.8% H	7.7% H	17.6% H
Births to women under 15	0.5% H	0.2% H	1.7% H
Births to women under 20 with parity of 1+	6.3% H	4.6% H	12.4% H
Births to women over 34	3.8% L**	4.0% L	3.2% L
Out of wedlock births	32.6% H	20.1% H	79.0% H
Less than H.S. education	38.1% H	36.0% H	46.2% H
Spacing less than 18 months	15.5% H	12.4% H	25.2% H
Parity 4+	4.7% H	2.6% H	12.2% H
Abortions	122.9 L	132.1 L	86.1 L
Abortions to women under 18	230.9 L	318.2 L	90.7 L

*H—significantly higher (p<.05) than the state rate
**L—significantly lower (p<.05) than the state rate
(Source: State Center for Health Statistics, Missouri Department of Health, 1990)

Births to women over age 34, known abortions and abortions to women younger than 18 years are significantly lower than the state rate. The abortion ratio is lower than the state average probably because of the unavailability of abortion providers in the area. An undercover network of lay abortion providers exists, but their impact is not known.

The population of the six counties was 158,674 in 1990; 111 practicing physicians served the area. Few of these physicians practice obstetrics, which creates an access problem — even when the families desire prenatal care and financial resources are available. It appears the culture of poverty together with poor education for a healthy lifestyle compounds the infant mortality problem as well as creates lifelong health problems such as diabetes, hypertension and heart disease and nutritionally-based disorders.

Sociology of Low Income Rural Single-Parent Families in the Missouri Delta

Poverty and problems affecting Single-Parent families are commonly associated with the urban areas. However, rural poverty is pervasive and is often viewed by the people it affects as hopeless. Such despair is particularly prevalent in areas such as the Missouri Bootheel, which has *never* seen a period of growth and prosperity since the beginning of the post-agricultural era following the mechanization of farms early in this century.

An underclass of poor people are descended from the sharecroppers and slaves who populated the area since the early 1800's. The economy largely resembles the southern, post-Civil War debtor's economy which developed as a response to an agrarian society with no infrastructure. Local resources (cotton, minerals and cheap labor) were sold to wealthy people in the north, or to local people of money and property. The economy is in the hands of those few people who control agriculture and the commercial enterprises. The influx of large dis-count stores has decimated small businesses and large, mechanized agribusiness has ruined small farms (Fitchen, 1991; Morrissey, 1990; Tickameyer & Duncan, 1990).

The area has no significant industry and lacks an infrastructure. Only one interstate highway transverses the area. Public transportation is virtually nonex-istent. The poor, elderly and disabled have few ways to get to larger towns for health care and other services for shopping.

Because of the stagnant economy, the tax base is relatively fixed and schools suffer as a result. Like inner-city schools, these rural schools cannot afford to provide a variety of courses, adequate computers or enrichment programs like those found in affluent suburban schools. These inequalities are evident on college admission test scores even for some highly achieving students. Students who do well in these schools generally come from professional or middle-class families who have the resources to supplement the curriculum (Pollard & O'Hare, 1990).

Drugs and other urban problems, including gang-like behaviors, are now entering in the rural schools. Urban youth who have been sent to relatives in the country for "straightening out", have imported gang culture. The amonie typical of disadvantaged urban youth is no less pervasive among disadvantaged rural youth. However, the small size of the communities make it more difficult to par-ticipate in illicit conduct without detection (Rath, Arola, Richter & Zahnow, 1991).

Only poor people with family or friendship ties tend to move into the area; it is not an area where one goes to look for good jobs. Unemployment and underemployment are high, with below-minimum-wage jobs in service or agriculture. Adequate and affordable housing is scarce. Formal social services are few, and health care is fragmented and difficult to obtain. Disadvantaged young people often move out of the communities to the city to better their lives and look for some excitement. Those who stay, or return, are often trapped in the same cycle of poverty as their parents, grandparents, great grandparents and the generations before them. Sometimes movement occurs between communities, to live with an aunt or cousin, but the economic deprivation and concomitant healthy lifestyle compromises follow the impoverished residents of the area from place to place as they do what is necessary to survive and make periodic attempts to try and better their lives (Deavers, 1989; Duncan, 1991; Gorham, 1990).

Not everyone in these communities is poor. A substantial middle class, (although less affluent than their urban counterparts) and a group of truly affluent people live in each community. Unlike urban areas, where people are often segregated economically and racially and have little day-to-day contact with one another, people in rural areas interact with people from various strata of society. Thus minority and poor people tend to be more visible than they are in cities; although they are perhaps equally ignored by the affluent unless some issue, usually unpleasant, forces notice.

Social stratification is relatively fixed. People are identified with their family of origin. This identification subtly defines appropriate friendship groups, church and social club memberships, entertainment and opportunities for advancement in education and jobs. Although it is possible to break free from this social ordering, doing so is difficult and can result in the breaking of bonds with friends, relations and colleagues. Upward mobility is often regarded as a fantasy one sees on television or in the movies but not obtainable by the average poor citizen. In fact, upward mobility is not always seen as desirable, with the exception of economic needs which must be met in order to survive.

The low-income residents of this area, like poor people everywhere, are survivors in the face of sometimes overwhelming odds. Natural helping networks consisting of stable, if poor, community members who can be counted on to provide emergency, and sometimes long-term, assistance. Some natural helpers are older, more established members of the family or close family friends who function as *de facto* family. Sometimes natural helpers are found in the churches, both in the poor and more affluent parts of town. The people who can be relied upon for emotional and substantive support are known in each community. These natural helpers view the people who come to them with troubles as survivors with strengths. These helpers often live and thrive in adverse conditions. They build community with the scarce physical resources at hand. Some of them escape and move into the middle class (Litwik & Szelenyi, 1969; Memmott & Brennan, 1988; Tracy, 1990).

Social workers and health care providers in the area confront the following problems:

1. Is there running water in the house? Is well water treated with chlorine? Availability and quality of water affect personal and household hygiene as well as physical health.

2. Although electricity is available even in the most rural areas through electrical cooperatives, is service connected to the client's home? If it is not, how is food preserved and stored, particularly milk and baby formula? Is the intense heat of a Delta summer a risk to elderly or chronically ill persons who do not have a fan? Water and electricity issues contribute to hygiene and health practices.

3. Lack of transportation is a major obstacle. Public transportation is not available. Family members or friends who have access to a car must often take off time from work without pay or lose their jobs entirely to provide transportation and other caretaking. Some rural areas and small towns have few or no paved streets, making driving in stormy weather more hazardous and causing wear on old cars at a fast rate.

4. In rural households, are chickens or other livestock brought into the house in cold weather? Heated hen houses and other live stock shelters are unusual this far south, especially among poor people. The presence of animals in the house is particularly worrisome when part or all of the house has a dirt floor which cannot be adequately cleaned of animal feces.

5. Is a pregnant woman eating clay? Nutritional deficiencies are common among persons who are poor; who often subsist on a diet of greasy, high-salt or high-sugar fast foods when money is available and a traditional, southern poverty diet of foods cooked in bacon grease when money is more scarce. Cheaper, fatty cuts of meat are fried or stewed with vegetables. Vegetables are generally canned and cooked with bacon grease for flavoring. Highly processed foods are favored. A family may barbecue, but rarely broil, and baking is reserved for deserts. Fresh fruits and vegetables are not only very expensive, they are not part of the culture.

6. Alcohol consumption is also problematic in an area that has little to offer in the way of affordable entertainment. Violence goes hand in hand with alcohol. Domestic violence and barroom brawls are common. As in many areas where hunting and fishing are not only recreational but necessary for putting food on the table, many citizens are armed. Crowded housing, lack of privacy at home and in the community, boredom, the ever present demands of poverty and Delta heat provide many opportunities for squabbles to violently erupt (Mookergee, 1984; Schorer, 1990).

Health Outreach

The Healthy Mothers/Healthy Fathers/Healthy Babies Prenatal Care Outreach Program in the Missouri Bootheel Region primarily serves female-headed, Single-Parent families; although the program also focuses attention on father involvement. Lay outreach workers, indigenous to their communities, identify pregnant women and assist them in accessing appropriate health education and medical services. This program targets African Americans, but all pregnant women are eligible for services. Families are followed from the time the pregnant woman registers in the program through the infant's first year of life. Babies younger than one year whose mothers were not part of the prenatal program are also eligible for services. Abysmal health-status indicators, for the Missouri Bootheel Region led to the development of this program.

Program History

In 1987 the governor of Missouri appointed a Minority Health Issues Task Force. Representatives included physicians, health administrators, educators and community representatives. One of its six subcommittees was devoted to the problem of infant mortality. This task force led to the creation of the Office of Minority Health in 1988 with HB1565. This office, funded by the state of Missouri through general revenue appropriations, monitors the progress of all programs in the Department of Health for their impact on eliminating disparities in health status among the African-American population, other minority groups and their White counterparts in Missouri.

As early as 1987, the Infant Mortality Subcommittee of the Minority Health Issues Task Force recommended community-based interventions be developed to address the high rates of infant mortality in the state of Missouri. In 1988, the Infant Mortality Subcommittee of the Office of Minority Health recommended the Missouri Department of Health respond to the appalling infant-mortality rates and other maternal- and child-health status indicators among African Americans in the Bootheel. The response was the development of the Healthy Mothers/Healthy Fathers/Healthy Babies Prenatal Outreach Program (HM/HF/HB). Planning began immediately, but the program was not funded until 1990 and not implemented until 1991.

Funding was originally sought from the state legislature to implement programs in the three areas of the state with the highest rates of Black infant mortality. General revenue funding was requested to implement this program. The legislature declined to provide this funding and suggested it be funded by the federal Maternal and Child Health Block Grant (Title V). Because of funding limitations, the Infant Mortality Subcommittee, in collaboration with the Missouri Department of

Health, recommended the Missouri Bootheel be the first site for program implementation.

The HM/HF/HB Program is operated under the purview of the Missouri Department of Health, Bureau of Perinatal and Child Health through the direct supervision of the Southeast District Office of the Department of Health. The Sub-committee on Infant Mortality, Minority Health Advisory Committee and the Chief of the Office of Minority Health serve as advisors to the project. Program implementation used local community- and county-based coalitions working with the county-based outreach workers to provided direction to the project.

Program Goals

The primary goal of the HM/HF/HB Program was to reduce minority infant mortality. To accomplish this goal, the program objective was to ensure all minority, high-risk pregnant women receive at least one prenatal care visit in the first trimester of pregnancy. The experience, data and literature on infant mortality consistently observes prenatal care in the first trimester of pregnancy is the most critical aspect of a successful pregnancy outcome, especially for high-risk mothers. To reduce infant mortality, the following objectives were established:

1. Reduce the rate of inadequate prenatal care.
2. Reduce the rate of pre-term and low-weight for gestational-age births.
3. Reduce the incidence of unplanned pregnancies.
4. Increase awareness of personal and family choices affecting one's health and total well being.
5. Increase male involvement in all aspects of reproductive and family health.

The target population for the program was minority high-risk pregnant women in five of the six Bootheel counties; although non-minority, high-risk, pregnant women were also served. The sixth county was not included in the project because of the very low proportion of births to African-American women. Primary high-risk criteria were African-American women younger than twenty years with less than a high-school education. Other risk factors included multiple pregnancies, poor diet, tobacco use, drug abuse or misuse (e.g., alcohol and illegal drugs), lack of proper exercise, major systemic diseases (e.g., diabetes, hypertension) and poverty. Most participants met several of these criteria.

Process and Program Implementation

The project director, a nurse, was hired and recruitment and training of outreach workers, who would have more intimate access to the target population, was begun. Care was taken to interact positively and establish relationships with the

171

existing official health care structures and social service agencies in each county to avoid ego and territoriality problems. It was important the program be seen as a help to existing services rather than as a force which would create dissatisfaction with existing providers of care. Under the auspices of the health department nurses, local health care providers as well as relevant politicians and other community leaders were contacted and provided with information about the program and its goals. Their assistance was solicited in locating women who could be trained to do the outreach, although churches and other natural helpers proved to be better resources for recruiting good outreach workers. The qualifications for the outreach workers included high-school education, long-time residence in the community and some record of being identified as a natural helper. Most of the women were mothers or grandmothers themselves.

Initially, one outreach worker was available for each of the five participating counties. Eventually, an additional outreach worker was hired in two of the counties. A total of fifteen outreach workers have been employed in this project, with a maximum of seven working at any one time. All outreach workers have been women. Although they are not handsomely paid, their employment adds to the economy of their families and provides status in the chronically impoverished, underemployed communities they served.

The program has operated with the cooperation of the local health department, which agreed to the following:
1. Commit existing resources to the project.
2. Provide office space and minimal supervision to the community outreach workers.
3. Assist outreach workers in identification and recruitment within the target population.
4. Assist outreach workers in establishing community coalitions and generally providing introductions with the middle-class professionals and organizations with whom they would be working.
5. Collaborate with other agencies and organizations identified through the project to help develop more integrated services.
6. Promote the involvement of their employees in training and workshops on cultural sensitivity in order to work better with the outreach workers and the target population.

The District Health Office (DHO), located in Poplar Bluff, Missouri (which is not in the five-county area but not far from it) provided supervision, office space, clerical staff and other resources to the project coordinator. The DHO staff assisted in training the outreach workers and helped identify appropriate strategies and resources, including culturally relevant educational materials. They also helped design and implement the project's record keeping and evaluation.

Finally, they kept the Infant Mortality Subcommittee and the chief of the Office of Minority Health informed on a monthly basis regarding the progress being made.

The first step in program implementation involved the actual location of the women at risk. All relevant health care providers and social service agencies were contacted early in the projects planning phase to elicit support. School administrators, teachers and PTAs were very influential in getting broad-based community support for the project. The Bootheel Black Mayors' Association, working with a supervisor at the Tri County Counseling Agency and the governor's Minority Health Task Force, not only helped gain support in the communities, but also influenced the legislature to provide funding. Other community organizations that proved influential included the Cardiovascular Coalition and the Minority Health Alliance.

In addition to agencies and formal organizations, all potential community contacts were used to locate potential clients. Day care providers, neighborhood "grandmothers", other indigenous providers of social and material support to poor Single-Parent families, ministers, women who provided leadership in the churches, African-American social clubs and identified unofficial leaders in the poor White and African-American neighborhoods in each county were contacted and asked to identify pregnant women, new mothers and children-at-risk. In addition, outreach workers approached pregnant women in the community and inquired if they needed assistance in receiving prenatal care and other related services. Families of low-birth-weight babies were also contacted to educate them about preventative health services and the need for close monitoring of their babies during the first year of life. Once the project became visible in the communities, referrals came steadily through both informal and formal channels.

The local media were very helpful in spreading the word about the program. In addition to ongoing publicity by the radio stations and newspapers serving the communities; the closest television station, KFBS, one hundred miles away in Cape Girardeau, provided excellent coverage both in public-service announcements and several interviews and news stories with the project coordinator. These programs often included local officials (the mayors and other influential community members) who offered public support to the program.

The program initially worked to improve the health awareness of the minority population to help assure pregnant women, corresponding fathers and women thinking of becoming pregnant had sufficient education to make responsible decisions with regard to delivering a healthy baby. Prospective mothers were referred to the health departments in Scott, New Madrid and Mississippi counties, which had established a cooperative program for the five-county catchment area. The goal of setting up an integrated services prenatal and postnatal care program in each county was not realized.

Home visiting was one of the most important facets of the program. Home visiting for health education is well documented as an economical and effective way to influence prenatal care as well as other health problems (Barnett, 1993; Gromby, Larson, Lewit & Behrman, 1993; Olds & Kitzman, 1993; Rogers, Peoples-Sheps & Sorenson, 1995). Each client was visited at least once a month, frequently more often, in her/his own home to see how s/he was doing and whether services were needed. Ongoing health education was provided and healthy behaviors were reinforced. This personalized interest in the client's welfare by a person perceived as both *of* the community *and* sympathetic to, as well as a knowledgeable, about the problems of the community seemed to be a critical factor in the client's compliance with the care plan.

Other facets of the program included health education programs for schools and other groups and "Teen Alert" meetings which provided health education in a social environment and structured activities for youth. Educational efforts included teen pregnancy prevention, sexually transmitted disease prevention, family planning and parenting skills. One-on-one counseling with identified teens was also provided on occasion.

Flyers announcing the "Teen Alert" program were placed in laundromats, grocery stores, and at the Housing Authority Office. Schools distributed flyers and children passed them out on the street corners on Saturdays. Local radio stations also gave publicity. Meetings were held twice a month in two communities. One group averaged twenty-five to fifty teens per meeting and the other averaged about thirty-five. Local businesses met the costs, which averaged approximately $25 per meeting plus the food donated by local stores. Some stores donated merchandise for door and game prizes.

Topics for educational programs were suggested by the teens themselves. Subject areas included: sexually transmitted diseases, HIV prevention, how to look for a job, parent education, college preparation, Pell grants and other scholarships, parenting classes and the services offered at the health department. A video was always shown and snacks were served. The "Just Say No" project made a presentation, and a buddy system was formed for peer support. "Teen Alert" was well received by the teens and the communities and could have become a significant factor in all the communities if adequate staffing and administrative support had been available. Instead, due to lack of funding, the program has languished.

The outreach workers were supported by the project nurse coordinator and a social worker. They provided health and psychosocial assessments and resource ideas for the outreach workers. Problems caused by poverty; particularly inadequate diet, lack of transportation for prenatal visits and lack of health insurance; were the major obstacles to prenatal and postnatal care. The issue of multigenerational, single, adolescent parenthood was difficult to address in a meaningful way.

Case Studies

The following case examples, illustrating the outreach worker's interventions, exemplify the process and results of the project (R. Williams, personal communication, February 14, 1996).

Jane

Jane, an African-American woman, was seventeen and pregnant for the first time. She was recruited by the project in her third month of pregnancy. She was living with her grandmother and had been referred because she had developed medical complications and was falling behind in school. Shortly after referral, she was put on complete bed rest for hypertension and edema in her feet and legs.

The outreach worker began working with Jane and her grandmother on diet and discovered a lot of salt was used in cooking. Jane's family had a history of high blood pressure and a tradition of eating rich, salty, home-cooked foods. In addition, Jane consumed much junk food. The outreach worker visited her everyday for three months with the objective of helping her change her diet. She also picked up her school assignments, provided some support for doing her homework and helped her catch up with her classes. As her eating habits improved, her blood pressure came under control, the edema disappeared and she was able to return to school. At that point, the focus of the visits shifted to family planning.

Even though Jane's condition improved, the baby arrived four to six weeks early. The outreach worker gathered information about premature babies, took Jane to the hospital to visit until the baby was released and provided monitoring and follow-up with the baby after Jane returned to school until the infant was six months old. Both baby and mother did fine and Jane was able, with the help of her grandmother, to finish high school. She decided not to have any more babies for a while and is using reliable contraception. She is employed as the manager of the deli department of a local supermarket.

Susie

Susie was 16 when she was referred to the project. The outreach worker met with her weekly at school during her physical education hour and worked on nutrition, prenatal care and future pregnancy prevention. Sue had a cesarean-section delivery with complications and was placed on bed rest by her physician. This development was not effectively communicated to the school and Susie was expelled from the tenth grade for excessive absence.

The outreach worker learned about her expulsion when she went to visit Susie at school after the delivery and was told that she had left town. When the outreach worker visited her home, Susie answered the door. The homebound teacher had not sent homework for Susie because she felt she had been out of school too long. When confronted by the outreach worker, the teacher related that after her own ceasarian-section delivery she had returned to work in less time. She felt that Susie's long absence was unacceptable. The outreach worker intervened with the principal and Susie was enrolled in summer school to make up for the work she missed, thus completing the tenth grade. She participated in the "Teen Alert" group and was followed by the outreach worker until she recently graduated from high school.

Mary and Bob

Mary was twenty-one years old and living with her baby's father, Bob, in an apartment provided by the Housing Authority. She was referred by the Housing Authority because they were about to be evicted. Mary confided she was having trouble with the Department of Family Services. She believed it was because she was White and the father was Black. They had been approved for AFDC because Bob was in an educational program to complete his Graduation Equivalency Diploma (GED) and had six quarters of previous employment. Mary was attending a post-high school refresher course, hoping to obtain a scholarship to the community college. Bob was getting ready to quit his GED program to look for work. The AFDC caseworker recently told Mary they did not qualify and discontinued both AFDC and food stamps. Mary said that they were told that they did not qualify and not to come back. They had no food and were about to be evicted for non-payment of rent.

The outreach worker called the AFDC worker who was not in. She spoke with the supervisor, who reviewed the case after the program was explained. Their benefits were reinstated. The outreach worker then referred them for family planning services. Bob finished the GED course and is now employed.

Terry

Terry's newborn baby had been sick for several days when the outreach worker went to visit. The outreach worker convinced Terry and her aunt the baby needed to go to the doctor immediately. She secured an appointment and took them to the office. The baby was seriously dehydrated and would have died in another day at home. Follow-up was provided for one year.

Belinda

Belinda contracted a sexually transmitted disease (STD) during her pregnancy and was referred by the emergency room doctor who treated her. She was not receiving prenatal care, was eating poorly and not taking her medication. The outreach worker arranged prenatal care and visited frequently to help her get in the habit of taking her medication. On the outreach worker's first post-partum home visit, the bedroom smelled badly and Belinda complained of severe pains in her back, side and legs. The outreach worker talked with the nurse, who suggested sitting in a tub of warm water. When the outreach worker assisted Belinda, she noticed an open, draining sore. She arranged a doctor's appointment immediately. Belinda was hospitalized and minor surgery was performed to drain an abscess. Home visiting continued with information and assistance in hygiene and prevention of pregnancy and STDs.

Program Results

Between January 1991, when the program began, and December 1994, when the program was discontinued, the rate of inadequate prenatal care decreased from 30.3% to 23.2%. Full staffing was available during the years 1991-3 and partial staffing in 1994. Several positions were vacant in 1994 because of administrative and organizational problems at the state and regional levels. The local departments of health were staffed by employees of Southwest Missouri State University (located in Springfield, Missouri, two hundred miles away). Turnovers occurred in the positions of the district administrator, perinatal nurse consultant, PACH bureau chief and associate bureau chief and MCFH division director and deputy director. The project coordinator resigned and the position was not filled for over a year.

Nevertheless, the results of the project were impressive: 1,451 mothers (1,119 single), 75 fathers and 772 babies were enrolled during the project's duration. About two-thirds of the participants were African American. Enrollment included 355 persons for family planning, 1,224 for prenatal care, and 450 for infant care. Other needs were discovered through assessment. In 1993, the last fully functioning year of the program, 624 clients were enrolled.

The evaluation components for the HM/HF/HB Program was based on health status indicators. Insufficient data precluded evaluation of infant-mortality reduction but evaluation measures included such factors as prenatal care utilization by the program participants as well as health care utilization rates for children. No attempt was made to conduct a qualitative evaluation, and indeed, many benefits of the program would be difficult to measure. The evaluation did not attempt to measure such factors as the impact of knowing someone cared enough about them to ask them to make positive lifestyle changes. Anecdotal reports indicated program participants told outreach workers they changed their behavior (by reducing or eliminating the use of tobacco, alcohol and drugs) because they knew the outreach worker would find out about it and the participants did not want to "get in trouble" with the outreach workers. Because the outreach workers were a part of their community and lived alongside the participants, they may have had more credibility than professional workers from outside the community would have had; although this was not evaluated. Participants were found by informal referral, in grocery stores and laundromats, and by word of mouth. Informal referrals were often made to the outreach workers by other community members. The outreach workers were often the first African-American employees of the county health department and provided a comfort zone allowing many women to use services at the health department for the first time.

The program was terminated in the summer of 1996. Lack of a qualitative evaluation made it impossible to demonstrate the positive impact the program had on participants. Quantitative evaluation measures for factors such as health-behavior change, staying in school or obtaining a GED were not measured either. This was a "feel good" program and was inspirational for those who had the opportunity to observe the work of the outreach workers. Program participants were often motivated to seek a better life for themselves because of the care and concern demonstrated. The participants were viewed in terms of their strengths. Education was provided to help them capitalize on those strengths and utilize existing resources to improve their health during pregnancy and the child's first year of life. Programs such as HM/HF/HB are destined to lose their funding if their worth is determined solely by outcome measures which do not measure the more subtle benefits.

Although the program was successful and economical, the emergence of Southwest Missouri State University staff as major players began a new era of professionalism. In December 1994, a new initiative, "Team for Resource, Advocacy and Care (TRAC)", was started. The team includes three registered nurses, a social worker, a health educator, a nutritionist and clerical support. They began seeing clients in July 1995 and had a caseload of 61 by the end of the year. They worked cooperatively with the remnants of the Program and used the outreach workers for case finding. The professional staff provides intervention and support services. The entire project is being renamed Healthy Families Resource Team (K. Kelly, personal communication, March 23, 1995).

Bibliography

Alessandri, S.M. (1992). Effects of maternal work status in single-parent families on children's perception of self and family and school achievement. *Journal of Experimental Child Psychology, 54,* 417-433.

Anthony, K.H. Weidemann, & S. Chin, Y. (1990). Housing perceptions of low-income single-parents. *Environment and Behavior, 22,* 147-182.

Barnett, W.S. (1993). Economic evaluation of home visiting programs. *The Future of Children, 3* (3), 6-24.

Bianchi, S.M. (1995). The changing demographic and socioeconomic characteristics of single-parent families. *Marriage and Family Review, 20,* 71-97.

Cowger, C.D. (1994). Assessing client strengths: Clinical assessment for client empowerment. *Social Work, 39,* 262-8.

Deavers, K. (1989) Rural American: Lagging growth and high poverty...do we care: *Choices, 2,* 4-7

DeJong, P. & Miller, S.D. (1995). How to interview for client strengths. *Social Work, 40,* 729-36.

DiLeonardi, J.W. (1993). Families in poverty and chronic neglect of children. *Families in Society, 74,* 557-62.

Donati, T. (1995). Single-parents and wider families in the new context of legitimacy. *Marriage and Family Review, 20,* 27-42.

Duncanm C. (1982). *Rural poverty in America.* New York: Auburn.

Fitchen, J. (1991). *Endangered spaces, enduring places: change, identity, and survival in rural America.* Boulder, CO: Westview.

Gelles, R.J. (1989). Child abuse and violence in single-parent families: Parent absence and economic deprivation. *American Journal of Orthopsychiatry, 59,* 492-501.

Greif, G.L. (1995). Single fathers with custody following separation and divorce. *Marriage and Family Review, 20,* 213-231.

Greif, G.L. & Demaris, A. (1990). Single fathers with custody. *Families in Society, 71,* 259-66.

Gromby, D.; Larson, C.; Lewit, E. & Behrman, R. (1993). Home visiting: Analysis and recommendations. *The Future of Children, 3* (3), 93-112.

Jackson, A.P. (1993). Black, single, working mothers in poverty: Preferences for employment, well-being, and perceptions of preschool-age children. *Social Work, 38,* 26-34.

Julian, D.J. (1995). Resources for single-parent families. *Marriage and Family Review, 20,* 499-512.

Kissman, K. (1991). Feminist-based social work with single-parent families. *Families in Society, 72,* 23-8.

Kissman, K. (1992). Single-parenting: Interventions in the transitional stage. *Contemporary Family Therapy, 14,* 323-33.

Lindblad-Goldberg, M. Dukes, J.L. Lasley & J.H. (1988). Stress in black, low-income, single-parent families: Normative and dysfunctional patterns. *American Journal of Orthopsychiatry, 58,* 104-20.

Lino, M. (1995). The economics of single-parenthood: Past research and future directions. *Marriage and Family Review, 20,* 99-114.

Litwik, E. & Szelenyi, I. (1969). Primary group structures and their functions: kin, neighbors and friends. *American Sociological Review, 34,* 465-81.

Memmott, J. & Brennan, E. (1988). Helping orientations and strategies of natural helpers and social workers in rural settings. *Social Work Research and Abstracts, 24* (2), 15-20.

Meyer, D.R. & Garasky, S. (1993). Custodial fathers: Myths, realities, and child support policies. *Journal of Marriage and the Family, 55,* 73-89.

Missouri Department of Health (1992). *Primary care planning areas and regional planning commissions.* Jefferson City, MO.

Missouri Department of Health (1990). *Missouri Maternal and infant health status indicators. Missouri Center for Health Statistics Publication No. 6.8,* (August). Jefferson City, MO.

Morrissey, E. (1990). Poverty among rural workers. *Rural Development Perspectives, (June-September),* 37-42.

Morrison, N.C. (1995). Successful single-parent families. *Journal of Divorce and Remarriage, 22,* 205-19.

Mookergee, H. (1984). Teenage drinking in rural middle Tennessee. *Journal of Alcohol and Drug Education, 29,* 49-57.

Mulroy, E. (1990). Single-parent families and the housing crisis: Implications for macropractice. *Social Work, 35,* 542-6

Nesto, B. (1994). Low-income single-mothers: Myths and realities. *Affilia, 9,* 232-46.

Neubauer, E. & Hormann, E. (1993). Economic and social support of single-parent families: Needs and reality. *Community Alternatives: International Journal of Family Care, 5,* 67-84.

Nichols-Casebolt, A.M. (1988). Black families headed by single-mothers: Growing numbers and increasing poverty. *Social Work, 33,* 306-13.

Olds, D. & Kitzman, H. (1993). Review of research on home visiting for pregnant women and parents of young children. *The Future of Children, 3* (3), 53-92.

Pollard, D. & O'Hare, W. (1990). *Beyond high school: The experience of urban and rural youth in the 1980s.* Washington, D.C.: Population Reference Bureau.

Rath, Q. Arola, T.; Richter, B. & Zahnow, S. (1991). Small town corrections: A rural perspective. *Corrections Today, 53,* 228-30.

Rogers, M.; Peoples-Sheps, M. & Sorenson, J. (1995). Translating research in MCH service: Comparison of a pilot project and a large-scale resource mothers program. *Public Health Reports, 110,* 563-9.

Sands, R.G. & Nuccio, K.E. (1989). Mother-headed single-parent families: A feminist perspective. *Affilia, 4,* 25-41.

Saleebey, D., ed. (1992). *The Strengths Perspective in Social Work Practice.* New York: Longman.

Saleebey, D. (1996). The strengths perspective in social work practice: Extensions and cautions. *Social Work, 41,* 296-305.

Schorer, F. (1990). Rural wife abuse. Des Moines Register, November 30, 1T-3T.

Steinbock, M.R. (1995). Homeless female-headed families: Relationships at risk. *Marriage and Family Review, 20,* 143-59.

Tickameyer, A. & Duncan, C. (1990). Poverty and opportunity structure in rural America. *Annual Review of Sociology, 16,* 67-86.

Tracy, E. (1990). Identifying social support resources of at-risk families. *Social Work, 35,* 252-8.

Thompson, M.S. & Peebles-Wilkins, W. (1992). The impact of formal, informal, and societal support networks on the psychological well-being of black adolescent mothers. *Social Work, 37,* 322-8.

Trent, K. & Harlan, S.L. (1994). Teenage mothers in nuclear and extended households: Differences by marital status and race/ethnicity. *Journal of Family Issues, 15,* 309-37.

Walters, L.H. & Abshire, C.R. (1995). Single-parenthood and the law. *Marriage and Family Review, 20,* 161-88.

Weick, A., Rapp, C.; Sullivan, W.P. & Kisthardt, W. (1989). A strengths perspective for social work practice. *Social Work, 34,* 350-4.

Zastowny, T.R. & Lewis, J.L. (1989). Family interactional patterns and social support systems in single-parent families. *Journal of Divorce, 13* (2), 1-40.

Empowerment and Collaboration with Single Parents of Children with Disabilities

Pauline Jivanjee, Ph.D.

A Parent's Story

TERRI IS A WHITE SINGLE MOTHER in her early forties who works as an occupational therapist in a public school system. Terri lives with her only child, Michael. Now aged fourteen, Michael has an auditory discrimination problem, resulting in a learning disability and behavioral disorder. Michael was born to Terri and her husband while Terri was completing a professional degree course in occupational therapy. Six months after the birth, Terri's husband (whom she describes as abusive and alcoholic) left the family, leaving her to care for Michael alone.

As a baby, Michael was very fussy and cried continually for hours at a time. When Terri sought assistance from her physician, she was told nothing was wrong, and he was simply "fooling her". By the time he began attending preschool, Michael was having frequent tantrums. Terri felt blamed by the preschool teachers, who recommended she seek help to improve her parenting skills. Together, Terri and Michael completed a parenting course and attended counseling sessions. Counseling ended after six sessions, when the counselor told Terri that she was unable to help Michael.

At the age of four, Michael was tested by the local school district and diagnosed with a speech and language disability. Weekly speech therapy did not improve his speech, so Terri took him for private testing and tutoring. Michael was diagnosed with a learning disability and an auditory discrimination impairment. Terri decided not to send Michael to the local public school because the staff was unresponsive and the teacher said she would call Terri and she would have to take him home for the rest of the day if there were any "problems". Terri felt she would not be able to work under these circumstances and she could not afford to give up work, so she sent him to a private school. Michael began to learn, but his behavior became increasingly problematic.

Two years later, Terri and Michael moved to another state and he was reevaluated by the new school district for special education services. Again, despite her own professional training and experience and the diagnostic documentation, Terri had difficulty convincing educators and service providers of Michael's needs. For years, Terri has had to negotiate with the school district to get appropriate services for Michael, on several occasions she has considered taking legal action against the district to have Michael's needs met. Terri describes her experiences as "unbelievably painful and life-consuming", not only because of the demands of caring for a child with a learning disability, but also because of the failure of professionals to listen to her and work in partnership with her.

To meet her son's needs for stability and structure, Terri has had to change her personality. She has learned to be extremely well-organized, to plan ahead and to always assess his mood before arranging activities. As a result, Terri has had to sacrifice many of her interests and social activities to provide a stable and consistent routine for Michael. During the last fourteen years, Terri has had several close relationships with men, but none who could endure Michael's difficult daily behaviors. At this time in her life, she chooses not to date.

Having no spousal support has been extremely difficult for Terri. Her ex-husband has only established telephone contact with Michael in the last year, after many years of no contact at all. He has never paid child support; she recently initiated child support proceedings against him, but has received nothing to date. Their lack of financial resources has prevented Terri and Michael from participating in activities and experiences. Because of Michael's behavioral problems and his need for consistency, respite care and babysitters have been difficult to find and Terri has had to either take him with her to social functions or stay home with him. Terri's employment in the school system has allowed her to spend summers with Michael, but without the financial resources to pay for activities, summers are stressful and exhausting. Michael attends a camp on occasional weekends and summer weeks which allows Terri some much-needed respite, while providing him with new experiences and opportunities. Having another adult to help raise Michael would have provided Terri with some relief and emotional support and she says this would also have helped Michael to cope with his self-doubt. Without the emotional and financial support of a spouse, Terri has relied on her family and friends for help. Her father, sister and several good friends have been supportive. Terri describes her mother as "unbelievably supportive" until her death three years ago which created a void that no-one can fill.

Due to the severity of Michael's behavioral problems and several incidents of violence, Terri has occasionally questioned whether they would both benefit from his placement in out-of-home care. She credits their ability to cope and to live together to her deep love of her son, her liking for his personality and caring qualities and their mutual respect.

Over the years, Terri's experiences working with service providers and educators have been quite negative. Terri has found few educators and practitioners willing to listen to her perspective or to follow her suggestions related to behavior management strategies she has found successful. Her employment has interfered with her ability to volunteer in her son's school and to work with service providers. She describes her experiences with the Individualized Education Process (IEP) as failing to consider Michael as a whole child. She has had little success in convincing school personnel of the advantages of a broader perspective. Terri's professional training, experience working in schools and personal strengths have enabled her to advocate strongly on behalf of her son. Terri believes her professional identity is a liability because educators and service providers are aware she knows the laws and she will challenge their decisions if they are not appropriate for Michael. School has been a negative experience, because Michael's progress is measured entirely in terms of criteria which does not fit for him and as a result his self-esteem has suffered.

During challenging times in their life together, Terri has periodically sought counseling to help her to cope, to learn strategies to deal with the challenges of parenting a child with a disability and to improve the relationship between herself and Michael. Some of these experiences have been positive, when the social worker or counselor listened and tried to understand their situation; others have been less helpful when the focus has been on Michael's failures and she has felt blamed for her son's difficulties.

In summary, Terri has demonstrated resources and strengths in dealing with the difficult challenges of being the Single Parent of a child with a learning disability and behavioral disorder. Her coping skills, creativity, emotional maturity and deep devotion to her son; together with practical and emotional support from her family and friends have carried her through the difficult times. Terri's skills in being assertive with educators and service providers and her ability to withstand criticisms of her decisions for Michael are particular strengths. Terri believes her parenting would have been enhanced by supportive, empowering professionals who recognized her strengths and collaborated with her to make appropriate decisions for herself and Michael.

Overview

Terri's story is a compelling account of the challenges faced by a Single Parent raising a child with a disability and her fortitude in meeting these challenges. Her account may or may not be representative of the experiences of Single Parents of children with disabilities, but it is included here as an illustration of the complexity of the issues related to parenting a child with a disability by oneself. Terri is remarkable for her emotional strength, her selflessness, her creativity, her strong informal support system and her deep love of her son. However, her story provides evidence of ways practitioners and service providers have failed to understand Terri's and Michael's needs, and insights into how professionals might have been more helpful. This chapter presents information and ideas about the experiences of Single Parents of children with serious emotional disorders intended to help social workers to be more responsive to the needs of Single Parents.

Social workers in a variety of settings, such as schools, health care, mental health and community-based social service agencies, are likely to encounter Single Parents whose children have disabilities and this chapter is intended to provide an overview of the issues facing such families and strategies for intervention. The chapter begins with an overview of childhood disability and Single Parenting. The effects of caring for a child with a disability or chronic illness, and Single Parents' use of coping strategies, social support and services are examined. Single Parents caring for children with disabilities are a diverse group in terms of culture and socioeconomic status and they have unique strengths and needs. At the same time, they have common concerns across disability groups related to providing the best care possible for all their children, while supporting the family and meeting their own needs. Services and supports most helpful to parents are reviewed and the recommendations for collaborative, family-centered approaches to social work practice, with the goal of empowering Single Parents of children with disabilities and chronic illnesses are provided.

Because over 90% of Single Parents taking care of a child with a disability are female, the pronoun "she" will be used throughout this chapter, and there will be special attention to the economic issues facing women parenting a child alone in inhospitable work environments and in a social and political context which does not place a high priority on financial and practical support for single women raising children with disabilities.

Children with many kinds of disabilities and chronic illnesses are over-represented among the population of Single-Parent families. Single Parents of children with a physical, emotional or behavioral disability or chronic illness are faced with a multitude of competing stresses and demands related to parenting alone, supporting their family, providing the specialized care their child requires, and negotiating complex and fragmented service systems. These pressures have a variety of negative effects on Single Parents and may result in fatigue, anxiety, depression, social isolation and family conflict which bring them to the attention of social workers. Despite the extraordinary difficulties of parenting alone, many Single Parents rise to the challenge, thrive and even find the strength to offer support to other parents.

Since the early 1980s, dramatic changes have occurred in the organization and delivery of services to families with children with disabilities. There has been a shift from the child being viewed as the focus of intervention, shifting from the child to the family and is guided by the families' needs and strengths, with professionals working in partnership with them (Garland, 1993; Szanton, 1991). Families are increasingly seen as able to perceive and articulate their own needs and aspirations, leading to changed approaches to service delivery which include: (a) parent-to-parent support and counseling, (b) parent involvement in professional training, and (c) political activism coordinated through parent advocacy organizations (Szanton, 1991). The provision of services to children with serious emotional and behavioral disorders is guided by a new emphasis on family support to keep families together and achieve balanced lives (Friesen & Wahlers, 1993). Increased attention is focused on family strengths, resources and coping capacities with professional efforts directed toward establishing relationships of trust with family members, providing family support, collaboration with families and family empowerment (Dunst, Trivette, & Deal, 1988).

Background

Nineteen and a half percent of children aged three to seventeen (10.7 million children) are affected by a chronic illness or disability (National Institute on Disability and Rehabilitation Research, 1992). Common physical disabilities include cerebral palsy, spina bifida, orthopedic disabilities, muscular dystrophy and visual and hearing impairments. Developmental disabilities are those which result in functional limitations in self-care, language, learning, mobility, self-direction and capacities for independent living and economic self-sufficiency (Friedman, Kutash & Duchnowski, 1996); disabilities include developmental delays, Down's syndrome, mental retardation and learning disabilities.

The most common chronic illnesses affecting children are asthma, congenital heart disease, seizure disorder and cerebral palsy. Approximately three million children in the United States have serious emotional and behavioral disabilities (Knitzer, 1982). Definitions of emotional disabilities focus on long-term impairments which substantially interfere with a child's functioning in family, school or community activities; they include schizophrenic, affective, anxiety, conduct and adjustment disorders (Friedman et al., 1996).

The rates of childhood disability are not evenly distributed among social groups. The rates of chronic illness and childhood disability in all disability groups are higher in single, female-headed families and are highly correlated with lower economic status (Garbarino, 1987; Jones, 1987; NIDRR, 1992; Sidel, 1986). For Single Parents the extraordinary costs of providing care to a child with a disability or chronic illness cause financial hardship which drive many families into poverty. Approximately 90% of children living with a Single Parent live with their mothers and the proportion of children with disabilities living with Single Mothers may be even higher (Wikler, Haack, & Intagliata, 1984).

Theoretical Frameworks Applied to Families and Childhood Disability

Single Parents represent a significant proportion of the respondents in studies of the effects of childhood disabilities on families, but few studies have focused on the particular needs and concerns of Single Parents of children with disabilities. There is, however, an extensive descriptive literature on the effects of a child with a disability or chronic illness on families generally. Ecological frameworks are helpful in providing understanding of the systemic influences within families and the reciprocal relationships between families and their environments. Stress and coping theory in addition to loss and grief frameworks have been applied to family responses to the presence of a child with a disability or chronic illness. Knowledge of these theoretical frameworks can help social workers to increase their understanding of the complexity and variability of family responses to childhood disability and to intervene appropriately and sensitively with Single Parents.

Ecological Perspectives

Family adaptations to the presence of a child with a disability vary widely and are affected by ecological influences within and beyond the family unit, including social support, locus of control, individual coping and problem solving capacities, socioeconomic status and income, self-concepts and personal beliefs and child characteristics (Dunst, Cooper, & Bolick, 1987; Mori, 1983). Factors associated with family adaptation include: the age of the child and parent at the onset of disability or illness, the severity, the social acceptability of the disability or illness, the manner in which the parent is informed (Mori, 1983), the effects of insensitive service providers and unpredictability and losses of relationships (Patterson, 1988). High rates of divorce, shifting currents in employment, new roles for women and men and rapid mobility affect the ways families respond to a childhood chronic illness (Burr, 1985; Hobbs, Perrin, & Ireys, 1985; Singer & Irvin, 1989).

Disabilities and chronic illnesses affect the quality of parent-child interactions, thereby increasing stress through a reciprocal process (Mori, 1983). For example, children with autism or pervasive developmental disorders often require extensive care similar to that needed by children with physical disabilities, but may show little positive affective responsiveness to the caregiving parent (Jones, 1987). Parents may reduce the amount of time they spend with infants who are passive or unresponsive, who in turn become even more withdrawn. In contrast, children who are socially responsive, despite severe physical disabilities, are likely to develop likeable attributes which facilitate bonding (Jones, 1987). Social workers should be careful to take into account these kinds of reciprocal effects within the family and avoid assuming linear, cause-effect relationships; e.g. the illness "caused" marital breakdown or marital breakdown "caused" exacerbation of the illness (Patterson, 1988).

Stress and Coping Theory

Common themes have emerged from research into the impact of childhood illness and disability on families: (a) a host of hardships and demands are associated with diagnosis of a chronic childhood illness; (b) capabilities of the child, parents, siblings, the family, and community mediate these demands; and (c) different meanings which are attributed to the chronic illness and its hardships and the family's capabilities shape their responses (Burr, 1985; Hobbs et al., 1985; Mori, 1983; Patterson, 1988; Singer & Irvin, 1989).

According to stress and coping theory, positive and negative family adaptations are the product of the interaction of intrafamily resources, community resources, stressors, the family's way of appraising stressors and resources and its repertoire of coping skills (McCubbin & Patterson, 1983; Patterson, 1988; Pearlin & Schooler, 1978; Singer & Irvin, 1989). The Double ABCX Model of family stress (McCubbin & Patterson, 1983) addresses A (the stressor event) interacting with B (the family's crisis meeting resources), and C (the family's definition of the event) to produce X (the crisis) with variables to describe family adaptation and resiliency over time. Patterson (1988) suggests families with a child with a chronic illness go through repeated cycles of adjustment/crisis/adaptation. Single-Parent families with a child with a disability may be more vulnerable to crisis because of the multiple, chronic hardships facing them. Conversely, families which develop the capabilities to meet the demands of caring for a child with a disability may be stronger and more resilient than other families.

Parents of children with disabilities or chronic illnesses experience a range of strains: cognitive demands such as the need to master knowledge about the condition and how to manage it and find competent service providers, emotional pain such as recurrent sorrow and worry and behavioral demands related to the tasks of caring for the child (Burr, 1985; Hobbs et al., 1985; Patterson, 1988; Singer & Irvin, 1989). Childhood chronic illness or disability may increase the accumulation of stressors and strains, creating a pileup of demands (Patterson, 1988). For example, financial worries are a major, constant burden for many families with a child with a chronic illness; that can aggravate tensions which are already high (Burr, 1985; Hobbs et al., 1985; Singer & Irvin, 1989). Expenses related to the child's illness are likely to limit the availability of resources for other needs, for example babysitting and respite care to provide emotional relief; vacations may not be possible because of limited finances. Day-to-day financial hassles create a background of strain which exacerbates parent stress (Singer & Irvin, 1989).

A disproportionate amount of time must be spent with children with chronic illnesses to maintain their health and this takes parents (especially Single Parents) away from other children, work and the possibility of leisure (Burr, 1985). Mothers of children with disabilities tend to limit their participation in the work force, resulting in reduced income and financial stress (Burr, 1985; Hobbs et al., 1985; Singer & Irvin, 1989). Financial difficulties are particularly acute for Single Mothers in the workforce, who must pay for additional expenses for caregiving (Singer & Irvin, 1989).

The demands of caring for a child with a disability or chronic illness may create or exacerbate conflict in the marital relationship. However, data on the relationship between childhood disability and divorce are sparse and contra-dictory (Burr, 1985; Hobbs et al., 1985; Patterson, 1988; Seligman & Darling, 1989; Singer & Irvin, 1990). The presence of a child with a disability can aggravate latent problems in the family unit (Jones, 1987; Seligman & Darling, 1989); that is the stresses of providing care to a child with a disability may contribute to other destructive processes, rather than being the sole cause of divorce. Further research is necessary to increase understanding of the reasons some families disintegrate under stress, while others thrive (Seligman & Darling, 1989).

Social support has been demonstrated to buffer the negative reactions of providing care to a family member with a disability (Pearlin & Schooler, 1978). Petr and Barney (1993) found both informal emotional support and formal services are important to parents. However, social support is not always helpful to families; support is unhelpful when it is accompanied by criticisms or suggestions which undermine the parent's self-esteem and sense of competence. For low-income, Single Mothers, women friends are a positive influence on functioning more often than any other resource, particularly in relation to parenting and self-care; but as women move into the instrumental roles of student and worker, friends become less important (Nesto, 1994). In view of the limited support networks available to many Single Mothers of children with disabilities, social workers may facilitate connections to effective informal and formal support systems.

Families with a child with a disability or chronic illness must have continuing contacts with a range of professionals which may include special educators, speech and language therapists, physical or occupational therapists, physicians, psychologists and social workers. While these experts can be helpful to families, there may be increased stress because of the time demands related to keeping appointments and providing personal information (Jones, 1987; Patterson, 1988). Parents who do not follow professional recommendations for treatment may be judged noncompliant and unconcerned about their child, whereas parents who do follow recommendations may neglect other family members (Jones, 1987). Single Parents are likely to respond positively when social workers are sensitive to these impacts and flexible about scheduling, when they limit requests for information to what is essential and when they elicit the parent's ideas about involvement in treatment. Social workers may need to utilize advocacy skills with larger systems when these systems are unresponsive to family needs and thus are part of the problem (Imber-Black, 1989).

The Effects of Stress

Acute depression, overeating, sleeplessness, irritability, school problems, marital tensions, social isolation, fatigue and a sense of helplessness are common problems for members of families with a child with chronic illness (Hobbs et al., 1985; Singer & Irvin, 1989; Zucman, 1982). Children with disabilities are more likely to come to the attention of social workers in child welfare settings because there is an increased incidence of abuse of children with disabilities. However, there may be difficulty determining whether the disability is an outcome of abuse, or whether children with disabilities are at increased risk of abuse by their parent(s) (Garbarino, 1987).

Risks in caring for a family member with a disability or chronic illness which have been identified include financial costs, stigma, time for personal care, difficulty with personal management, interruptions with sleep, social isolation, limitations in recreational opportunities, behavioral problems, sibling distress, difficulty in shopping and other normal household routines, and limited prospects for the future (Burr, 1985; Hobbs et al., 1985; Mori, 1983; Moroney, 1980; Singer & Irvin, 1989). Caregiving burden varies with the type of disability, the kind of care provided and the supports available. Hobbs and co-workers (1985) note these negative effects and add lives are made more burdensome by policies ill-suited to their needs and the presence of myths and prejudices in communities.

The time demands associated with the care of a child with a disability are highly associated with negative reactions by parents (Dunst et al., 1987). In addition, by focusing on managing the disease, parents may lose the benefit of social support and the opportunity to share the burden of care (Burr, 1985). Chronic illness of a child is distinguished from other sources of stress by its constancy, by the increased possibility of an early death, by an often unpredictable but usually deteriorating course of illness and by the demands of the illness itself, including both hospitalization and routine care (Hobbs et al., 1985). Parents must also deal with their child's physical and psychological pain, boredom and frustration.

Characteristics of some children with a disability or chronic illness, such as fussiness, a need for special care and delinquent or aggressive behavior may make them challenging to care for and at risk of maltreatment (Garbarino, 1987). Other factors associated with maltreatment are negative interactions between the parent and child – either escalating conflict or progressive withdrawal, isolation from sources of social support and cultural values which promote or permit physical discipline (Garbarino, 1987). Dunst and colleagues (1987) suggest a handicapping condition *per se* is not an elicitor of abuse, but it may constitute a predisposing factor, with behaviors associated with the disability (such as excessive time demands) functioning as precipitating events which adversely affect personal and family well-being. Regardless, social workers should be alert to the possibility of abuse in families of children with disabilities and be prepared to work with families to alleviate their stress.

Capabilities and Coping

In addition to knowledge and understanding of specific disabilities and chronic illnesses on Single-Parent families, social workers need to have awareness of the strengths, resilience and coping capacities of families. Focusing on families' strengths and capacities for growth, the strengths perspective of social work practice offers a model for supporting and empowering families through collaborative relationships (Saleebey, 1992, 1996). According to the Family Adjustment and Adaptation Research (FAAR) Model, family adaptation is influenced by capabilities: resources; what the family has and coping behaviors; which are what the family does to manage demands (McCubbin & Patterson, 1983; Patterson, 1988). Self-esteem of the child and parent, the parent's intelligence, education, health and financial state are personal resources associated with well-being in families with members who have a disability (Patterson, 1988). Aspects of the family system – such as clear rules and expectations, generational boundaries, shared responsibility, cohesion and an atmosphere of normalcy – may also contribute to positive adaptation to chronic illness (Patterson, 1988).

Support from other parents who are coping with similar conditions is a resource which helps families to adapt. Mutual support is often found through support groups; although not all parents choose to use this form of support.

Coping behaviors are directed at maintaining or restoring the balance between demands and resources by: (a) reducing the number or intensity of demands, (b) increasing or maintaining the family's resources, (c) altering the meaning of the situation to make it more manageable and/or (d) managing the tension associated with unresolved strain (McCubbin & Patterson, 1983; Patterson, 1988). Examples of coping strategies which alter the meaning of the situation include believing in the child's and family's capabilities, using positive comparisons and having realistic attitudes about treatment (Patterson, 1988). Parents may enhance their coping with stress through the use of positive illusions, in which they: (a) appraise negative events in terms of challenges rather than threats, (b) actively try to alter stressful situations, (c) use cognitive reinterpretation to construe stressful events in a way that makes them less threatening and (d) are more able to manage emotional distress (Taylor, 1989; Brown, 1993).

Since the late 1970s, family researchers have demonstrated growing interest in what Antonovsky (1993) calls "a salutogenic orientation" to studying disabilities in families. This approach shifts the emphasis from family pathology to what promotes health, in particular the family's sense of coherence and use of a range of cognitive, affective and instrumental coping strategies (Antonovsky, 1993). Despite recurrent periods of crisis, many families with a child with a chronic illness or disability are able to sustain themselves, rise to the occasion and live a quality life (Hobbs et al., 1985).

Families may find a greater closeness in a mutual commitment to caring for their ill child; There have been reports religious beliefs have been strengthened by having a child with a chronic illness (Hobbs et al., 1985; Patterson, 1988). A supportive community of relatives and friends are variables which contribute to a sense of greater closeness (Hobbs et al., 1985). For some Single Mothers, the child's father may be a source of assistance in caring for a child with a disability (Jones, 1987). Other young, Single Mothers may gain support and assistance from their own mothers; although there are mixed findings related to the relief they gain and the power struggles and sense of incompetence which may ensue (Jones, 1987). If relatives, friends and community members are disparaging or critical of the Single Mother's efforts, her self-esteem is undermined and support may be experienced as negative. Careful assessment increases the social worker's understanding of the needs for support and the positive and negative effects of support received by the Single Parent caring for a child with a disability.

Social work assessment and interventions which take account of Single Parents' coping capacities and resilience and build upon their strengths are likely to be most helpful. The strains experienced by Single Parents of children with disabilities are not to be minimized; but people have skills, abilities, knowledge and insight which accumulate over time as these parents struggle to surmount adversity and meet challenges (Saleebey, 1996). Strengths-focused interventions center on recognizing and fostering family strengths and resilience within a collaborative, empowering relationship and making use of available resources (Saleebey, 1992; 1996).

Effects on Siblings

Siblings of children with disabilities are believed to be at risk psychologically and their adjustment is influenced by family strengths and supports, including both psychological strengths and financial resources (Atkins, 1989; Mori, 1983). The internal structure and functioning of the family may be changed to accommodate the needs of the child with a disability, thus placing increased demands on siblings to contribute to meeting the family's needs (Hobbs et al., 1985; Patterson, 1988). A disproportionate share of the family's resources – time, energy, money – are devoted to the child with a chronic illness and the needs of siblings may take second place (Hobbs et al., 1985). Sisters and brothers, particularly sisters, may be compelled to take on extra chores and a Single Parent may use a healthy sibling as an emotional support. Siblings may present health and behavior problems as a way to get attention, which is more likely to occur in Single-Parent families (Zucman, 1982). The financial burden associated with caring for a child with a chronic illness increases family stress and may lead the parent to work longer hours, resulting in children being unsupervised for longer periods of time.

Siblings may experience a variety of feelings such as anger, resentment, embarrassment and guilt (Atkins, 1989). Positive effects have also been noted and characteristics such as sensitivity, warmth and understanding have been observed (Atkins). Siblings have gained by the experiences of having a brother or sister with a chronic illness, becoming by their own accounts more sensitive and caring adults (Burr, 1985; Hobbs et al., 1985). Some parents believe having a child with a chronic illness has made them stronger or helped their other children develop more patience, tolerance and empathy (Zucman, 1982). Siblings of children with long-term illness or disability may be more socially competent than siblings of normal controls and have more compassion and sensitivity to the needs of others (Patterson, 1988; Hobbs et al., 1985).

Atkins (1989) recommends professionals working with children with disabilities and their families focus attention on the non-disabled siblings. Social work intervention should be guided by assessment of risk factors, the quality of relationships and the issues, concerns and feelings of these children within the family context (Atkins, 1989). Parents may need to be encouraged to be open and honest with their healthy children about the child's disability, to allow them to be involved in the child's care to the extent they desire and to plan quality "alone time" with them (Mori, 1983). Supportive interventions, such as sibling groups may be offered to help to normalize the experiences of siblings and to assist them in working through their feelings of resentment, fear, embarrassment and shame (Mori, 1983).

Grief and Loss

The responses of parents of children with disabilities are diverse and complex, but theorists have observed parents tend to pass through a number of stages of grief and loss with some predictability (Mori, 1983). Researchers opinions differ on the number and names of the stages, the sequence of stages and the precise nature of parental concern at each stage, but several consistent themes have been identified. Knowledge of the stages which families pass through is helpful to social workers so they can validate parents' feelings, normalize their reactions and help them to manage their grief and achieve personal growth (Powers, 1993).

The initial stage is characterized by parents' severe psychological disorganization: initially, parents experience shock, disbelief, hopelessness, mourning and sorrow (Mori, 1983). Denial may occur in the middle stages, with the parent refusing to talk about the problem and avoiding intervention for the child. With acceptance, in the final stage parents seek ways to establish a nurturing relationship with their child (Mori, 1983). The use of a grieving framework for examining the losses experienced by the family at the birth of a child with disabilities may be useful for social workers helping families deal with the grief process (Ellis, 1989). Ellis presents a six-stage model for professionals: (a) initial awareness, (b) strategies to overcome loss, (c) awareness of loss, (d) completions, (e) resolutions and reformulations and (f) transcending loss. Social workers can help families to understand the grief process, and the ways they may go back and forth through stages (Ellis, 1989).

Social work intervention at the time of diagnosis may help families to deal with the developmental challenge of creating meaning for the disability which preserves a sense of mastery (Jones, 1987; Rolland, 1993). Parents of children with a chronic illness seek knowledge in three areas: the basic physiology, course and treatment of the illness; the workings of the health care system and related services and the management of the strong emotions which the illness arouses (Hobbs et al., 1985). Social workers can provide information and both practical and emotional support at this critical stage – they can also assist Single Parents negotiating systems. Jones (1987) recommends professionals exercise care in presenting clear, understandable information about diagnosis to the parent and be prepared to facilitate gradual understanding of the child's condition.

Parents of children with a disability or chronic illness do not necessarily move linearly through the stages of grief; instead they may repeat stages with critial transitions or events. After moving through the stress and grief associated with the initial identification of a disability, parents may confront these same issues when the child enters a school program, reaches puberty, and with vocational planning and when the parent begins to worry about who will care for the child when she is too old to provide care (Mori, 1983). Social work support may be particularly important at these stages, to help Single Parents obtain information and resources and cope with their own emotional reactions.

Social workers may be helpful to Single Parents dealing with disability-related grief by letting families tell their story; helping them process their loss through the use of rituals; promoting self-care and skill-building; helping families to develop and maintain support networks and facilitating the development of new meanings through reflection (Powers, 1993). Awareness of the ways family beliefs about health and illness are influenced by ethnicity, race and religion will be helpful for social workers planning interventions with Single Parents of children with a disability (McGoldrick, Pearce & Giordano, 1982). Cultural beliefs about health vary in terms of the appropriate role of the patient, the kind and degree of communication about the illness or disability, who assists the primary caregiver and the kinds of rituals associated with different stages of the illness (Rolland, 1993). Social work interventions that consider the Single-Parent family's cultural identity and beliefs, such as their use of spirituality as a coping mechanism, are most likely to be experienced as helpful.

Issues for Single Mothers of Children with Disabilities

Most assumptions about the Single Parents of children with disabilities are intuitive, because the compounding nature of having a child with a disability and being a Single Parent has not been the subject of much systematic research (Deiner, 1987; Jones, 1987; Seligman & Darling, 1989). The type of disability (physical, developmental or emotional), its severity and time of onset; and factors such as the degree to which the child can assist in her/his own care, the child's level of social responsiveness and the kinds of unusual behaviors the child exhibits affect the Single Parent's level of stress (Jones, 1987).

Single Mothers of children with developmental disabilities reported greater stress and more social isolation than their counterparts in dual-parent families, less help with caregiving activities and burden related to heavy time demands (Beckman, 1983). However, based on their review of fifteen studies in the research literature, Boyce et al. (1995) reported the findings across studies that

Single Parents of children with disabilities are more stressed than mothers in two-parent families are inconsistent. Single Mothers across a number of studies were found to be younger and have less education and/or income than mothers in two-parent families (Boyce et al., 1995). Boyce and colleagues suggest it is not the presence of a child with a disability *per se* that results in increased stress. Instead, the social and economic problems associated with Single Parenthood are so overwhelming they gravely complicate the effects of having a child with a disability in the family (Boyce et al., 1995).

Other findings affirm the interaction of Single Parenthood, childhood disability and economic status. For example, Single Mothers with a child with a disability are less likely to be employed, more likely to be on welfare and more likely to believe they will not remarry than Single Mothers of healthy children (Wikler, 1981; Wikler et al., 1984). When asked to rank their needs, Single Parents of children listed respite care, financial needs and personal/ social needs as most important (Wikler et al., 1984).

The double duty of Single Mothers exacerbates the problems which all employed parents have in balancing the responsibilities of work and family (Knitzer & Aber, 1995; McLanahan, Garfinkel & Ooms, 1987; Sidel, 1986). In addition, many poor women must deal with low educational levels, depression and role strain (Belle, 1982). Single Mothers' inflexible work schedules and inability to lose income, combined with daytime scheduling at schools and medical and social service offices make it difficult for them to participate in appointments, meetings and conferences. These parents lack of involvement may be interpreted by professionals as lack of interest (McLanahan et al., 1987).

The child care needs of Single Parents with a child with a disability have not been studied systematically, but it is likely they have even greater needs and concerns than other Single Parents in the workforce, because of the special care needs of their child. Although there are a few exemplary organizations, many employers are not aware of, or responsive to work/family strain and conflict. Galinsky and Stein (1990) These authors identified sources of childcare-related stress for employees: childcare is difficult to find and expensive, latchkey arrangements are less satisfactory and parents are forced to put together a patchwork system of care which tends to fall apart. Anecdotal evidence from Single Parents suggests the lack of appropriate after-school care for children with disabilities leaves many of them at home unsupervised, while mothers complete their working day and maintain contact by telephone. This type of arrangement not only puts the child and siblings at risk, but increases the Single Mother's anxiety and reduces her productivity.

The assumption women balancing work and family responsibilities are always more stressed than women without these competing demands is not always

195

borne out by research. Galinsky (1994) suggests the benefits of multiple roles may outweigh the problems and women with multiple roles are less depressed, happier and have higher self-esteem. Single Parents of children with serious emotional disorders working outside the home reported stress related to home and family, but also reported pleasure related to work and even perceived work as a coping mechanism (Brennan & Poertner, 1997). Thorough assessment enhances the social worker's understanding of the Single Parent's perspective on employment on her life with a child with a disability, since it appears personal and monetary rewards may counterbalance the stressful aspects.

Caregivers who remain at home to provide care to a child with a disability or chronic illness do so at the cost of a higher standard of living. For many Single Parents, staying at home to care for a child with a disability results in welfare dependence, together with interference in their lives designed to push them into the workforce (Sancier & Mapp, 1992; Singer & Irvin, 1989). Recent legislative changes in income support programs for Single Parents have a punitive tone, and it is not possible at this time to speculate about their impact on the well-being of Single Parents with children with a disability. Advocacy efforts may help to bring about compassionate responses.

Single-Parent families with children with disabilities are a diverse group; they vary in their race and ethnicity, socioeconomic status, developmental status within individual and family life cycles, cause of Single Parenthood, type of disability and gender of Single Parent (Boyce et al., 1995; Jones, 1987). Social work interventions designed to take account of each family's unique needs and builds upon their strengths in the context of their own community and helping network are most likely to be experienced as helpful.

Practice with Single Parents of Children with Disabilities

Identifying Needs

Parents of children with disabilities and chronic illnesses have indicated their greatest needs are help with the pragmatic aspects of daily living (Jones, 1987). Professionals who assist in locating financial resources, babysitters, respite care and information about handling issues related to the child's condition are most helpful. Children with disabilities and their families want to be included in ordinary activites like Little League, Girl Scouts and church outings; social workers can help families find opportunites to be included in such activities (Hobbs et al., 1985). Collaborative relationships, rather than inappropriate offers of therapy, are most likely to empower parents to care for their children (Jones).

Participants in focus groups for parents of children with disabilities expressed needs for information about, access to and competent provision of services (Petr & Barney, 1993). Parents said they need an array of services including respite care and supportive, preventive services to help them avert crises (Petr & Barney). Financial needs related to the expenses of caring for a child with a disability were mentioned by some parents. The most important source of emotional support mentioned by parents was from other parents of children with similar disabilities (Petr & Barney, 1993).

Studies of help-giving suggest the ways in which the help-giving interaction are structured as well as the interpersonal skills of the professional helper are important to families (Dunst et al., 1988). In a study by Huang and Heifetz (1984, cited by Singer & Irvin, 1989) mothers of young children with mental retardation identified four general factors which characterize helpful professionals. The first factor, personal relatedness, was exemplified by professionals described as warm, supportive, enthusiastic, likable and open-minded. Competence, the second factor, was characterized by professionals who were generally well-informed and specifically well-informed about their child's condition. Third, helpful professionals were characterized by their work in creating collaborative working relationships in which parents perceived they were treated as equals, their suggestions were taken seriously and they were involved in decision making. Finally, helpful professionals were described as efficient, talking to the point and focusing on practical goals and management issues (Huang and Heifetz, 1984 cited by Singer & Irvin, 1989).

Parents in different disability groups in Petr and Barney's (1993) study offered different perspectives on the qualities most important to the parent/professional relationship. Parents of children with emotional disorders emphasized personal qualities such as listening, showing respect for parents and being flexible in scheduling appointments. In the same vein, Friesen, Koren and Koroloff (1992) reported that parents of children with serious emotional disorders considered professionals' honesty, non-blaming attitude, supportiveness and inclusion in decision-making as most important. Parents of children with developmental disabilities wished for more professional commitment from workers and felt workers were often overwhelmed by large caseloads and could only see them in a crisis (Petr & Barney, 1993). Parents of medically fragile children wanted more information about and access to programs. Petr and Barney conclude parents want professionals to: appreciate the positive things in their lives and relate to them as peers and collaborators; adopt family-centered values and address their financial needs and seek regular input from families in the design, implementation and evaluation of interventions.

The ways in which agencies structure the relationships between service providers and clients also affects the quality of help received. Help is most beneficial when it is offered proactively, when the recipient perceives it is needed, when there is no stigma attached and when it emphasizes family strengths (Singer & Irvin, 1989; Saleebey, 1992). Parents of children with emotional disabilities complain about states' requirement that they relinquish custody in order to receive services funded by the state, although this has been changed in some states in response to parent advocacy (McManus & Friessen, 1989). Agency administration and management can influence the degree to which services are perceived as supportive and family-centered (Singer & Irvin). Social work practitioners may influence ways their agencies provide services by educating program planners and administrators about the needs of parents. They may also advocate for parents of children with disabilities to be involved in the design and planning of services through membership on boards and advisory committees.

The Context of Practice

In the last fifteen years, significant changes in the organization and delivery of educational, health, mental health and social services to the families of children with all kinds of disabilities have resulted in new roles for social workers and other professionals working in these systems. Increased attention is being focused on family-centered services, rather than child-centered services; such services are individualized to meet the unique and diverse needs of families. They are focused on family strengths and insist on family involvement in the planning and delivery of services. These changes have been demanded by family advocacy organizations such as the Federation for Children with Special Needs and the Federation of Families for Children's Mental Health which have become increasingly vocal at state and national levels. The changes are required by federal law, although it should be noted implementation varies across the country. A summary of some of the key legislation and its effects for families is presented here.

In 1975, the Education for All Handicapped Children Act (Public Law 94-142) introduced mandated individualized education plans (IEPs) for all children with disabilities. The Education of the Handicapped Act Amendments (Public Law 99-457 of 1986) called for mandatory individualized family plans. Part H of this law was reauthorized as PL 102-119, the Individuals with Disabilities Education Act (IDEA) Amendments in 1991. Passage of these laws is considered revolutionary because of the emphasis on building collaborative relationships among families, professionals, disciplines, agencies and institutions (Winton, 1996). The dual expectations that families will be an integral part of planning for children with disabilities and that comprehensive services require interprofessional collaboration means social workers will be more involved with families whose children have disabilities (Cole, Pearl & Welsch, 1989). Unfortunately, these laws do not generally extend to meeting the needs of children with a chronic illness (Hobbs et al., 1985).

These legislative changes in educational planning were paralleled by major changes in mental health and related services for children with serious emotional and behavioral disorders. The introduction of the Child and Adolescent Service System Program (CASSP) in 1984 was guided by a set of principles focused on providing individualized, comprehensive, culturally competent services to meet the broad range of children's and families' needs; which are coordinated and family-centered, and with families involved in decision making (Stroul & Friedman, 1988). Practice associated with the idea of individualized care to meet the unique needs of each child and family is most clearly represented in the concept of "wraparound" services developed by VanDenBerg (1992). Wraparound services are community-based, coordinated, highly individualized, unconditional services centered on the strengths of the child and family and developed by an interdisciplinary team (Lourie, Katz-Leavy, & Stroul, 1996).

Federally funded maternal and child health programs have a long tradition of providing primary and preventive health services to mothers and children, particularly those with low incomes or limited access to health services. Like other service systems, maternal and child health programs have in recent years developed a family-centered, community-based, coordinated context for providing care for children with special health care needs and their families, although considerable local variation exists (Simeonsson, 1994). These developments have been accompanied by growing awareness that the quality and utilization of services is enhanced when families play a significant role in their design, delivery and evaluation (Shelton, Jeppson, & Johnson, 1989).

The shifts to family-centered, community-based care have introduced new demands for greater integration and coordination of services for families whose children have disabilities. Traditionally, specialized agencies have provided narrowly defined services according to the child's diagnosis and funding constraints. The evolution of family-centered approaches is associated with growing recognition of the importance of interagency and interprofessional collaboration (Duchnowski & Friedman, 1990; Jivanjee, Friesen, Schultze & Hunter, 1993). By gaining understanding and respect for the roles, methods and expertise of other professions, social workers can enhance the coordination and individualization of services for families. Further, interagency collaboration can allow professionals to overcome agency limitations and provide truly integrated services (Barth, 1986).

In educational, health, mental health and other kinds of social service settings, professionals have a responsibility to help Single Parents develop the skills required to obtain the services they need and to refuse services they do not need (Jones, 1987). IEP meetings are often intimidating to parents who do not understand the professional jargon used by staff. Parents can become empowered when professionals prepare them with questions and explain the options generally available to them in school settings (Jones, 1987).

The Strengths Perspective

The strengths perspective of social work practice (Saleebey, 1992, 1996; Weick, 1992) offers a model for practice with Single Parents of children with disabilities which builds upon what we know about the resilience of human beings to rise above difficult circumstances. Despite overwhelming stresses and serious challenges of all kinds, many people survive, thrive and go on to help others (Saleebey, 1992, 1996). The strengths perspective offers a framework for viewing people holistically; as made up of interacting physical, social, mental and spiritual dimensions; with emphasis on the inherent capacity of humans for healing and regeneration (Weick, 1992). Focusing on the strengths, capacities and resilience of families; social workers share power with them in collaborative, egalitarian relationships based on mutual respect and trust (Saleebey, 1992).

Although the strengths perspective is in an early stage of development as a model of practice, a set of assumptions has been proposed to guide practice.

1. Families' abilities, resources, and aspirations are recognized and respected – with parents perceived as experts in their own situation.
2. Family strengths and competencies are utilized in the process of growth and change.
3. Motivation to change is fostered by attention to family strengths.
4. The social worker's role is that of a collaborator or consultant, rather than an "expert".
5. By "avoiding the victim mindset" social workers gain understanding of the challenging environments within which families live and the ways they have survived and coped.
6. Untapped resources and supports in the environment are identified and used.

The strengths perspective, as conceptualized by Saleebey (1992) rests upon a number of key concepts: empowerment, in which parents are helped to discover the power within themselves, their families and their communities; membership, the entitlement of all parents to dignity, respect and responsibility; regeneration, the capacity of individuals and groups for healing and transformation from within; synergy, the possibility for people interacting together to create new energy and ideas; dialog within a relationship of mutual trust and inclusion in which collaboration and negotiation become possible and suspension of disbelief which requires social workers to set aside their efforts to be objective, to encourage the emergence of the parent's truth and meaning (Saleebey, 1992).

As a framework for viewing the situations of Single-Parent families of children with disabilities and a model for practice, the strengths perspective lends itself to new ways of addressing family concerns. The strengths perspective has been used as a lens to examine the strengths and coping capacities of the families of children with physical and emotional disabilities and to develop and implement family support services (Poertner & Ronnau, 1992; Singer & Powers, 1993). However, there continues to be dissonance between social work practice from a strengths perspective and the dominant modes of thinking in many agencies and organizations, which are driven by a focus on diagnosing and treating individual and family failures and dysfunction.

Family-Centered Care

A core value of the system of care in children's mental health is services must be driven by the needs of the child and family (Stroul & Friedman, 1996). The commitment is to adapting services to the child and family, rather than expecting children and families to conform to pre-existing service configurations (Stroul & Friedman, 1996). Further, family-centered services respect the wishes and goals of children and families and maximize opportunities for involvement and self-determination in the planning and delivery of services (Stroul & Friedman, 1996).

Key elements of family-centered care have been identified by the National Center for Family-Centered Care (1990) and they include valuable guidelines for practitioners working with Single-Parent families. Family-centered interventions: (a) recognize that the family is the constant in the child's life, while the services systems and personnel within those systems fluctuate; (b) facilitate parent/professional collaboration at all levels of care; (c) honor the racial, ethnic, cultural and socioeconomic diversity of families; (d) recognize family strengths and individuality and respect different methods of coping; (e) share with parents, on a continuing basis and in a supportive manner, complete and unbiased information; (f) encourage and facilitate family-to-family support and networking; (g) understand and incorporate the developmental needs of infants, children, and adolescents and their families into health care programs. Additional elements focused on the organizational contexts of family-centered practice address comprehensive policies and programs to provide emotional and financial support for families and accessible service systems which are flexible, culturally competent and responsive to family-identified needs (National Center for Family-Centered Care, 1990).

Even though family-centered care is established as both law and practice, comprehensive implementation is still developing (Simeonsson, 1994). Issues such as flexible scheduling of meetings, representativeness of families involved and lack of payment for family involvement continue to create barriers. Further, Simeonsson (1994) notes the inaccessibility of services is a problem for many families with a child with a disability. Families without transportation, child care, information and other resources are at a disadvantage if services are located outside their community. Service coordination for families who require assistance in gaining access to services they need, public awareness activities, and support services such as respite and transportation , may facilitate Single Parents' use of community-based services. Koroloff, Elliott, Koren & Friesen (1994) describe a successful innovative program in rural areas in which parents without professional mental health training act in the role of "family associates", providing emotional and practical support to help low-income families to access mental health services for their children.

Family-centered services for children with serious emotional disorders and their families have been slower to develop than in other areas of childhood disability because of the stigma and blaming associated with early beliefs that children's emotional disorders were the result of inadequate, inappropriate or poor parenting (Caplan & Hall-McCorquodale, 1985; Collins & Collins, 1990; Friesen & Koroloff, 1990; Wahl, 1989). With the advent of interactive conceptions of childhood development (Thomas & Chess, 1984) and evidence from studies which disconfirmed beliefs about parents' contributions to childhood pathology (for example, Erickson, 1968; Waxler & Mischler, 1972), new approaches to strengthening families' formal and informal supports in the community have emerged (Weiss & Jacobs, 1988). Despite these developments, parents of children with serious emotional disorders still complain about the lack of support and prevalence of blaming attitudes (Friesen & Huff, 1996).

Culturally Competent Practice

There is increasing awareness of the cultural diversity of our communities, which has resulted in efforts across the country to design and deliver culturally competent services to families with children with a disability. Cultural competence is defined as a set of congruent behaviors, attitudes, practices and policies enabling agency systems and professionals to work effectively in cross-cultural situations (Isaacs-Shockley, Cross, Bazron, Dennis, & Benjamin, 1996,). Culturally appropriate treatment strategies are based on the cultural values of families served and reflect families cultural attitudes, expectations, norms and preferences (Isaacs-Shockley et al., 1996).

Cross, Bazron, Dennis and Isaacs (1989) proposed a philosophical framework and five elements of culturally competent practice which are gradually being incorporated into systems of care for children with serious emotional disabilities.

Culturally competent practice and culturally competent systems of care possess the following attributes: they value the richness of diverse cultures; they incorporate cultural self-awareness and understanding of the ways that cultural values and beliefs influence the behaviors of client families; they understand the dynamics of difference when cultures interact; they have developed specific mechanisms to gain cultural knowledge for effective interactions with parents; and they have developed adaptations to diversity in practice, for example focusing on strengths, accepting families' own definition of their family and changing the types of services that are offered (Cross et al., 1989; Isaacs-Shockley et al.). Specifically, cultural competence involves working in conjunction with natural, informal support and helping networks within the community, such as neighborhood organizations, churches, spiritual leaders, healers and community leaders (Isaacs-Shockley et al., 1996).

Family Support

New approaches to providing services to Single-Parent families with a child with a disability are focused on identifying the needs and strengths of the family and facilitating support to enable them to care for children. Family support is defined by the Federation of Families for Children's Mental Health (1992) as consisting of formal and informal services and goods which enable a family to care for a child with an emotional, behavioral or mental disorder; to maintain close ties with a child in out-of-home placement and to help families when their child is ready to return home. In other words, family support is "whatever it takes" for a family to care for and live with a child who has an emotional, behavioral or mental disorder (Federation of Families for Children's Mental Health, 1992).

The key element of family support is it must be family-centered, with what is needed and acceptable to the family defined by each of its members (Friesen & Koroloff, 1990). Family support builds on family strengths, acknowledges families as the primary source of information about their child and the family's needs, tailors services to fit the family's needs and preferences, focuses on the whole family; is appropriate for the family's culture and traditions; utilizes informal helping networks and formal supports and respects the family's choices about the nature, timing and location of services (Friesen, 1993). Best practices in family support include treating families with respect and involving them as partners, providing up-to-date and complete information, providing emotional and tangible support, providing assistance so parents can be employed if they choose and working to change policies and funding approaches which mitigate against families staying together (Friesen, 1993). Positive outcomes were reported for families participating in a model of family support comprised of case management, support groups, respite care, volunteers assisting children to join in community activities, behavioral counseling and coordination with the public school district (Singer & Irvin, 1989).

Family-Professional Collaboration

In response to the demands of parents to be actively involved in making decisions about the care of their children; professionals have begun to shift their practice toward more collaborative, empowering relationships with families of children with disabilities (Collins & Collins, 1990; Bryant-Comstock, Huff, & VanDenBerg, 1996). Four key elements of family-professional collaboration have been identified: supportive relationships; practical service arrangements; forthright information exchange and a flexible, shared approach to measuring failure and success (DeChillo, Koren & Schultze, 1994). Parent-professional collaboration is characterized by mutual respect for skills and knowledge; honest and clear communication; two-way sharing of information; mutually agreed upon goals and shared planning and decision making (Vosler-Hunter, 1989).

Collaborative relationships between parents and professionals are believed to lead to better outcomes for families of children with special needs (Bishop, Woll, Arango, 1993). Principles of family-professional collaboration have been developed to guide the practice of social workers and other professionals working with children with special needs and their families. Family-professional collaboration:

1. Promotes relationships in which family members and professionals work together to ensure the best services for the child and the family;
2. Recognizes and respects the knowledge, skills and experience families and professionals bring to the relationship;
3. Acknowledges the development of trust is an integral part of a collaborative relationship;
4. Facilitates open communication so families and professionals feel free to express themselves;
5. Creates an atmosphere in which cultural traditions, values and diversity of families are acknowledged and honored;
6. Recognizes negotiation is essential in a collaborative relationship;
7. Brings to the relationship the mutual commitment of families, professionals and communities to meet the needs of children with special health needs and their families (Bishop et al., 1993,).

Parents and professionals who participated in training workshops on collaboration agreed the most frequent barriers to collaboration were: professionals' lack of sufficient time to spend with families, high caseloads and families' previous

204

negative experiences with professionals (Williams-Murphy, DeChillo, Koren, & Hunter, 1994). Other barriers identified by parents were professionals' beliefs families cause emotional disorders; the inherent power imbalance between professionals and parents, lack of administrative support for collaboration and state custody relinquishment policies. The majority of professionals and parents who participated in training for collaboration rated the training as a major contributor to their ability to collaborate (Williams-Murphy et al.). Clearly, practitioners in many agencies have time constraints related to high caseloads. However, by participating in training to enhance collaborative skills and devoting time to building empowering, collaborative relationships with Single Parents; social workers may be better able to support and build upon the strengths, resources and capabilities of families.

Family Empowerment

Family-centered care is associated with empowerment approaches to practice which emphasize family strengths, resilience and competencies and promote collaborative working relationships between parents and professionals (Collins & Collins; Singer & Powers, 1993; Solomon, 1976). Empowerment is defined as "a process though which clients obtain resources — personal, organizational and community — that enable them to gain greater control over their environment and to attain their aspirations" (Hasenfeld, 1987, p. 478-9). It is described as both an individual and collective phenomenon by which people "become active participants in the creation and implementation of policies, decisions and processes which affect them" (Staples, 1990, p. 31). Elements of empowering relationships identified by African-American mothers of children with disabilities included workers' responsiveness to needs for emotional support and specific services; and their ability to establish rapport by being conversational, interpreting what the mothers said, sharing relevant experiences, recognizing the mothers' care for their children, and attention to cultural differences (Kalyanpur & Rao, 1991).

To advance an empowerment agenda, Saleebey (1992) suggests practitioners discover the power within people by trusting their accounts and perspectives and providing opportunities for families to make connections with each other and with communities. Conditions which are necessary for empowerment to occur are a personal attitude which promotes active social involvement, capacity for critical analysis of social and political systems, an ability to develop strategies and obtain resources to achieve goals and an ability to act with others to define and attain collective goals (Kieffer, 1981). These are skills which social workers must cultivate if they are to be effective partners in family empowerment processes. However, Staples (1990) makes the case that resources and opportunities are necessary for empowerment to occur. Clearly social workers have an advocacy role in promoting the development of resources and opportunities for family empowerment.

An aspect of family empowerment which has recently become a focus of family advocacy efforts is family involvement in services at the individual, program/agency, community and society levels. Moxley, Raider, and Cohen, 1989 identified five family member roles: treatment agent, planner, advocate, evaluator and consultant/educator. Family can be involved in designing and evaluating services, setting policy and providing services (Bryant-Comstock, Huff & VanDenBerg, 1996). In other areas, parents do not have opportunities for involvement and some parents channel their ideas through family advocacy-organizations such as the Federation of Families for Children's Mental Health and the Federation for Children with Special Needs.

Barriers to involvement include: (a) resource barriers such as time, opportunities and supports for involvement; (b) training and skill barriers; and (c) communication barriers between families and professionals. Family involvement is a laudable goal, but requires resources which Single Parents may not have. In educational settings, professionals need to be cognizant of the other demands on a Single Parent's time when making requests for parental treatment efforts or school involvement (Jones, 1987). Social workers working with low-income, Single-Parent families who wish to promote family involvement in services must examine whether Single Parents have the time to become involved, whether they will lose pay for time taken away from work and the availability of transportation and child care so Single Parents can attend meetings (Moxley et al., 1989). If resources are not available, social workers may need to advocate for them so child care and transportation can be made available and parents can be compensated for their time.

Supportive Services

Dunst and colleagues (1988) suggest family-level assessment include identification of: (a) family needs and aspirations, (b) intrafamily strengths and capabilities, and (c) resources for meeting needs and aspirations. Professionals who function in a number of roles – empathetic listener, teacher/therapist, consultant, resource, enabler, mobilizer, mediator and advocate – are more likely to enable the family to become competent in mobilizing resources to meet its needs and achieve desired goals (Dunst et al., 1987).

Promising approaches for enhancing the well-being of families with a child with a disability include teaching children socially adaptive behaviors to replace aversive behaviors, such as fussiness and crying; teaching problem solving and coping strategies to parents; promoting positive interactions between parent and child; making respite care available and helping low-income, Single-Parent families to access resources and informal support (Dunst, Cooper & Bolick, 1987). These authors recommend supporting and strengthening families with a child with a disability through the use of informal sources of support in the family and community, reducing excessive time demands through the use of respite and child care and ensuring that families are able to meet their basic needs.

Respite services may provide relief for parents from the continuous provision of care to a child with disabilities; these services may also be a positive, supportive force in the prevention of placement outside the home (Salisbury & Intagliata, 1986; Singer & Irvin, 1989; Starker & Sarli, 1989). Respite care is highly valued by many families with a child with serious disabilities; however, the availability of respite varies widely and the types of respite available are not always geared to meeting family needs (Starker & Sarli, 1989). Not all families who have access to respite care choose to make use of it and Singer and Irvin (1989) suggest respite care is most likely to help families when it is one part of a comprehensive package of supports.

Mutual assistance groups can help people to find meaning in challenging circumstances (Singer & Irvin, 1989). Parents of children with a disability or chronic illness benefit from contacts with similar others, opportunities to express feelings and expressions of concern. Parents are empowered through group participation when they can reciprocate as well as receive aid (Singer & Irvin, 1985). A benefit of support groups may be sharing strategies to bypass bureaucratic obstacles to appropriate care (Hobbs et al., 1985).

Professionally led psychoeducational groups providing information about specific disabilities and their treatment while teaching coping strategies may be particularly helpful to parents if they are also designed to encourage mutual sharing and support. Mutual aid organizations are better suited to helping parents deal with the long-term, stressful circumstances of childhood disability than short-term interventions.

Measures such as the Impact-on-Family Scale (Stein and Riessman, 1980) and the Family Empowerment Scale (Koren, DeChillo, & Friesen, 1992) can be useful assessment tools for social workers. Four dimensions of family functioning are measured by the Impact-on-Family Scale (Stein and Riessman): financial burden, familial/social impact, personal strain and psychological burden. The Family Empowerment Scale (Koren et al., 1992) measures empowerment in terms of attitudes, knowledge and behaviors at three levels: family, service system and community. These instruments are also useful in evaluating the outcomes of social work interventions with families.

Conclusion

This chapter has presented an overview of the stresses and challenges experienced by Single Parents of children with disabilities, theoretical frameworks for increasing understanding of their experiences, recent changes in ways the services are delivered to families and a discussion of approaches to social work practice designed to support, strengthen and empower families. Single Parents of children with disabilities are a diverse group; they are faced with complex demands related to supporting and caring for their children. Although research evidence is limited, it is clear that many Single Parents demonstrate incredible resilience and coping capabilities in dealing with the extraordinary challenges of parenting a child with a disability. Emerging models of social work practice focus on family-centered services, family support tailored to meet the unique needs and preferences of families. Social work interventions which build on the informal helping networks in the community and incorporate collaboration and empowerment are recommended as being most helpful to families.

Clearly, the research base reveals there is an inadequate base of research knowledge on the needs and strengths of Single-Parent families with children with disabilities, particularly culturally diverse families, is inadequate.Interevention studies will increase our understanding of the kinds of social work interventions most helpful to Single-Parent families. Serious attention must be paid to the design and implementation of policies and programs to support Single Parents of children with disabilities — in particular to address Single Parents' financial difficulties and work-related concerns. Professional training to prepare social workers to collaborate with parents and other professionals involved in family-centered services has received some attention and there are efforts beginning to involve parents of children with disabilities in professional training (Jivanjee, Moore, Friesen & Schultze, 1995).

The chapter began with the account of Terri, a parent of a child with a learning disability, of her experiences raising her child and dealing with unresponsive systems and professionals. It is hoped that some of the suggestions, ideas and recommendations presented here will help social workers to understand and respond to the needs of Single Parents in ways which are strengths-oriented, collaborative, and empowering.

Bibliography

Antonovsky, A. (1993). The implications of salutogenesis: An outsider's view. In A.P. Turnbull, J.M. Patterson, S.K. Behr, D.L. Murphy, J.G. Marquis, & M.J. Blue-Banning (Eds.) (1993). *Cognitive coping, families and disability* (pp. 111-22). Baltimore, MD: Paul H.Brookes.

Atkins, S.P. (1989). Siblings of handicapped children. *Child and Adolescent Social Work, 6*(4), 271-82.

Barth, R.P. (1986). *Social and cognitive treatment of children*. San Francisco: Jossey-Bass.

Beckman, P.J. (1983). Influence of selected child characteristics on stress in families of handicapped infants. *American Journal of Mental Deficiency, 88,* 150-6.

Belle, D. (1982) *Lives in stress: Women and depression.* Newbury Park, CA: Sage Publications.

Bishop, K.K., Woll, J., & Arango, P. with Families and Professionals. (1993). *Family/professional collaboration for children with special needs and their families.* Burlington, VT: Department of Social Work, University of Vermont.

Boyce, G.C., Miller, B.C., White, K.R., & Godfrey, M.K. (1995). Single parenting in families of children with disabilities. *Marriage and Family Review (The Haworth Press, Inc.), 20*(3/4), 389-409. Also in S.M. Hanson et al. (Eds.), (1995). *Single parent families: Diversity, myths, and realities* (pp. 389-409). New York: The Haworth Press, Inc.

Brennan, E.M. & Poertner, J. (1997). Balancing the responsibilities of work and family life: Results of the family caregiving study. *Journal of Emotional and Behavioral Disorders, 5* (3) 239-49.

Brown, J.D. (1993). Coping with stress: The beneficial role of positive illusions. In A.P. Turnbull, J.M. Patterson, S.K. Behr, D.L. Murphy, J.G. Marquis, & M.J. Blue-Banning (Eds.), (1993). *Cognitive coping, families, and disability* (pp. 123-33). Baltimore, MD: Paul H.Brookes.

Bryant-Comstock, S., Huff, B., & VanDenBerg, J. (1996). The evolution of the family advocacy movement. In B.A. Stroul (Ed.), *Children's mental health: Creating systems of care in a changing society* (pp. 359-74). Baltimore, MD: Paul H. Brookes.

Burr, C. (1985). Impact on the family of a chronically ill child. In N. Hobbs & J.M. Perrin (Eds.) *Issues in the care of children with chronic illness* (pp. 24-40). San Francisco: Jossey-Bass.

Caplan, P.J. & Hall-McCorquodale, I. (1985). Mother blaming in major clinical journals. *American Journal of Orthopsychiatry, 55,* 345-53.

Cole, B.S., Pearl, L.F., & Welsch, M.J. (1989). Education of social workers for intervention with families of children with special needs. *Child and Adolescent Social Work, 6*(4), 327-38.

Collins, B. & Collins, T. (1990). Parent-professional relationships in the treatment of seriously emotionally disturbed children and adolescents. *Social Work, 35*(6), 522-27.

Cross, T.L., Bazron, B.J., Dennis, K.W., & Isaacs, M.R. (1989). *Towards a culturally competent system of care: A monograph on effective services for minority children who are severely emotionally disturbed.* Washington, DC: CASSP Technical Assistance Center, Georgetown University Child Development Center.

DeChillo, N., Koren, P.E., & Schultze, K.H. (1994). From paternalism to partnership: Family and professional collaboration in children's mental health. *American Journal of Orthopsychiatry, 64* (4), 564-76.

Deiner, P.L. (1987). Systems of care for disabled children and family members: New paradigms and alternatives. In M. Ferrari & M.B. Sussman (Eds.), *Childhood disability and family systems* (pp. 193-211). NY: Haworth.

Duchnowski, A.J. & Friedman, R.M. (1990) Children's mental health: Challenges for the nineties. *Journal of Mental Health Administration, 17* (1), 3-12.

Dunst, C.J., Cooper, C.S., & Bolick, F.A. (1987). Supporting families of handicapped children. In J. Garbarino, P.E. Brookhouser, K.J. Authier, & Associates (1987). *Special children – Special Risks: The maltreatment of children with disabilities* (pp. 17-46). NY: Aldine de Gruyter.

Dunst, C.J., Trivette, C.M. & Deal, A.G. (1988). *Enabling and empowering families: Principles and guidelines for practice.* Cambridge, MA: Brookline Books.

Ellis, J.B. (1989). Grieving for the loss of the perfect child: Parents of children with handicaps. *Child and Adolescent Social Work, 6* (4), 259-70.

Erickson, M.T. (1968). Comparisons between parents of young emotionally disturbed and organically retarded children. *Journal of Consulting and Clinical Psychology, 32,* 701-6.

Federation of Families for Children's Mental Health (1992). *Principles on family support.* Alexandria, VA: Federation of Families for Children's Mental Health.

Friesen, B.J. (1993). *Family support in child and adult mental health.* Paper presented at Conference on Family Support, Hanover, New Hampshire, June 18-20, 1993.

Friesen, B.J. & Huff, B. (1996). Family perspectives on systems of care. In B.A. Stroul (Ed.), *Children's mental health: Creating systems of care in a changing society* (pp. 41-67). Baltimore, MD: Paul H. Brookes.

Friesen, B.J., Koren, P.E,. & Koroloff, N.M. (1992). How parents view professional behaviors: A cross-professional analysis. *Journal of Child and Family Studies, 1* (2), 209-31.

Friesen, B.J. & Koroloff, N.M. (1990). Family-centered services: Implications for mental health administration and research. *The Journal of Mental Health Administration, 17* (1), 13-25.

Friesen, B.J. & Wahlers, D. (1993). Respect and real help: Family support and children's mental health. *Journal of Emotional and Behavioral Problems, Winter,* 12-15.

Friedman, R.M., Kutash, K., & Duchnowski, A.J. (1996). The population of concern: Defining the issues. In B.A. Stroul (Ed.), *Children's mental health: Creating systems of care in a changing society* (pp. 69-96). Baltimore, MD: Paul H. Brooke.

Galinsky, E. (1994). Families and work: The importance of the quality of the work environment. In S.L. Kagan & B. Weissbourd (Eds.), *Putting families first: America's family support movement and the challenge of change* (pp. 112- 36). San Francisco, CA: Jossey-Bass.

Garbarino, J. (1987). The abuse and neglect of special children: An introduction to the issues. In J. Garbarino, P.E. Brookhouser, K.J. Authier, & Associates (1987). *Special children – Special Risks: The maltreatment of children with disabilities* (pp. 3-14). NY: Aldine de Gruyter.

Garland, C.W. (1993). Beyond chronic sorrow: A new understanding of family adaptation. In A.P. Turnbull, J.M. Patterson, S.K. Behr, D.L. Murphy, J.G. Marquis, & M.J. Blue-Banning (Eds.), (1993). *Cognitive coping, families, and disability* (pp. 67-80). Baltimore, MD: Paul H.Brookes.

Hasenfeld, Y. (1987). Power in social work practice. *Social Service Review, 61,* 467-83.

Hobbs, N., Perrin, J.M., & Ireys, H.T. (1985). *Chronically ill children and their families.* San Francisco, CA: Jossey-Bass.

Imber-Black, E. (1989). Women's relationships with larger systems. In M. McGoldrick, C.M. Anderson & F. Walsh (Eds.), *Women in families* (pp. 335-53). New York: Norton & Co.

Isaacs-Shockley, M., Cross, T., Bazron, B.J., Dennis, K., & Benjamin, M.P. (1996). Framework for a culturally competent system of care. In B.A. Stroul (Ed.), *Children's mental health: Creating systems of care in a changing society* (pp. 23-39). Baltimore, MD: Paul H. Brookes.

Jivanjee, P., Friesen, B.J., Schultze, K.H., & Hunter, R.W. (1993), *Principles of collaborative practice in children's mental health: Spanning family, professional, and agency boundaries.* Unpublished manuscript, Portland, OR: Portland State University, research and Training Center on Family Support and Children's Mental Health.

Jivanjee, P., Moore, K.R., Friesen, B.J., & Schultze, K.H. (1995), *Interprofessional education for family-centered services: A survey of interprofessional/interdisciplinary training programs.* Portland, OR: Portland State University, research and Training Center on Family Support and Children's Mental Health.

Jones, C.W. (1987). Coping with the young handicapped child in the single-parent family: An ecosystemic perspective. In M. Lindblad-Goldberg (Ed.), *Clinical issues in single-parent households* (pp. 85-100). Rockville, MD: Aspen Publications.

Kalyanpur, M. & Rao, S.S. (1991). Empowering low-income black families of handicapped children. *American Journal of Orthopsychiatry, 61* (4), 523-32.

Kieffer, C.H. (1981). *The emergence of empowerment: The development of participatory competence among individuals in citizen organizations.* Department of Psychology, University of Michigan.

Knitzer, J. (1982). *Unclaimed children.* Washington, DC: Children's Defense Fund.

Knitzer, J. & Aber, J.L. (1995). Young children in poverty: Facing the facts. *American Journal of Othopsychiatry, 65* (2), 174-6.

Koren, P.E., DeChillo, N., & Friesen, B.J. (1992). Measuring empowerment in families whose children have emotional disabilities: A brief questionnaire. *Rehabilitation Psychology, 37* (4), 305-21.

Koroloff, N.M., Elliott, D.J., Koren, P.E., & Friesen, B.J. (1994). Connecting low-income families to mental health services: The role of the family associate. *Journal of Emotional and Behavioral Disorders, 2* (4), 240-6.

Lourie, I.S., Katz-Leavy, J., & Stroul, B.A. (1996). Individualized services in a system of care. In B.A. Stroul (Ed.), *Children's mental health: Creating systems of care in a changing society* (pp. 429-52). Baltimore, MD: Paul H. Brookes.

McCubbin, H.I. & Patterson, J.M. (1983). Family transitions: Adaptation to stress. In H.I. McCubbin & C.R. Figley (Eds.), *Stress and the family* (pp. 5-25). NY: Brunner/Mazel.

McGoldrick, M., Pearce, J.M., & Giordano, J. (Eds.). *Ethnicity and family therapy.* New York: Guilford Press.

McLanahan, S.S., Garfinkel, I., & Ooms, T. (1987) Female-headed families and economic policy: Expanding the clinician's focus. In M. Lindblad-Goldberg (Ed.), *Clinical issues in single-parent households* (pp. 1-17). Rockville, MD: Aspen Publications.

McManus, M.C. & Friesen, B.J. (1989). Barriers to accessing services: Relinquishing legal custody as a means of obtaining services for children who have serious emotional disabilities. *Focal Point, 3* (3).

Mori, A. (1983). *Families of children with special needs: Early intervention techniques for the practitioner.* Rockville, MD: Aspen Publications.

Moroney, R. (1980). *Families, social services and social policy: The issue of shared responsibility.* Rockville, MD: National Institute of Mental Health.

Moxley, D.P., Raider, M.C., & Cohen, S.N. (1989). Specifying and facilitating family involvement in services to persons with developmental disabilities. *Child and Adolescent Social Work, 6*(4), 301-12.

National Center for Family-Centered Care (1990). *What is family-centered care?* Bethesda, MD: Association for the Care of Children's Health.

National Institute on Disability and Rehabilitation Research (NIDRR) (1992). *Digest on persons with disabilities.* Washington, DC: U.S. Department of Education.

Nesto, B. (1994). Low-income single mothers: Myths and realities. *Affilia, 9* (3), 232-46.

Patterson, J.M. (1988). Chronic illness in children and the impact on families. In C. Chilman, E. Nunally, & F. Cox (Eds.), *Chronic illness and disability* (pp. 69-107). Beverly Hills: Sage Publications.

Pearlin, L.I. & Schooler, C. (1978). The structure of coping. *Journal of Health and Social Behavior, 19* (March), 2-21.

Petr, C.G. & Barney, D.D. (1993). Reasonable efforts for children with disabilities: The parents' perspective. *Social Work, 38* (3), 247-54.

Poertner, J. & Ronnau, J. (1992). A strengths approach to children with emotional disabilities. In D. Saleebey (Ed.), *The strengths perspective in social work practice* (pp. 111-21). New York: Longman Publishing Group.

Powers, L.E. (1993). Disability and grief: From tragedy to challenge. In G.H.S. Singer & L.E. Powers (Eds.), *Families, disability, and empowerment: Active coping skills and strategies for family interventions* (pp. 119-149). Baltimore, MD: Paul H. Brookes.

Rolland, J.S. (1993). Mastering family challenges in serious illness and disability. In F. Walsh (Ed.). *Normal family processes* (pp. 444-73). New York: Guilford Press.

Saleebey, D. (1992). Introduction: Power in the people. In D. Saleebey (Ed), *The strengths perspective in social work practice (*pp. 3-17). New York: Longman Publishing Group.

Saleebey, D. (1996). The strengths perspective in social work practice: Extensions and cautions. *Social Work, 41* (3), 296-305.

Salisbury, C.L. & Intagliata, J. (Eds.) (1986). *Respite care: Support for persons with developmental disabilities and their families.* Baltimore, MD: Paul H. Brookes.

Sancier, B. & Mapp, P. (1992). Who helps working women care for the young and old? *Affilia, 7* (2), 61-76.

Seligman, M. & Darling, R.B. (1989). *Ordinary families, special children: A systems approach to childhood disability.* NY: The Guilford Press.

Shelton, T., Jeppson, E., & Johnson, B.H. (1989). *Family-centered care for children with special health care needs (2nd. ed.).* Bethesda, MD: Association for the Care of Children's Mental Health.

Sidel, R. (1986). *Women and children last: The plight of poor women in affluent America.* New York: Penguin Books.

Simeonsson, R.J. (1994). *Risk, resilience, and prevention.* Baltimore, MD: Paul H. Brookes.

Singer, G.H.S. & Irvin, L.K. (1989). Supporting families of persons with severe disabilities: Emerging findings, practices, and questions. In L.H. Meyer, C.A. Peck, & L. Brown (Eds.), *Critical issues in the lives of people with severe disabilities* (pp. 271-312). Baltimore, MD: Paul H. Brookes.

Singer, G.H.S. & Powers, L.E. (1993). Contributing to resilience in families: An overview. In G.H.S. Singer & L.E. Powers (Eds.), *Families, disability, and empowerment* (pp. 1-25). Baltimore, MD: Paul H. Brookes.

Solomon, B.B. (1976). *Black empowerment: Social work in oppressed communities.* New York: Columbia University Press.

Staples, L.H. (1990). Powerful ideas about empowerment. *Administration in Social Work, 14* (2), 29-42.

Starker, J. & Sarli, P. (1989). Respite and family support services: Responding to the need. *Child and Adolescent Social Work, 6* (4), 313-326.

Stein, R.E.K. & Riessman, C.K. (1980). The development of an impact-on-family scale: Preliminary findings. *Medical Care, XVIII* (4), 465-72.

Stroul, B.A. & Friedman, R.M. (1988). Principles for a system of care. *Children Today, 17* (4), 11-15.

Stroul, B.A. & Friedman, R.M. (1996). The system of care concept and philosophy. In B.A. Stroul B.A. (Ed.), *Children's mental health: Creating systems of care in a changing society* (pp. 3-21). Baltimore, MD: Paul H. Brookes.

Szanton, E.S. (1991). Services for children with special needs: Partnerships from the beginning between parents and practitioners. In D.G. Unger & D.R. Powell (Eds.), *Families as nurturing systems: Support across the life span* (pp. 87-97), New York: Haworth Press.

Taylor, S.E. (1989). *Positive illusions: Creative self-deception and the healthy mind.* NY: Basic Books.

Thomas A. & Chess, S. (1984). Genesis and evolution of behavioral disorders: From infancy to adult life. *American Journal of Psychiatry, 141,* 1-9.

VanDenBerg, J. (1992). Individualized services for children. *New Directions for Mental Health Services, 54,* 97-100.

Vosler-Hunter, R.W. (1989). *Changing roles, changing relationships: Parent-professional collaboration on behalf of children with emotional disabilities.* Portland, OR: Portland State University, Research and Training Center on Family Support and Children's Mental Health.

Wahl, O.F. (1989). Schizophrenogenic parenting in abnormal psychology textbooks. *Teaching of Psychology, 16,* 3-33.

Waxler, N.E. & Mischler, E.G. (1972). Parental interaction with schizophrenic children and well siblings: An experimental test of some etiological theories. *Annual Progress in Child Psychiatry and Child Development,* 568-86.

Weick, A. (1992). Building a strengths perspective for social work. In D. Saleebey (Ed.), *The strengths perspective in social work practice* (pp.18-26). New York: Longman Publishing Group.

Weiss, H.B. & Jacobs, F.H. (1988). *Evaluating family programs.* New York: Aldine de Gruyter.

Wikler, L. (1981). Chronic stresses of families with mentally retarded children. *Family Relations, 30,* 281-8.

Wikler, L..; Haack, J. & Intagliata, J. (1984). Bearing the burden alone? Helping divorced mothers of children with developmental disabilities. In E.I. Coopersmith (Ed.), *Families with handicapped members* (pp. 44-62). Rockville, MD: Aspen.

Williams-Murphy, T.; DeChillo, N.; Koren, P.E. & Hunter, R.W. (1994). *Family/professional collaboration: The perspective of those who have tried.* Portland, OR: Portland State University, Research and Training Center on Family Support and Children's Mental Health.

Winton, P.J. (1996). Foreword. In P. Rosin, A.D. Whitehead, L.I. Tuchman, G.S. Jesien, A.L. Begun, & L. Irwin (Eds.), *Partnerships in family-centered care* (pp. xi-xii). Baltimore, MD: Paul H. Brookes.

Zucman, E. (1982). *Childhood disability in the family.* New York: International Exchange of Information in Rehabilitation, World Rehabilitation Fund, Inc.

When Fathers Raise Children Alone

Geoffrey L. Greif, DSW

THE END OF THIS CENTURY marks a sharp increase in the number of fathers who have gained custody of their children following separation and divorce. As an emerging family structure, the Single-Father family offers many intriguing issues for the social work practitioner to consider. This chapter considers potential reasons for the increase, describes the nature of these families, presents case studies and suggests practice implications.

Background

Between 1970 and 1994, the percent of children in the United States living with a Single-Father tripled while the percent living with both parents declined (U.S. Bureau of the Census, 1996). The number of Single-Fathers raising children under eighteen years of age increased from 341,000 to 1,314,000 (U.S. Bureau of the Census, 1995.) During this same period the number of widowers decreased. As is well known, the number of divorces also increased precipitously, thereby increasing the pool of families which could be headed by fathers. We are now living in a culture which has become accustomed to the notion of divorce. Some would argue we have become too comfortable with divorce and we should make it harder to end a marriage. Others bemoan the increase but believe restricting the ease with which one can get a divorce is not the answer. The culture's view of divorce is important to consider because it sets the context for how we view these fathers' and children's experiences.

Fathers raising children alone has an historical precedent; although not in recent history. Prior to the twentieth century, women and children had few rights and, in the rare case of divorce (most marriages ended by the death of one of the parents), the father would usually gain custody of the children. With the Industrial Revolution, men were pulled away from the home and women assumed a caretaker role. By the 1920s, and with the ascendancy of the "best interests of the child" notion and the "tender years" doctrine (which refers to the presumption children need to be with the mother) the mother's role in the family became increasingly important (Hanson, 1988). The mother's role was further buttressed by a burgeoning psychology movement which highlighted the early mother/child bond. During the next fifty years, the mother held the upper hand in seeking custody after divorce.

With the women's movement of the 1960s and 1970s the push for equal rights for women engendered, partly by way of a backlash, a push for "men's rights" as well. States' custody and child-support laws were altered to "sex-neutral" criteria. By the early-1980s, mothers were no longer favored with post-divorce custody to the extent they had been in the previous decades. Women were entering the job market in greater numbers – though at lower salaries than men. The potential developed for women to define themselves beyond motherhood (Greif, 1995); and, as mothers were spending more time away from home, the potential developed for a shift in the role fathers were playing in the home. As some fathers became more involved in family life, the door opened for them to gain greater access to their children if the marriage failed.

By the mid-1980s, a "fathers' movement" was also developing. Fathers were being chastised in many quarters for their historic lack of involvement in child-care and the family. Some men sought redefinition as househusbands. Others were glorified as representing the "new man" – someone who was sensitive and caring. The media began to feature fathers in active parenting roles which went beyond the "Honey, I'm home" days of the 1950s television show to sitcoms showing fathers who were raising children with no women present. The rise in joint custody has also led to greater father involvement in the family. With joint custody, fathers share parenting and remain more involved with their children after marital dissolution than they would have in the traditional mother-custody arrangement. As a joint-custody relationship evolves, the father may achieve even greater involvement with his children. All these factors (an increased number of divorces, traditional gendered inequalities in income, the women's movement and the resulting backlash, changing custody laws, a friendlier work-place for women, more father/child time and a desire by the fathers for greater involvement) have contributed to the growth of Single-Father-headed families.

The Nature of the Single-Father Family

Until recently, the specter of a father raising children alone following marital dissolution was unusual. The socialization of males in the United States has mitigated against males performing the daily childcare chores needed to maintain a family. Boys are not encouraged to play with dolls; neither are they reared to be caretakers of infants nor to visualize themselves as homemakers. In marriage, childcare responsibilities usually fall to the mother. Even if both parents work full time outside of the home, such tasks tend to remain the mother's responsibility. When fathers assume full custody, they are often unprepared psychologically for the role and are unclear how to perform the requisite tasks.

Most fathers have no role model to show them how to be a nurturer. For many fathers playing catch after work is easier to envision than changing diapers, planning a menu, shopping for clothes or operating a vacuum cleaner and washing machine simultaneously. Most fathers are not prepared to talk to children about feelings or to process emotions at different developmental stages. Even those who gain custody after divorce are likely to have been minimally involved in these tasks before the divorce. Thus, at the very beginning of their solo parenting, many Single Fathers are often a step behind. They face a family landscape rife with landmines.

In the best scenario, a father gains custody after discussing and planning the arrangements with the mother and children. Optimally, the mother stays involved with child-rearing responsibilities. The father, however, may have gained custody having had little warning or after a protracted legal battle. Some fathers gain custody precipitously, with the unexpected departure or death of the mother. In such cases, the father must care for children who may be extremely upset emotionally. Court battles often pit parents against each other and place the child in the middle. A child may overtly or covertly be asked to choose between parents. For example, in an attempt to ascertain which parent is more nurturing, judges sometimes take children into chambers and ask them which parent they go to when they are hurt. A perceptive child is likely to interpret this question as an attempt to determine where the child wants to live.

Child rearing is made more difficult when the child is in emotional pain. Children may blame themselves for the failure of their parents' relationship. If the parent has a typical and normally inconsequential conflict with a child in the evening then leaves the next morning, the child may associate the parent's departure with his or her behavior the night before. In cases in which the mother leaves and ceases contact with the child, the child is even more likely to feel unloved and believe if he or she was more loveable, the mother would visit. The child absorbs the conflictual feelings and lack of love in the household. If the parents are angry, depressed or anxious; the child may assume those moods, also.

The father's own emotional state may interfere with the tasks of raising children. An embattled or deserted father is likely to feel emotionally unprepared to handle the needs of his children as he struggles with his own conflicts and turmoil. In effect, when the child needs him the most, he may be the most unavailable. Finally, a mother who remains in contact with the child and the father may be an unstable influence. She may withhold child-support, contest custody or present herself as depressed and anxious when visiting the child. In such a case, the newly forming family system must struggle with multiple issues.

A Brief Look at the Literature

Research on Single Fathers is relatively recent, beginning in the United States only in the 1970s. Early efforts to understand the population were largely exploratory and descriptive and involved small samples of White, middle-class fathers (see, Bartz & Witcher, 1976; Chang & Deinard, 1982; Gasser & Taylor, 1976; Gersick, 1979; Hanson, 1981; Orthner, Brown & Ferguson, 1976; Rosenthal & Keshet, 1981). By the mid-1980s, larger samples were studied, but the approach was still descriptive (see, Greif, 1985; 1990; Meyer & Garasky, 1993.) In recent years, increasingly sophisticated research techniques have been used to analyze the data (Greif & DeMaris, 1990, 1995.)

Results have been fairly consistent across studies. Fathers are found to be viable Single Parents, with only a minority (5% to 25% depending on the sample) experiencing significant problems. Fathers tend to gain custody because of their stronger financial position and because of the mother's questionable psychological status or parenting abilities. This is not just the fathers' view. Research asking mothers without custody why they do not have custody offers similar reasons (Grief, 1997; Greif & Pabst, 1988.) In fact the body of literature on this group of mothers can help inform practice with fathers with custody. Fathers usually gain custody by mutual agreement with the mother, rather than after a court battle. In addition, child support is ordered less often for custodial fathers than for custodial mothers. Fathers worry, because of a perceived bias in the courts towards mothers, they will lose custody to the mother at some future date if she contests the arrangement.

Other specific research findings are also instructive. Housework is not described as a problem, arranging childcare often is. Fathers reported the most satisfaction raising preadolescent daughters. The fathers most likely to report a high level of adjustment to their roles were those who had sole custody for a few years, had a satisfactory social life, were not religiously affiliated, were experiencing an increase in their income, expressed satisfaction with their relationship with their children and felt visitation with the noncustodial mother was being handled amicably (Greif, 1995).

Finally, Single-Parent fathers have been studied longitudinally. In a two-year, follow-up study of 173 fathers who participated in a questionnaire survey (Greif & DeMaris, 1995), various characteristics were compared between time one and time two, including the quality of the father's relationship with the child as measured by Hudson's Index of Parental Attitudes, satisfaction with the children's progress, the father's self-rating as a Single Parent, the difficulty of combining work and child-care, frequency of dating, frequency of sexual relations, satisfaction with social life, extent of conflict with the ex-wife, support from significant others regarding the father's having custody, frequency of the ex-wife's visitation with the children, whether the ex-wife is under court order to pay child support, the amount of child support paid and the father's income. Only the frequency with which the mother was ordered by the court to pay support changed over time (it increased.) An earlier study (Greif, 1987) found an increase only in frequency of the visits by the mother over time.

Case Studies

The following two case examples depict different aspects of Single-Father headed families. The first illustrates an acrimonious family situation and the second is a model of how father-custody situations can evolve in the course of time.

Mark and Ellen

Mark, a 37-year-old, White, Single Father was raising four children alone when we first met. He gained custody when his wife, Ellen, left him for his best friend the same day he came home after being laid off from his job. The children ranged in age from eight weeks to six years of age. He had little parenting experience at the time and struggled with the childcare demands as would any parent in this situation. Six months later, Ellen returned and demanded custody. He fought her in court and won, but a ten-year battle for custody of the children ensued. During those years, the children went back and forth between parents. First the oldest, a girl, left Mark, saying with the onset of puberty she felt uncomfortable living with him. Mark claimed she left because he set stricter rules than Ellen. Then a second daughter left, only to return to Mark's house six months later after she tired of constantly fighting with her older sister.

Counseling attempted through the school system failed because the animosity between the warring parents was too great when they were in the same room together. Finally, as the children grew older and after spending extended periods with each parent, they either graduated or dropped out of school and moved out on their own. Age quieted the custody battles. However, the children were left confused, hurt and distrustful. Each child, all of whom I have interviewed over the course of ten years, has been left with some emotional scar. Both Mark and Ellen have stopped communicating with at least one of the children for extended periods.

Mark was supported by the courts in his attempts to gain custody. But he eventually became fatigued with trying to retain custody and allowed the children to choose where they wanted to live. When the children wanted to experiment with life with their mother, he relented. The "back and forth" between the homes took its toll on everyone. Such wars between parents often result in unhappy children and leave them bereft of any sense of stability in their life. The children's prognosis for establishing healthy, intimate relationships in the future is not good.

Susan and Joe

In contrast to Mark and Ellen, Susan and Joe agreed Joe should have custody of their then ten-year-old son, Bill. The parents, whose marriage had been shaky for years, divorced following the untimely death of a younger son. The marriage could not sustain the trauma as they pulled apart rather than together. Susan first had custody, as mothers frequently do, but found herself seeking too much support from her then-six-year-old son who she treated as a peer instead of a child. As she recalled, "He came to me one day, and said he wanted to divorce me. I had been acting like he was an adult and had been talking with him about adult stuff. He was right to want to leave."

Joe had remained involved with Bill as a noncustodial parent and agreed to move into the home as Susan moved out. Four years after this switch, the parents have been able to sustain a model parent-to-parent relationship even though their spousal relationship ended. Susan visits frequently. They consult each other about how to raise Bill, speak about personal issues with each other (Susan has remarried) and have begun to plan financially for Bill's college education. Today they see each other as friends now who just were not happy while married to each other.

Susan and Joe have been able to keep the boundaries in their relationship clearly demarcated. Even in this situation, all is not perfect – Bill still wonders why, if his parents can get along so well now, they could not have stayed married.

Implications for Practice

As the number of fathers with custody grows, the demands on practitioners to handle cases like these will increase. The following issues could be considered when working with the fathers and their children:

Feeling out of place. Some Single Fathers feel out of place. One father asked me when he gained custody, "How many freaks are there out there like me?" The men, despite their success in coping with their new role, felt they did not fit in anywhere. Single Mothers with custody, the more common arrangement after separation and divorce, often have other women in their community whom they can rely on or use as role models. Fathers often do not have similar support. In fact, it is not uncommon for jokes to be made about how incompetent men are with children.

The practitioner needs to cautiously ask the father his feelings about the uniqueness of his situation. Some fathers, when seeking help for their children, deny they are experiencing any difficulties themselves. Other fathers will appreciate the recognition of the role conflict they are experiencing. Unless the context in which the father is parenting is appreciated, the chance to align with the father will be missed.

Divorce related trauma. Fathers and children commonly experience specific divorce-related traumas. Desertion, court battles, money, visitation disputes and loss of neighborhood and home take their toll on family members as well. Different therapeutic approaches with adults and children, family therapy for example, can be utilized. The principles of structural family therapy (Minuchin, 1974), with its emphasis on boundaries and hierarchy, can be easily grasped by the father seeking short-term help and provide a template for interacting with the noncustodial mother.

Joe and Susan, for example, were clear about communicating with each other as parents but not as spouses. This dichotomy of roles must be clarified when working with divorcing parents. On the one hand, the therapist can speak to them as parents and, on the other, as divorcing people no longer a "couple". The mother and father may need to be coached on ways to avoid letting their conflictual marital relationship affect their parental responsibilities. Lingering or active disagreements can taint the difficult task of meeting the emotional and physical needs of the children.

Family-of-origin issues may need to be explored. These fathers were raised during a time when women performed the traditional caretaking roles in the family. Group therapy with children of divorce (Bonkowski, Bequette & Boomhower, 1984) can also be an effective approach, particularly if the father is not interested in treatment for himself. Individual time-limited work may be especially attractive to the fathers.

Long-term problems. Fathers often look for specific, short-term answers to problems which may require a long-term, process-oriented approach. Accustomed to "getting to the point and getting things done", many men have trouble engaging in therapy which goes beyond a few sessions. For example, a typical father may believe if the reason for the divorce has been explained to his child once, no further explanation is needed. He may not understand the child's ability to grasp the meaning of the divorce varies by age and developmental level and environmental events (seeing a movie about divorce, having a friend whose parents divorce) may trigger a new series of questions. Explaining to the father he will need to continue to engage the child in discussions about the divorce helps protect the father from being caught off-guard and unprepared for such questions. It also places him in the role of nurturing parent, a role he may not believe he is capable of fulfilling.

Advocacy. Advocacy for fathers, from legal referral to specific services for men, is often necessary. Having a list of "father-friendly" lawyers and mediators helps reassure fathers their concerns are important. Agencies sponsor men's groups, workshops for fathers, seminars (Frieman, Garon & Mandell, 1994) and other targeted services send positive messages to fathers. Mark, in the first case example, would have been a good candidate for a support group.

Relationship with the children's mother. The importance of the father's on-going relationship with the children's mother cannot be overemphasized. Although attention needs to be focused to the issues of child support, visitation and co-parenting; the feelings of the father toward the mother (anger, resentment, love, longing) must also be attended to. Divorces are often messy because of the feelings ex-spouses continue to hold for each other. These feelings need to be addressed directly so that attempts can be made to resolve them and understand how they may be affecting the co-parental relationship.

Triangulation. Children become triangulated in conflicts between parents when they are asked to show favoritism, spend more time with one parent than the other or to spy on the other parent. Even the best intentioned may have confusion about boundaries. Parents should be informed about behaviors which may cause potential problems for children and where lines and boundaries should be drawn in their own development as Single Parents.

Custodial parents generally act as gatekeepers in their children's contact with the visiting parent. (Mark and Ellen blocked each other for years.) The clinician should explore various questions: Does the father encourage the child to call the mother? Does he help the child prepare for visitation in a timely fashion? Does he denigrate the mother to the child as some research suggests fathers do (Smith & Smith, 1981)? How are other women in the father's life introduced to the mother? Are they described as having traits the father stated the mother did not possessed? Does the father forget about visitation or openly discourage it? Such actions place the child in an awkward and painful position between the parents and can drive a wedge between the parent and child.

Involving the mother. Generally, the better the child feels about the mother, the better the child will feel about him/herself. To that end, consideration should be given to including the mother if the children are in therapy. Mother-child communication may be one focus of treatment. Including the mother in therapy may resurrect the child's fantasy of a reconciliation (as occurred when Bill wondered why his parents could not have reconciled). Communication also can become quite volatile (as with Mark and Ellen). Nonetheless, if the mother is integral to the child's life, her involvement can benefit the child and the father. The situation should be carefully assessed.

Relatives. Maintaining connections with relatives can ease transitions. Extended family are an important source of support to both the father and the children. Grandparents in particular can offer stability and love during a vulnerable time for family members.

Although paternal grandparents usually do not pose a problem, in-laws can be problematic for the father. A father may need to strike a delicate balance between his feelings toward the mother of his children and his feelings toward her parents. Just as a father can look in his children's eyes and see his ex-wife, he can also look in his in-laws' eyes and see her. The clinician's task is to help him untangle his feelings for the sake of his children as well as himself.

The father's in-laws generally take one of three positions after a divorce: they side with their daughter, they side with the father or they attempt to remain neutral. Obviously, the father will find it easier to involve his in-laws in the children's lives in the latter two situations. However, if the in-laws side with him, the children will likely sense that everyone believes that something is wrong with the mother, which in turn may serve to alienate them from their mother. The same principles of boundary marking and guarding against triangulation should be applied in work with the father so the children can continue to benefit from contact with this older generation and not experience another loss.

Work and home. The father may need assistance balancing work and home needs. In most families, mothers are more apt to subordinate their work aspirations to the needs of the children than fathers are. A father who has maintained a high level of career involvement with the assumption his children are being well cared for by the mother will have to learn how to juggle these competing demands as a Single Parent. Because men's self-esteem is frequently tied to their work life, the new focus on family at the expense of work may be a significant blow to their ego. If the father's work environment is not supportive, the situation can be even more problematic. The father may have to mourn the loss of his career aspirations before he can set new priorities involving the children.

New Relationships. The father may be ambivalent about starting new relationships. Research shows that fathers tend to wait approximately six months after the breakup before dating again when their social life may become active. Nearly half the fathers in one survey were dating at least once a week, though there was a high level of dissatisfaction with it (Greif, 1990). Their dissatisfaction may result in part from unclear expectations. They may be unable to articulate whether they are interested in a friend, a sexual partner or someone who can be a mother to the child. In turn, their date may not be able to accurately interpret the father's behavior.

If a new relationship is established, the children may feel distressed their father's new "friend" might replace their mother. Or they may express strong preferences regarding their father's selection of a companion, making new relationships even more difficult to establish. Despite these obstacles, fathers should be encouraged to socialize. The father who remains home and uninvolved with new friends sends a message that his children should not socialize.

Conclusion

The picture for the future is not clear. The standards fathers from the 1970s and the preceding decades had to achieve in order to win custody are no longer operable. As the numbers of Single-Father families increase, more men who are unprepared for the rigors of Single Parenting will be parenting alone. These fathers, however, will find a changed attitude along with more support and information about fathering. Social workers are being called upon to work with these families. This chapter provides an overview of the issues with a description of the current context and suggestions for practice which will help fathers cope with the demands of child rearing.

Children in Single-Father families do not see their families as unusual as did children in recent generations. Almost every child has a friend whose parents are divorced and most are familiar with someone who spends a lot of time with her/his father. It is difficult to predict how social trends and parent preparedness may buffer or exacerbate the impact divorce has on most families and the individuals within them. Regardless, such transitions remain terribly painful for everyone involved, despite the best intentions of well-meaning parents.

Bibliography

Bartz, K.W. & Witcher, W.C. (1978). When father gets custody. *Children Today, 7* (5), 2-6, 35.

Bonkowski, S.E., Bequette, S.Q., & Boomhower, S. (1984). A group design to help children adjust to parental divorce. *Social Casework, 65,* 131-7.

Chang, P. & Deinard, A.S. (1982). Singlefather caretakers: Demographic characteristics and adjustment processes. *American Journal of Orthopsychiatry, 52,* 236-42.

Frieman. B.B., Garon, R., & Mandell, B. (1994). Parenting seminars for divorcing parents. *Social Work, 39,* 609-13.

Gasser, R.D. & Taylor, C.M. (1976). Role adjustment of single parent fathers with dependent children. *The Coordinator, 25,* 397-401.

Gersick, K. (1979). Fathers by choice: Divorced men who receive custody of their children. In G. Levenger & O.C. Moles (Eds), *Divorce and separation* (pp. 307-23). New York: Basic Books.

Greif, G.L. (1985). *Single fathers.* New York: MacMillan/Lexington Books.

Greif, G.L. (1987). A longitudinal examination of single custodial fathers: Implications for treatment. *American Journal of Family Therapy, 15*, 253-260.

Greif, G.L. (1990). *The daddy track and the single father.* New York: MacMillan/Lexington.

Greif, G.L. (1995). Single-fathers with custody following separation and divorce. *Marriage and Family Review, 20* (1/2), 213-31.

Greif, G.L. (1997). Working with noncustodial mothers. *Families in Society, 78*, 46-51.

Greif G.L. & DeMaris, A. (1990). Single fathers with custody. *Families in Society, 71*, 259-266.

Greif G.L. & DeMaris, A. (1995). Single fathers with custody: Do they change over time? In W. Marsiglio (Ed.) *Fatherhood: Contemporary theory, research, and social policy* (pp. 193-210). Thousand Oaks, CA: Sage.

Greif, G.L. & Pabst, M.S. (1988). *Mothers without custody.* New York: MacMillan/Lexington.

Hanson, S.M.H. (1981). Single custodial fathers and the parentchild relationship. *Nursing Research, 30*, 202-4.

Hanson, S.M.H. (1988). Divorced fathers with custody. In Bronstein, P. & Cowan, C.P. (Eds.) *Fatherhood today: Men's changing role in the family* (pp. 166-94.) New York: John Wiley.

Meyer, D.R. & Garasky, S. (1993). Custodial fathers: Myths, realities, and child support policy. *Journal of Marriage and the Family, 55*, 73-89.

Minuchin, S. (1974). *Families and family therapy.* Cambridge, MA: Harvard University Press.

Orthner, D.K.; Brown, T. & Ferguson, D. (1976). Single-parent fatherhood: An emerging family life style. *The Family Coordinator, 25*, 429-37.

Rosenthal, K.M. & Keshet, H.F. (1981). *Fathers without partners,* Totowa, NJ: Rowman and Littlefield.

Smith, R.M. & Smith, C.W. (1981). Childrearing and single parent fathers. *Family Relations, 30*, 411-17.

U. S. Bureau of the Census. (1995). *Household and family characteristics: March 1994. Series P20-483.* Washington, DC: Government Printing Office.

U. S. Bureau of the Census. (1996). *Marital status and living arrangements: March 1994. Series P20-484.* Washington, DC: Government Printing Office.

Grandparents Parenting Grandchildren of Drug-Abusing Children

Faye Y. Abram, Ph.D.

MOST OF THE PRACTICE LITERATURE on Single Parents focuses on young, Single Mothers ignoring middle-aged and elderly grandparents who, often alone, are raising their at-risk grandchildren. Only recently has this literature begun to focus on grandparents who serve as primary caregivers for their grandchildren. Many of these grandparents are older, Single Parents and many are also struggling to solve drug abuse-related problems within their family system.

The term "Single-Parent family" generally refers to a household unit consisting of one parent and at least one dependent child who are related. For this chapter, however, the term is broadened to include families consisting of one grandparent and at least one grandchild or other child from outside the immediate family. The term "Single Parent" herein refers not only to a parent functioning as the "sole executive" (Mendes, 1979) in a household with children younger than eighteen years but also to three distinct types of Single Grandparents functioning as solo surrogate parents of grandchildren: custodial grandparents, living-with grandparents and day-care grandparents (Jendrek,1994a, 1994b) The custodial grandparent has legal custody of a grandchild through adoption, full custody, temporary custody or guardianship. The living-with grandparent raises a grandchild in his or her home but does not have a legal custodial relationship with the grandchild. The day-care grandparent provides regular day care at home to a grandchild who lives elsewhere.

227

Single-Parenting by custodial, living-with, and day-care grandparents does not capture the variety of child-rearing functions carried out by older, single adults. For example, an adult relative (such as an aunt, uncle or other adult) may live with and provide regular care to at least one related or unrelated minor child. A Single-Parent family with an unrelated child might consist of one adult and a child who is "fictive kin" (Stack, 1974), that is, a non-blood-related child whom family members treat as kin.

This chapter focuses on older Single Parents and Grandparents raising at least one minor child or grandchild. A case illustration presents a grandparent who has primary responsibility for the care of a grandchild as well as some involvement with the drug-abusing parent of that child. The case illustration captures the diversity among older Single-Grandparent families as well as the variety of family systems; living arrangements; parenting behaviors and human interactions among children, adults and others (Bianchi, 1995; Morrison, 1995; Nesto, 1994; Trent & Harlan, 1994). The chapter aims to sensitize those in the helping professions to the realities, strengths, and service needs of Single Grandparents raising children and to challenge misconceptions and assumptions about Single Parents, the peripheral role of grandparents and the pathology of families effected by abuse.

Demographics

Although grandparents are not mentioned or explicitly identified in the United States census definition of parents, census data on Single-Parent families include information about Single-Parent families with children or grandchildren younger than eighteen years. Single-Grandparent families, like Single-Parent families, often maintain strong extended family ties beyond the household unit and include not only families with custodial arrangements but also families with noncustodial arrangements (Kissman & Allen, 1993; Trent & Harlan, 1994). However, census data on Single-Grandparent families provide information only about families in which grandchildren live with a grandparent house-holder, that is, the grandparent who owns or rents the home or housing unit. Consequently, these data do not provide good information about the range of Single-Parent or Grandparent families and do not capture the extent of kinship bonds in families. Census statistics do provide good data about the number and percent of children who are raised in grandparent households.

Many children are being raised by a Single Grandparent. Census data reveal 3.7 million grandchildren younger than eighteen years (5% of all children younger than eighteen) lived in the home of their grandparent(s) in 1994. Of the children living with a grandparent, 36% had neither parent present in the grandparents' home (U.S. Bureau of the Census, 1994a).

Census data also provide information about the sex, race and economic status of grandparent householders with children younger than eighteen years. Grandparents who are alone and raising grandchildren, like other Single Parents, include women and men of all socioeconomic classes and ethnic groups. These parents, however, disproportionately represent populations commonly regarded as oppressed women; persons of color and poor people (Sands & Nuccio, 1989).

Most Single Grandparents raising children are women. Most children (87%) living with a Single Grandparent in 1991 lived with their grandmother only. Similarly, in that same year, more children lived in grandmother-only households than in households with both grandparents and households with only the grandfather present combined. In 1991, more than half (55%) of all children living with at least one grandparent lived in grandmother-only households (U.S. Bureau of the census, 1944b).

Minority children constitute a disproportionately large share of children living in grandparent families. In 1993, of all children living in grandparent households, 12% were Black and 4% White. Nearly 40% of Black children, compared with 26% of non-Hispanic White children who were living with at least one grandparent, had neither parent present in the household. Some of the children who lived with neither parent were living with more than one grandparent. However, a census report on the diverse living arrangements of children in 1991 disclosed 729,000 Black children compared with 1,394,000 non-Hispanic White children lived with a Single Grandparent (U.S. Bureau of the Census, 1994c). Proportionally, 66% of the Black children compared with 60% of the non-Hispanic White children in grandparent households lived with a grandmother or grandfather only. In these instances, a Single Grandparent (most often the grandmother) had sole responsibility for the care of a grandchild or grandchildren.

For poor, Single Parents or Single Grandparents, raising children can be difficult. The combined effects of ageism and sexism may suppress the income of elderly Single Grandmothers. In 1993, almost one third (30%) of all grandparent householders with grandchildren younger than eighteen years living in their home had incomes below the poverty level. In that same year, 17% of the non-Hispanic, White, grandparent householders with children were poor, and 44% of the Black grandparent householders with children were poor (U.S. Bureau of the Census, 1995). The risk of being poor may be greater in elderly (and perhaps very young) Single-Parent families than in families headed by middle-age Single Parents. Also, the scarce resources of Single-Grandparent families may be stretched to support "official" as well as "unofficial" dependents. Official dependents of Single Grandparents include dependent minors such as custodial grandchildren or children younger than eighteen years. Unofficial dependents include noncustodial grandchildren, day-care grandchildren, unrelated minors or dependent adults. These dependents receive support and care from a grandparent but are not recognized as legitimate dependents because "on paper" they live elsewhere or are older than eighteen years and are therefore considered an independent adult.

Grandparent families with children younger than eighteen years are quite diverse in term of their ages, living arrangements and other factors. Census data on grandparent householders do not separate Single-Grandparent households from households with two grandparents or intergenerational households with children. Nevertheless, many grandparents of various circumstances are busy parenting grandchildren. Some of these grandparents are very young grandparents; others are quite old. Approximately half are employed. Most live in metropolitan areas.

In 1993, the median age of grandparent householders with grandchildren younger than eighteen years living in their home was fifty-six years. These grandparent householders, however, include approximately 5,000 grandparents who were younger than thirty years and approximately 17,000 grandparents who were eighty-five years of age or older (U.S. Bureau of the Census, 1995). These data indicate that some relatively young grandparents are raising grandchildren and their own children simultaneously in the same household. Some middle-aged grandparents have the additional responsibility of caring for a frail, elderly parent. Many elderly grandparents are raising grandchildren long after their traditional child-rearing years have passed and when they are in the midst of declining health.

Many Single Grandmothers raise their grandchildren without help from a parent or other adults in the home. Almost half (49%) of all grandparent householders with live-in grandchildren were employed. According to 1993 data, slightly more than half of all grandparent heads of household with grandchildren had at least a high school education and approximately 9% had at least a bachelor's degree. Most (80%) of the grandparent householders with live-in grandchildren lived in metropolitan areas; 40% of these householders lived in inner-city areas (U.S. Bureau of the Census, 1995).

Review of the Literature

Recent studies of grandparents parenting their grandchildren (e.g., Jendrek, 1994a; Joslin & Brouard, 1995; Pope et al., 1993; Roberto, 1990; Solomon & Marx, 1995) tend to focus on the grandparents' involvement with grandchildren and to examine the effects of later-life parenting on grandparents or grandchildren. Solomon and Marx (1995), for example, examined the link between grandparent(s) characteristics and the health and well-being of grandchildren.

Using data from a national children's health survey, they studied 17,110 children raised solely by a grandparent, reporting most (60%) of the grandparent households with children were without grandfathers present. Most grandparent households with children are single-grandmother households. Solomon and Marx (1995) also reported their general finding in terms of health and school adjustment "children raised solely by grandparents… fare quite well relative to children in families with one biological parent present; a category which includes both single-parent and blended families" (p. 386).

In some studies, it is not always reported nor clear whether the grandchild(ren) is cared for by a Single Grandparent or two grandparents. Studies reporting the marital status of the grandparent householder or the number of grandparents in the household show quite a range – from a low of 11% Single Grandparents within a sample of predominately White day-care grandparents in one study (Jendrek, 1994a), to a high of 65% Single Grandparents in a study of African-American grandmothers raising grandchildren whose parent or parents were crack-cocaine addicted (Minkler, Roe & Price, 1992; Minkler, Roe & Robertson-Beckley, 1994).

It is not clear whether Single-Grandparent families with children younger than eighteen years are more or less stressed than families with two grandparents or with more than one adult. The presence of two grandparents or another adult in the household suggests the second grandparent or adult could provide additional resources (income, time or energy) toward the care of the children. However, the other/second adult in the home could be a dependent (disabled, frail, chronically ill or drug-abusing) adult who requires more resources or care than the grandparent can provide (Jennings, 1987). In such instances, the other adult may contribute to the burden of the grandparent who is raising the children and maintaining the home.

Raising Children of a Drug-Abusing Parent

Several recent studies describe grandparents who are parenting grandchildren of a drug-abusing adult son or daughter. Burton's (1992) research focused on sixty Black grandparents rearing children of drug-addicted parents in a drug-infested environment. Smith (1994) studied sixteen African Americans rearing their cocaine-addicted daughters' children and participating in a grandmothers' support group they had organized as a self-help group for grandparents waging a war against the crack-cocaine epidemic in their community. Similarly, Minkler and associates' (1994) research focused on seventy-one grandparents rearing young children because of the children's parents' involvement with crack cocaine. Jendrek's (1994a, 1994b) research on 114 grandparents (primarily White, middle-class grandparents) providing regular care to their grandchildren

231

found that "more than half of the white custodial grandparents report that they had a legal relationship with their grandchild because of parental drug abuse" (p. 214). More than a third (35.7%) of the grandparents across all types of care (custodial, living-with and day-care grandparents) identified the grandchild's mother or father as having a drug problem as one reason for providing regular care. Jendrek's research helps to counter the stereotype that surrogate parenting is a Black-grandmother issue and to correct the erroneous perception only a small percent of parenting grandparents are responding to the problems of drug-abusing adult children.

Studies which focus heavily on grandparents' involvements with their grandchildren lead some to assume parenting grandparents are only marginally involved or generally uninvolved with adult children; they dissociate themselves from and shun adult children who are abusing drugs. These assumptions, however, may not be well grounded and may have even less validity for Single Grandparents. Kaufman's (1982) study of the family ties of drug abusers, for example, suggests that "contrary to the conventional assumption that addicts are peer-oriented sociopaths, accumulating evidence shows that they maintain close family ties" (p. 889). Madanes, Duke, and Harbin (1980) found many drug abusers reside with or have weekly to daily contact with their parents (usually mothers) and they use the parental home as a constant reference point in their lives. Moreover, in a recent study of grandparents parenting grandchildren of a drug-abusing adult son or daughter, many grandparents reported they try to maintain ties with the grandchild's parent because "they want the parent to be present in the child's life and in their lives" (Jendrek, 1994a, p. 214). In contrast, other parenting grandparents who interact with a drug-abusing parent of the children have reported they dread repeated contact with the parent because of the drug abuse-related problems which accompany the parent.

Studies of Single-Grandparent families, like studies of Single-Parent families, tend to explore and provide information about the problems or difficulties of these families, especially those Single Grandparents affected by drug abuse within the family system. When Single Grandparents are raising a grandchild of a drug-abusing adult son or daughter, these grandparents often must deal with the added burden of being blamed for the "addictive family systems" (Sullivan, 1993, Ziegler-Driscoll, 1981) and their helping behavior is often labeled as pathological "co-dependency" (Cermak, 1986; Schaef, 1992; Wegscheider-Cruse & Cruse, 1990; Whitfield, 1989).

Similarly, Single Grandparents heading families are often described as too old to be raising children or as overly involved in the parental role because they are inappropriately trying to fill a void or their own need for companionship as a result of the lack or loss of a relationship with a spouse or adult partner (Lewis, 1990; Roberto, 1990).

The reality of the drug world and culture and how it touches and affects parenting grandparents, the lives of their grandchildren and other members of their family system need to be understood. In one study (Burton, 1992), a majority of the grandparent respondents rearing children of drug-abusing parents

expressed concern and fear about the burglaries, drive-by shootings, and increased automobile traffic in their neighborhoods as a result of drug trafficking [and] indicated that the timing of drug trade in their community had an impact on how they organized daily activities such as grocery shopping, paying bills, and letting their grandchildren go outside to play. (p. 748)

Some grandparents feel as though they are raising grandchildren in environments filled with "mine fields" (Hines, 1990). Many worry about the recruitment or lure of school-age grandchildren into the drug trade.

The Impact of the Drug Environment

The absence or presence of economic, physical and other resources in the social environment can make parenting more or less stressful. It is difficult to raise a child in high-unemployment, poverty, crime and drug-abuse areas. Some parenting grandparents and grandchildren live in communities which are part of the drug world and thus are affected directly by the dangers associated with the neighborhood drug trade. Those living outside or adjacent to these communities are indirectly affected by drug traffic.

Other grandparents with children of a drug-abusing son or daughter do not live in a drug-plagued environment but have episodic encounters with the drug world when they visit places where the drug-abusing parent stays or when the parent visits them. These grandparents and children fear being victimized by unknown predators in an unsafe neighborhood, by the drug-abusing parent or by associates of that parent who come into the grandparent's home. Grandparents sometimes have to contend with persons exhibiting the behavioral effects of continued drug use – irritability, sleeplessness, delusions, hallucinations and psychological damage associated with crack cocaine use. These grandparents and children experience more than their share of crises, crime, health and legal problems.

In addition to the direct and indirect effects of the neighborhood as a source of stress; other contextual factors, such as time, development and ethnicity or race may influence the surrogate-parenting role of grandparents (Burton, Dilworth-Anderson, & Merriwether-de-Vries, 1995). Often grandparents have little advance notice before they are forced to assume the surrogate-parent role.

Developmental and intergenerational issues may arise. Also, ethnicity or race relates not only to certain health and poverty risks but also to the amount of help that is needed or available. Ethnicity and race also relate to cultural norms that influence the grandparent's decision, which is often a non-decision or "impulse to care" (McGrew, 1991) for one's at-risk grandchildren.

Intervention From a Position of Strength

Saleebey (1996) notes the accentuation of problems tends to undermine clients' self-esteem by speaking to and about clients in a way which debases, belittles or discounts them; and to create a web of negative expectations about clients, their environment and problem-solving capacities and to foster the victim mindset as well as conflict between clients and workers. In contrast to a problem-focused perspective on Single Grandparents, a strengths perspective directs attention to the important role women's relationships and sense of connectedness to others, plays in shaping a positive view of themselves – as women, mothers and grandmothers (Collins, 1993).

The strengths perspective enables practitioners to build on grandparents' caring skills and encourages the empowerment of grandmothers as women and mothers (Cowger, 1992, 1994; Freedberg, 1993). A strengths perspective fosters discovery of unrecognized potential as well as the power and capacity which Single Grandparents (and other members of the client system) have to continue to learn, grow and change (Saleebey, 1992).

Similarly, it shifts attention from environmental deficiencies, hazards and obstacles to existing community resources which can be mobilized to combat social, political and economic factors which make parenting difficult (Sullivan, Wolk & Hartmann, 1992; Weick, Rapp, Sullivan & Kisthardt, 1989). This perspective enables practitioners to capitalize on factors and resources which support "wellness amidst distress" (Tweed & Ryff, 1991). For all the above reasons, a strengths perspective is the preferred approach to guide practice interventions with Single Grandparents raising grandchildren.

The strengths perspective directs attention to the critical role of the social environment in clients' lives. An advocate of this approach asserts that "no matter how a harsh environment tests the mettle of inhabitants, it can also be understood as a lush topography of resources and possibilities" (Saleebey, 1992, p. 7). From this perspective, grandparents who are raising a grandchild of a drug-abusing parent are seen as a special population with resources as well as needs defined and maintained by the social context in which they live.

Kretzmann and McKnight (1993) point out the benefits of viewing neighborhoods in terms of their community assets. These include resources such as the gifts and talents of its residents as well as its churches, block clubs, cultural groups, citizens' associations and local institutions. Neighborhoods; even those with high rates of unemployment, child abuse, illiteracy, crime, broken families, alcoholism and drug abuse; have assets which can be mobilized to build stronger, more self-reliant, better functioning families and communities. Although some Single Grandparents raising grandchildren are aware of important resources within their communities, most are more aware of community problems and needs.

Case Example

To understand the realities, strengths and service needs of Single Grandparents and their families, it is helpful to share their stories. The following case example includes bits and pieces of the stories of various Single Grandparents raising their grandchildren. It presents the concerns of these grandparents who live in or just outside a large metropolitan area. Parenting grandparents living in rural areas have concerns which are similar to and different from grandparents parenting in the inner city.

The case illustration is drawn from my work with grandparents caring for their grandchildren. Some of these grandparents are struggling to get the children's parent into a drug-treatment program. Some are trying to raise their grandchildren within a public housing complex. One family is a member of a church-based support group for grandparents raising grandchildren. The following case exemplifies the diversity within Single-Grandparent families and captures various realities confronting Single Grandmothers.

Harriet

Harriet Jackson is 68-year-old, African-American, Single Grandmother caring for her grandson, Willie, who lives with her. She is recently widowed and has been caring for Willie since Willie's father (her 32-year-old son, LW) rescued him from a crack house where Willie's mother was then living. The mother's current whereabouts are not known. Harriet knows that LW "has a drug problem" and she explained she keeps Willie and will continue to care for her grandson until her boy "gets through this", which according to her "is no more and no less" than what she has done for her other children. Harriet is the mother of seven adult children, LW and six daughters, and the grandmother of a host of grandchildren. Her daughters are all older than LW, doing well, and show no drug-abuse problems. Harriet has extensive contact and good relationships with all her children and grandchildren. However, the more she tries to help LW, the more strained her relationships with her other children, relatives and friends become.

A retired career nurse, Harriet describes herself as "fairly healthy". Her husband, William Sr. also known as Big William, "drank too much" and died of colon cancer three years ago. Harriet owns and lives in a nice home in a working-class neighborhood. She also owns income property (an apartment building and two small frame houses), one of which she has let LW live in rent free "until he gets himself straight". The apartment building was badly damaged recently by a fire that was started in retaliation for a drug deal that went bad. It is now vacant and in need of major repairs. One of the frame houses, which had earlier been overtaken by drug dealers, is now so deteriorated and unsafe that LW convinced his mother he could not live there any longer and she should let him stay at the other small house she owns just two blocks away from her home.

Willie, Harriet's grandson, is now ten years old. He has been living with Harriet since his father brought him to her at age five. Willie's mother had not registered him to begin kindergarten. Weeks after the start of school, Harriet registered Willie in a school in her neighborhood. She recalls that she had "lots of hassles" with school officials, welfare case workers and the staff at medical clinic because she was not Willie's legal guardian. At first, Willie did poorly in school. His teachers described him as "fidgety, impulsive and developmentally delayed". Willie's grades and behavior started to improve and he continued at an "above average" level through the fourth grade.

Harriet describes Willie as a "pretty self-sufficient kid". He, for example, often makes his own breakfast and gets himself off to school, goes grocery shopping for Harriet and does yard work and snow shoveling in the neighborhood for spending money. But Willie has begun to "hang out" with some boys who tease him about the "chump change" he is earning and being a "mama's boy". These boys have a reputation for "skipping school, being disrespectful toward grown-ups, and getting into trouble". When Willie started fifth grade, he began to run with these boys, to "talk back" to Harriet and his aunts, to show up with "things that they gave" him and to be in the middle of arguments between Harriet and LW about house rules, curfew and who's allowed to discipline him when he's bad or disobedient. Harriet adds that Willie had Ds on his report card for the past two semesters and several after-school detentions for misbehavior. She states, with some resignation, Willie is "getting to be more than a handful" and that "he may now need to be with his father". Harriet also admits to asking herself several times if she's too old to be raising her active grandson.

Recently, Harriet confided in her pastor the trouble she was having with Willie and LW. She also told him LW stole from her repeatedly; pawned her car for $50; wrote checks on her credit union accounts and called many times in the middle of the night for money, first aid or to be rescued or sheltered from someone who was after him. She also told her pastor she had tried unsuccessfully to get LW into or to complete various drug-treatment programs. Harriet complained she was tired and frustrated because she didn't know what else she could or should do. Her pastor prayed with her and then encouraged her to contact the family-development center and a drug-treatment program in the area for help.

LW is a welfare recipient and the legal custodial parent for Willie. The welfare check replaces the wages he used to earn from work with a janitorial company his father had started and had planned to pass along to him. However, LW hated his father's business and joined the air force to pursue a career in aviation mechanics, which was his love. When he was discharged, he slowly realized the airlines were not hiring blacks in that capacity. Anger and rage set in. He began working at the janitorial company and using drugs. When LW's abuse of crack cocaine got worse, the janitorial business started to lose money. Harriet hired a manager to prevent the business from going under. LW stated he "stopped working to take care of Willie". He applied for welfare.

Currently, LW is still using drugs and using his welfare check and petty theft to support his habit. He visits Harriet's home several times a week for food, money, clean laundry, things to take and pawn and to see Willie. LW also has a pattern of disappearing for weeks. The last time he disappeared, he took Harriet's car. Harriet called the drug treatment center for help but was told LW should contact them. She called repeatedly until she finally got someone who listened to her story and asked what she should do.

Harriet's Strengths

From a strengths perspective, it is easy to see Harriet as a heroine and savior of her grandchild. She and other grandparents like her can be viewed as "the system balancers" (Pinderhughes, 1986, p. 51) within their families and communities. Harriet can also be viewed as a catalyst for change, a significant other who, like many Black grandmothers, feels obligated to ensure the intergenerational survival of her family (Kivett, 1993; Timberlake & Chipungu, 1992); to reduce the risks of out-of-home placement, abuse or neglect of grandchildren and to prevent the replication of drug abuse and other problems among children of succeeding generations.

A summary review of Harriet's personal strengths shows she is an educated woman in fair health who thinks clearly and rationally. She owns her home as well as income property and appears to have sufficient retirement income to sustain a moderate standard of living. Harriet has nursing and parenting skills. She has raised seven children, six of whom are successful adults with no apparent drug-abuse problems. She has successfully raised and generally had no problems with Willie for four of the five years he has lived with her.

Harriet is able to consider and weigh alternatives in problem solving and to realize some success (albeit short-lived) she has had with getting LW into drug

237

treatment in the past. She is emotionally stable and not easily unnerved by recurrent crises in LW's life. Harriet's commitment to do all she can for LW "until he gets himself straight" is indicative of the hope she has for her son as well as her generally positive attitude toward life and people's capacity to grow, mature and better themselves. Harriet shares her concerns about LW and her situation with her other adult children as well as her pastor and acts on his suggestion that she contact a drug-treatment program. Thus, she is willing to seek help and to verbalize her troubles with persons whom she trusts. Harriet has friends and good relationships with family members. She makes sacrifices for her family and gives time and money to help meet some of the needs of her dependent adult children as well as her grandchildren. Harriet's efforts to get LW into various drug-treatment programs and her repeated calls to the drug-treatment center and community agencies suggest she is highly motivated, resourceful and persistent in her search to find help for LW as well as answers to her questions regarding what should she do about drug-abuse-related problems.

Harriet's understanding of racial oppression, another strength, justifies her need to protect LW. She is aware of the social and economic injustices many African Americans experience as well as the need to combat various forms and effects of racism, discrimination and oppression. Harriet, for example, knows LW was not able to get a job as an aviation mechanic because "the airlines were not hiring blacks in that capacity" and LW had been assaulted several times by drug dealers.

Beyond Harriet's intellectual, emotional, coping, motivational and inter-personal strengths; she has resources in her family system and environment. She is part of a relatively large extended-family system within which most family members are healthy, well-adjusted and mutually supportive of one another. Even Willie contributes to the strengths and functioning of the family system. Because Willie, like other children of Single-Parent households, is generally more autonomous and self-sufficient than same-age children in two-parent families (Amato, 1987); Harriet does not feel that she has to pay someone to "baby-sit" him, to run errands or to do certain housekeeping chores for her. Willie also provides Harriet, an elderly widowed woman, with some companionship.

LW exhibits some important strengths as well. He had technical training and job skills even though currently he is unemployed. He has demonstrated his caring and concern for Willie by removing him from the crack house where the boy's mother was living. It appears as though LW wants Willie to be with Harriet because he wants to do what is best for the boy.

Important resources within the community include Harriet's church and her pastor. Both appear to be part of her social and spiritual support system. The family janitorial business, which is now solvent and has growth potential, is also an asset. Although LW may view the family business as low-status domestic or maintenance work for unskilled Black laborers, a strengths-focused practitioner might reframe this type of work and help LW reenvision it as a self-employment opportunity for a skilled entrepreneur. Family service agencies in the community have demonstrated knowledge of African-American culture and families and have realized some success using culturally specific interventions with children, parents and grandparents in drug-affected families.

Common Strengths of Single-Grandparent Families

Harriet's family system and her community, as well as Single-Grandparent families in general, have strengths not initially apparent which appear later as treatment proceeds. In Harriet's case, an expected or potential strength is that Harriet, as a Single Grandmother, will show greater responsiveness to (as well as better utilization of) extrafamilial support systems than do mothers in two-parent families (Marlow, 1994; Walters, 1988). Older Single Grandparents may also have strengths or resources which accompany their age and life experience – a solid sense of place which comes from years of maintaining themselves in their own homes within a familiar community; wisdom, patience and good judgment gained from years of work and life experiences and the respect, honor and deference traditionally accorded to elders in ethnic-minority communities.

Many Single-Grandparent families have characteristics Hill (1992) and others (Hurd, Moore & Rogers, 1995; Littlejohn-Blake & Darling, 1993; Thomas & Daneby, 1985) identify as strengths in Black families; including strong kinship bonds, strong work orientation, flexible family roles, emphasis on educational and occupational achievement and a strong spiritual or religious orientation. In addition to these strengths, many Black grandparents are aware they must raise their children in a "hostile environment" (Chestang, 1972) and they have an ability to teach their grandchildren the values and mores of the Black culture while equipping them with attitudes and skills to confront individual as well as institutional racism (Hurd et al., 1995; Logan, Freeman & McRoy, 1990; Norton, 1978). A self-identified strength of African-American parents is that they "recognized the need to prepare their children to survive in a racist society... to cope with discrimination, sometimes through assertiveness and sometimes through superior effort" (Hurd et al., 1995, p. 440).

In identifying and building upon the strengths of Single-Grandparent families, practitioners are wise to engage the client system in joint assessment, goal setting and decision making. Programs and services which elicit the input of workers and clients have greater potential to succeed. Single Grandparents need to be given the opportunity to contribute information about what they see as a problem and desire as outcomes and, on the basis of what they have tried and experienced, about what they think will work or bring about change.

Supportive Services and Programs

Grandparent Support Groups

Grandparent support groups can be very helpful to Single Grandparents raising children. In Harriet's case, a group called Proud Grandparents began when an outreach worker encouraged several parenting grandparents who visited the church's food pantry and clothing store weekly to meet with other grandparents and to share their parenting stories over coffee. The group has a positive focus as members share pictures of children and grandchildren as well as proud moments. Often participants reserve a few minutes of their meetings for what Harriet calls "bragging time", which seems to be an important, affirming feature of older Single-Parent and grandparent groups. Such activities help offset negative comparisons of Single-Parent or grandparent families with "intact" families (Kissman, 1991) or of "being treated as second-class citizens vis-à-vis both public and private programs and services" (Minkler & Roe, 1993, p. 194). Activities reinforce the view that older, Single-Grandparent families are normal, healthy and well-functioning. Consistent with practice wisdom (Donati, 1995; Kissman, 1991; Young, 1994), affirmation of the Single-Parent or Grandparent family as legitimate and viable is a first step in normalizing the lives of Single Mothers and grandmothers and their children.

Group members also share their successes with legal aid attorneys or getting adult children into treatment. Initially, members of grandparent groups seem more comfortable discussing their grandchildren. After a sense of trust and safety is realized within the group, members begin to share problems and difficulties they experience in their role as parents to their grandchildren and in their seemingly never-ending role as parents of dependent adult children.

Successful support groups invite speakers to provide useful information about medical coverage, ensuring that children will not be refused medical treatment because the grandparent is not the grandchild's legal guardian. Speakers also discuss legal issues such as the implications of obtaining guardianship versus temporary custody, legal custody or the formal or informal adoption of the grandchild and coping with the announcement in court that one's adult son or daughter is an unfit parent.

Grandparent groups typically are composed of members who are parenting school-age children or who have major concerns about their adult children.

Some groups divide into two subgroups when the larger group includes members with different concerns. Members may attend meetings of one or both groups. Grandparent groups also accommodate a wide range of ages and family types. Their membership may include custodial as well as noncustodial grandparents, who in some groups are nonvoting members. Typically, a few members of the grandparent support groups are keenly aware of community resources which are particularly useful to them, other grandparents or their grandchildren (Julian, 1995). Many grandparents, however, have questions about their new parenting role (Lott, 1993; Roberto, 1990) and are more focused on their problems and needs than on community resources. Consequently, grandparents who are struggling to fulfill the demands of Single-Parenting welcome and appreciate practitioners who help them dissect and reenvision problems which seem overwhelming, as well as practitioners who facilitate pooling and sharing individual members' knowledge of community resources (Kissman, 1991).

Church-based grandparent groups typically incorporate spirituality and prayer; although they rarely evolve into twelve-step groups. Several feminist critiques of twelve-step groups such as AA (e.g., Abbott, 1995; Bepko, 1991; Collins, 1993) suggest women, and by extension mothers and grandmothers, may reject twelve-step programs because they do not want to view themselves as powerless. Grandmothers are less likely to call upon God or a higher power to help them passively accept things beyond their control than to ask for strength, affirm their own inner wisdom and magnify their power to choose and do what they believe is right. For example, one grandmother often quotes the Bible (Nehemiah 4: 9, 14) which say: "We prayed to our God and posted a guard"… "Remember the Lord…and fight", as proof that we are to combine prayer and action; as instruction we are to work and fight for what we pray for. The spiritual focus is on empowering grandparents to make changes in their lives. Some members have specifically asked for information about professional helpers who have an appreciation for the spiritual dimension of their lives or of recovery programs. Single Grandparents establish rapport quickly with practitioners who recognize the importance of spirituality. Similarly, several contributors to practice journals describe the benefits of using spirituality as a tool in the assessment and treatment of drug-abusing clients and their families (Boyd-Franklin, 1989; Knox, 1985). Morrell (1996) argues that social workers connecting treatment, spirituality and politics can radicalize recovery.

> Whether thought of as God or as the vitality that results from communing with other, spirituality can inspire and sustain people to move beyond external and internalized oppression. Many people in substance abuse treatment are dispirited. Beliefs and experiences that connect them to others and challenge discouragement can be thought of as spiritual; they invigorate and empower people. (p. 309)

Social workers supportive of parenting Single Grandparents show respect for diversity by honoring the important role spirituality plays in the lives of people of all cultures and by integrating spiritual traditions and activities of particular clients and family systems into their practice with them.

Parents and Grandparents as Educators

A parents-as-educators program, modeled after the parents-as-teachers program, helps grandparents as well as parents teach drug-abuse prevention to their grandchildren and reinforce the nonabuse of drugs with their adult children. Family-life-education programs help grandparents and parents learn how to better raise children and incorporate drug-abuse education and prevention modules which enhance parents' and grandparents' own knowledge and understanding of drugs, signs of drug abuse, the link between drug use and health risks and ways to discourage their children and grandchildren from trying illicit drugs. Programs such as this extend the primary-prevention focus beyond the general population of children and youth who are least at risk to address the specific concerns of a population at greater risk: members of families with a drug-abusing, young adult member. Programs using parents and grandparents to educate family members about drug abuse seem to thrive at such sites as parents' homes, churches, community centers and cultural organizations. In these settings, parents may be less threatened by teachers or others with "expert knowledge" and may feel more empowered to share what they have learned and know.

Community Interventions

Social workers have helped Single Grandmothers recognize many of their personal troubles and concerns are political in nature and related to key public policy issues. Members of grandmother support groups have come to recognize their own and others' efforts to help them cope with their new caregiving roles "cannot take the place of policy-level changes that would supplement support on the individual level with broad-based societal support for such caregivers and their families" (Minkler et al., 1994, p. 27). They begin to recognize policymakers need to develop and implement child-support policies which provide parity for relatives who provide care for children. Most grandmothers acknowledge their income is inadequate to meet their own and their grandchildren's needs. Practitioners who provide information about the inequity in child support to relative caregivers help politicize grandparents. For example: "In all but a few states grandparents who are raising grandchildren and eligible for government assistance generally receive AFDC, rather than the more generous foster-care payments, and are denied such additional foster care benefits as mental health counseling and a children's clothing allowance" (Minkler et al., 1994, p. 28).

With greater political awareness, members of grandparent support groups are joining with citizen groups to advocate for progressive welfare reform to ensure their state's plan for the use of federal block grants to provide Temporary Assistance to Needy Families (TANF), specified in the federal Personal Responsibility and Work Opportunity Reconciliation Act of 1996, is responsive to their needs. Some are working with the Older Women's League and the legislative committee of their state chapter of the American Association for Retired Persons, advocating not only for equal income support for relative caregivers, but also for affordable or free and high-quality, respite care and for abolishing the discriminatory denial of assistance to unmarried teens and denial of TANF federal cash assistance, Food Stamps and medical assistance to anyone convicted of a felony drug charge (i.e., possession, use or distribution).

Practitioners can help parenting grandparents crystallize their concerns, connect them to local groups and organizations which advocate for low-income families and involve them in local efforts to influence the legislative process and state welfare reform strategies. Grandparents express concern if they are helped financially and their drug-abusing children or unmarried teens are not helped, then they will have to share even more of their scarce resources with family members, who with few exceptions are denied any and all types of government financial assistance. Grandparents also worry if needy drug abusers and unmarried parenting teens are not helped, these persons are more likely to prey on them and others in their community. They are also concerned that dependent adult children and unmarried teen mothers are less likely to resume parenting of their children at some point in the future because their poverty, dependence or personal problems will likely persist if they do not receive assistance or intervention.

Social workers can empower grandparents by supporting the social actions they initiate. For example, a grandmothers' walk "consisted of a five-mile walk through their drug-infected neighborhood, demonstrating their fight against crack cocaine. It was a very powerful act, and with the children accompanying them, their message was profound, especially to their grandchildren" (Smith, 1994, p. 30). In another community action, grandmothers stood with picket signs on the corners of an intersection that was known as a place to buy stolen merchandise. Their signs read, "We Are Against Crack" and "We're Taking Our Neighborhood Back." Single Grandmothers raising children of drug-abusing parents view as helpful practitioners who support efforts to identify and resist activities within their communities that collude with the drug culture. When grandmothers organized against drug abuse and picketed activities which allowed and perpetuated the presence of drugs in their community, one practitioner recruited a few retired police officers and off-duty firemen to provide a volunteer patrol for the demonstration.

243

Community-based, family-focused, intergenerational drug education and drug-prevention programs are also supportive of Single Grandparents' efforts to raise their grandchildren. Black Family Development, Inc. (BFDI), a family service agency created by a local chapter of the National Association of Black Social Workers, for example, has worked quite effectively with families like Harriet's. Successful family outcomes are in part due to BFDI, which trains social workers and educates family members of all ages about various forms of collusion with the drug culture within African-American communities. Participants in the training learn the drug culture is supported when people do the following:

- Excuse drug dealing as a viable means of making money because few good-paying jobs are available.
- Buy stolen goods.
- Accept money from children with the full knowledge it came from selling drugs or some other type of involvement in drug-related activities.
- Accept cash for expensive automobiles or as a down payment on a home from anyone.
- Patronize business establishments primarily devoted to, and supported by, the illicit drug trade or individuals trying to emulate persons who are drug dealers.
- Allow children to be in the company of drug dealers or those involved in drug-related activities.
- Rent property with the certain knowledge it will be used to sell drugs or for drug-related activities.
- Adopt the same materialistic values as the drug culture (Black Family Development, Inc., 1990).

Participants in community-based, family-focused and intergenerational drug-abuse-education programs like the BFDI training program comment training helps them identify and confront attitudes, beliefs, behaviors, values and life philosophies which support the drug culture. One participant said she was able to get rid of some of her negative views about Black people and the Black community because she learned that the drug culture is totally separate from the African-American culture and diametrically opposed to it.

Trainers help grandmothers and others develop strategies to resist the drug culture. They also point out the sole purpose of the drug culture is to derive monetary gain from the community via the illicit sale of drugs or accouterments of the drug life. Grandparents learn key questions to ask and signs to watch for to recognize drug abuse in a family member. Harriet, for example, confronted Willie about a gold chain, compact disks and a pager he said a neighborhood boy gave him. Training helped her recognize this as a sign of possible gang or drug involvement. Grandparents also learn it is important to share what they learn with their children and grandchildren.

Unilateral Family Treatment and Family-Focused Treatment

Grandparents frequently express the view that all family members need to be involved in the treatment of substance abuse within the family. After searching for an appropriate drug-treatment program, however, many report being disappointed most programs provide only individual treatment to drug abusers or their co-dependent spouses and most "family" treatment models focus either on parents involved with adolescent drug abusers or adolescents dealing with a parent who is an alcoholic or a drug abuser. Harriet reported the programs she contacted discouraged her from getting involved in drug-prevention efforts targeted at her grandson and urged her not to be "the monkey-in-the-middle" between a drug-treatment programs and her drug-abusing son. Some clinical staff may give grandmothers their unsolicited professional opinion nothing can be done to help and nothing anyone does will help if the drug-abusing family member is not ready to change or to come in for treatment.

An encouraging exception to such nonresponsiveness is the Unilateral Family Treatment (UFT) program. Thomas (1994) described UFT as an intervention directed toward changing the behavior of an uncooperative family member through working with a cooperative family member as a mediator. The program has been used primarily with noncooperative alcoholics and cooperative, non-alcohol-abusing spouses. The UFT literature does not discuss its applicability to Single-Parent families. In applying UFT to an out-of-treatment, drug-abusing adult son or daughter, the cooperative non-drug-abusing parent, grandparent or other family member is helped to influence the drug-abusing family member to stop or reduce use of illegal drugs, to enter treatment or both. The drug-abusing family member does not participate in the UFT program. This approach does not assume the cooperative family member is to blame for drug abuse within the family. Instead, it directs practitioners to view a cooperative spouse, parent, grandparent, sibling or other family member as a vital and potentially crucial point of leverage who may be the main or only rehabilitative influence accessible to the family practitioner. This approach is somewhat similar to the family-intervention approach advanced by Casolaro and Smith (1993), which aims to get alcohol abusers and drug abusers into treatment by working with their family members.

The unilateral family treatment approach has three foci of intervention: an individual focus, an interactional focus and a third-party focus. The cooperative individual focus emphasizes coping by reducing stress and anxiety through affordable respite-care services for parenting grandparents and caregivers, wellness interventions which address self-care and self-protection strategies to prevent financial and material exploitation. The interactional focus entails mediating behavior among family members, helping members substitute any nagging, disparaging or enabling behavior with positive actions. The third-party focus involves work to bring about change in the uncooperative family member, such as getting the family member to assess his or her readiness to change, providing information about new programs which make both child welfare and substance abuse treatment services available. These models help the family discuss obstacles which block pathways into treatment for the alcohol- or drug-abusing parent as well as ways to overcome these obstacles and to educate the drug abuser about risks of HIV/AIDS.

The UFT approach is not explicitly intergenerational. It does not specify whether or how children, grandchildren, grandparents or other family members are to be involved. However, practitioners who aim to form empowering relationships, to build on clients' strengths, to respect and incorporate diversity and to carry out gender-sensitive interventions will certainly want to include grandmothers and others in unilateral family treatment plans.

Kinship-Care and Foster-Family-Care Programs

Perhaps the most important action which practitioners can take to help Single-Parenting grandparents is to advocate for child and family welfare policies that support kinship care. Historically, an informal kinship system has served as the African-American community's response to ensuring the preservation of Black families. A system of formal kinship care has only recently surfaced as a response to the increase in children entering the foster-care system and at risk of out-of-home placement because of parental drug abuse or multiple environmental stressors. Scannapieco and Jackson (1996) describe formal kinship care as a system through which the state or county has custody of the child but a relative takes care of the child. For policymakers, program developers and social work practitioners to be responsive to kinship-care systems, they need to do the following:

- Recognize children in kinship care are predominately African American and a culturally based perspective is therefore needed.
- Affirm Black kinship care as a system of care which is historically strong, intact, resilient and adaptive.
- Work with the "kinship triad" made up of children, biological parents and the caregiver relatives and direct services at this union of three.
- Include all family and kin (all possible caregivers) in the development of the case plan and decision making.

- Be mindful the relative caregiver does not consider herself or himself to be a foster parent in the traditional sense.
- Speak out against policies or practices which might undermine or destroy indigenous kinship care arrangements (Scannapieco & Jackson, 1996).

Several authors (Barth, Ramler, & Pietrzak, 1993; Daley & Raskin, 1991; Woodruff & Sterzin, 1993) have described foster-family-care and shared-family-care programs which could also support Single Grandparents' efforts to parent their grandchildren and help drug-abusing adult children. These programs are designed to provide child protection without parent/child separation. Foster-family care permits a family consisting of one or more children and a dependent parent (who may be drug addicted, mentally retarded, physically challenged, emotionally disturbed or health impaired) to be fostered and cared for by a family, a family member or multiple family caregivers. Foster-family care systems function well when child and family welfare systems provide counseling, financial assistance and other services to strengthen both the parent/child family and the newly formed foster family of which it becomes a part or a subfamily. Similarly, shared family care is the "planned provision of out-of-home care to parent(s) and children so that the parent and host caregivers simultaneously share the care of the child and work toward independent in-home care by the parent(s)" (Barth, 1993, p. 273). Both shared family care and foster care for families have been in operation for centuries in Europe. However, these programs have been largely unavailable throughout the United States and have been neglected by the social work community. Today they are increasingly recognized as potentially very responsive to the needs of Single Grandparents, parents, children and grandchildren in drug-affected family systems.

Thus, Single-Grandparent families with children of a drug-abusing parent not only need to be supported as kinship-care systems but also as promising foster- or shared-family-care systems. Practitioners are able to plan more appropriate family interventions by employing assessment knowledge, techniques and tools which examine intergenerational relationships across cultures (Hines, Garcia-Preto, McGoldrick, Almeida & Weltman, 1992), sharpening skills for assessing drug-involved clients in nonspecialized programs (Griffin, 1993) and adapting imaginative family-care programs to the needs of Single-Grandparent families.

Conclusion

Practitioners who work with children and Single-Grandparent families affected by drug abuse have learned an individual-client focused, problem-oriented approach is not very effective. Clearly, a full continuum of assistance is needed including not only social services for individual families but basic social provisions for all families such as adequate income, employment opportunities, decent and affordable housing, acceptable and accessible child care and education.

Without these basic supports both child welfare staff and substance abuse treatment providers will continue to be hampered in their ability to respond to the pressing needs of their client. Without working to correct the racism and sexism that feed stereotypes about substance-abusing [and single-grandparent families], it will be difficult to develop the base of support necessary to put in place the services these families need. (Azzi-Lessing & Olsen, 1996, p.21)

Thus, social work and other human service practitioners who wish to help Single-Grandparent families affected by drug abuse within the family system need to work on several levels. They must support the well-functioning and competence of Single-Grandparent families, strengthening those families which are overwhelmed with their responsibilities. Further they need to foster collaboration and coordinated service delivery between child welfare and substance-abuse-treatment providers; closing the gaps in services to nontraditional families and challenging societal oppression that limits opportunities for families.

Bibliography

Abbott, A.A. (1995). Substance abuse and the feminist perspective. In N. Van DenBergh (Ed.). *Feminist practice in the 21st century* (pp. 258-77). Washington, DC: NASW Press.

Amato, P.R. (1987). Family processes in one-parent, stepparent, and intact families: The child's point of view. *Journal of Marriage and the Family, 49,* 327-37.

Azzi-Lessing, L. & Olsen, L.J. (1996). Substance abuse affected families in the child welfare system: New challenges, new alliances. *Social Work, 41,* 15-23.

Barth, R.P. (1993). Shared family care: Child protection without parent/child separation. In R.P. Barth, J. Pietrzak, & M. Ramler (Eds.), *Families living with drugs and HIV: Intervention and treatment strategies* (pp. 272-95). New York: Guilford.

Barth, R.P., Ramler, M., & Pietrzak, J. (1993). Toward more effective and efficient programs for drug- and AIDS-affected families. In R.P. Barth, J. Pietrzak, & M. Ramler (Eds.), *Families living with drugs and HIV: Intervention and treatment strategies* (pp. 337-53). New York: Guilford.

Black Family Development, Inc. (1990). *Drug culture collaboration. Training series: Drug abuse.* Detroit, MI: Author.

BepRo, C. (Ed.). (1991). *Feminism and addiction.* New York: Haworth.

Bianchi, S. M. (1995). The changing demographics and socioeconomic characteristics of single-parent families. *Marriage and Family Review,* 20, 71-97.

Boyd-Franklin, N. (1989). Religion, spirituality, and the treatment of Black families. *In Black families in therapy: A multisystems approach* (pp. 78-91). New York: Guilford.

Burton, L. (1992). Black grandmothers rearing children of drug-addicted parents: Stressors, outcomes and social service needs. *Gerontologist, 32,* 744-51.

Burton, L.; Dilworth-Anderson, P. & Merriwether-de-Vries, C. (1995). Context and surrogate parenting among contemporary grandmothers. *Marriage and Family Review, 20,* 349-66.

Casolaro, V. & Smith, R.J. (1993). The process of intervention: Getting alcohol and drug abusers into treatment. In S.L.A. Straussner (Ed.), *Clinical work with substance abusing clients* (pp. 105-18). New York: Guilford.

Cermak, T.L. (1986). *Diagnosing and treating co-dependency.* Minneapolis, MN: The Johnson Institute.

Chestang, L. (1972). *Character development in a hostile environment. Occasional Paper No. 3.* Chicago: University of Chicago School of Social Service Administration.

Collins, B.G. (1993). Reconstructing codependency using self-in-relation theory: A feminist perspective. *SocialWork, 38,* 470-6.

Cowger, C.D. (1992). Assessment of clients strengths. In D. Saleebey (Ed.) *Strengths perspective in social work practice* (pp. 139-47). New York: Longman.

Cowger, C.D. (1994). Assessing client strengths: Clinical assessment for client empowerment. Social Work, 39, 262-8.

Daley, D.C. & Raskin, M.S. (Eds.) (1991). *Treating the chemically dependent and their families.* Newbury Park, CA:Sage Publications.

Donati, T. (1995). Single parents and wider families in the new context of legitimacy. *Marriage and Family Review, 20,* 27-42.

Freedberg, S. (1993). The feminine ethic of care and the professionalization of social work. *Social Work, 38,* 535-40.

Griffin, R.E. (1993). Assessing the drug-involved client. In Rauch, J.B. (Ed.), *Assessment: A sourcebook for social work practice.* Milwaukee, WI: Families International (pp. 173-84).

Hill, R. (1972). *The strengths of black families.* New York: Emerson Hall.

Hines, P. (1990). African American mothers. *Journal of Feminist Family Therapy, 2* (2). 23-32.

Hines, P.M., Garcia-Preto, N., McGoldrick, M., Almeida, R., & Weltman, S. (1992). Intergenerational relations across cultures. *Families in Society, 73,* 323-38.

Hurd, E.; Moore, C. & Rogers, R. (1995). Quiet success: Parenting' strengths among African Americans. *Families in Society, 76,* 434-43.

Jendrek, M.P. (1994a). Grandparents who parent their grandchildren: Circumstances and decisions. *Gerontologist, 34,* 206-16.

Jendrek, M.P. (1994b). Policy concerns of white grandparents who provide regular care to their grandchildren. *Journal of Gerontological Social Work, 23,* 175-200.

Jennings, J. (1987). Elderly parents as caregivers for their adult dependent children. *Social Work, 32* (5), 430-3.

Joslin, D. & Brouard, A. (1995). The prevalence of grandmothers as primary caregivers in a poor pediatric population. *Journal of Community Health, 20,* 383-401.

Julian D.J. (1995). Resources for single-parent families. *Marriage and Family Review, 20,* 499-512.

Kaufman, E. (1982). Family structures of narcotic addicts. *International Journal of Addictions, 16,* 105-8.

Kissman, K. (1991). Feminist-based social work with singleparent families. *Families in Society, 72,* 23-8.

Kissman, K. & Allen, J.A. (1993). *Single-parent families.* Newbury Park, CA: Sage Publications.

Kivett, V.R. (1993). Racial comparisons of the grandmother role: Implications for strengthening the family support system of older black women. *Family Relations, 42,* 165-72.

Knox, D.H. (1985). Spirituality: A tool in the assessment and treatment of black alcoholics and their families. *Alcoholism Treatment Quarterly, 2* (3/4), 31-44.

Kretzmann, J.P. & McKnight, J.L. (1993). *Building communities from the inside out: A path toward finding and mobilizing a community's assets.* Chicago: ACTA Publications.

Lewis, R.A. (1990). The adult child and older parents. In T.H. Brubaker (Ed.), *Family relationships in later life* (2nd ed., pp. 68-85). Newbury Park, CA: Sage Publications.

Littlejohn-Blake, S.M. & Darling, C.A. (1993). Understanding the strengths of African American families. *Journal of Black Studies, 23*, 460-71.

Logan, S.M.L., Freeman, E.M., & McRoy, R.G. (1990). *Social work practice with Black families: A culturally specific perspective.* New York: Longman.

Lott, J.G. (1993). Here come the grandmothers: Where's the rite of passage? Where's the book of rules? *Ms, 3* (5), 94-5.

Madanes, C., Duke, M., & Harbin, H. (1980). Family ties of heroin addicts. Archives of *General Psychiatry, 37*, 889-94.

Marlow, C. (1994). Ex-partner, family, friends, and other relationships: Their role within the social network of long-term single mothers. *Journal of Applied Social Psychology, 24*, 60-81.

McGrew, K.B. (1991). *Daughters' decision making about the nature and level of their participation in the long-term care of their dependent elderly mothers: A qualitative study.* Oxford, OH: Scripps Gerontology Center.

Mendes, H.A. (1979). Single-parent families: A typology of lifestyles. *Social Work 24*, 193-220.

Minkler, M. & Roe, K.M. (1993). *Grandmothers as caregivers: Raising children of the crack cocaine epidemic.* Newbury Park, CA: Sage Publications.

Minkler, M., Roe, K.M., & Price, M. (1992). The physical and emotional health of grandmothers raising grandchildren in the crack cocaine 'epidemic'. *Gerontologist, 32*, 752-61.

Minkler, M., Roe, K.M,. & Robertson-Beckley, R.J. (1994). Raising grandchildren from crack cocaine households: Effects on family and friendship ties of African-American women. *American Journal of Orthopsychiatry, 64*, 20-9.

Morrell, C. (1996). Radicalizing recovery: Addiction, spirituality, and politics. *Social Work, 41*, 306-12.

Morrison, N.C. (1995). Successful single-parent families. *Journal of Divorce and Remarriage, 22*, 205-19.

Nesto, B. (1994). Low-income single mothers: Myths and realities. *Affilia, 9*, 232-46.

Norton, D.C. (1978). *The dual perspective.* New York: Council on Social Work Education.

Pinderhughes, E. (1986). Minority women: A nodal point in the functioning of the social system. In M. Ault-Riche (Ed.), *Women and family therapy.* Rockville, MD: Aspen System Corp.

Pope, S.K., Whiteside, L., Brooks-Gunn, J., Kelleher, K.J., Rickert, V.I., Bradley, R.H., & Casey, P.H. (1993). Low-birthweight infants born to adolescent mothers: Effects of coresidency with grandmothers on child development. *Journal of the American Medical Association, 269*, 1396-400.

Roberto, K.A. (1990). Grandparent and grandchild relationships. In T.H. Brubaker (Ed.), *Family relationships in later life* (2nd ed., pp. 100-12). Newbury Park, CA: Sage Publications.

Saleebey, D. (Ed) (1992). *The strengths perspective in social work practice.* New York: Longman.

Saleebey, D. (1996). The strengths perspective in social work practice: Extensions and cautions. *Social Work, 41*, 296-305.

Sands, R.G. & Nuccio, K.E. (1989). Mother-headed single-parent families: A feminist perspective. *Affilia, 4*(3), 25-41.

Scannapieco, M. & Jackson, S. (1996). Kinship care: The African-American response to family preservation. *Social Work, 41* (2), 190-6.

Schaef, A. W. (1992). Co-dependence: Misunderstood-Mistreated. New York: Harper Collins.

Smith, A. (1994). African-American grandmothers' war against the crack cocaine epidemic. *Arete, 19*(1), 22-36.

Solomon, J.C. & Marx, J. (1995)." To grandmother's house we go": Health and school adjustment of children raised solely by grandparents. *Gerontologist, 35*, 386-94.

Stack, C.B. (1974). *All our kin: Strategies for survival in a Black community.* New York: Harper & Row.

Sullivan, M.A. (1993, Spring). Addictive family systems: No home for vulnerable Black women. *Black Caucus: Journal of the NABSW*, 11-l9.

Sullivan, W.P., Wolk, J.L., & Hartman, D.J. (1992) Case management in alcohol and drug treatment: Improving client outcomes. *Families in Society, 73*, 195-2O3.

Thomas, E.J. (1994). The unilateral treatment program for alcohol abuse: Background, selected procedures, and case applications. In J. Rothman & E.J. Thomas (Eds.), *Intervention research: Design and development for human service* (pp. 427-47). New York: Haworth.

Thomas, M.B. & Dansby, P.G. (1985). Black clients: Family structures, therapeutic issues, and strengths. *Psychotherapy, 22*, 398-406.

Timberlake, E.M. & Chipungu, S.S. (1992). Grandmotherhood: Contemporary meaning among African-American middle-class grandmothers. *Social Work, 37*, 216-22.

Trent, K. & Harlan, S.L. (1994). Teenage mothers in nuclear and extended households: Differences by marital status and race/ethnicity. *Journal of Family Issues, 15*, 309-37.

Tweed, S.H. & Ryff, C.D. (1991). Adult children of alcoholics: Profiles of wellness amidst distress. *Journal of Studies in Alcohol, 52*, 133-41.

U.S. Bureau of the Census. (1994a). *Marital status and living arrangements: March 1994. Current Population Reports*, pp. 20-484. Washington, DC: U.S. Government Printing Office.

U.S. Bureau of the Census. (1994b). *The diverse living arrangements of children: Summer 1991. Current Population Reports*, pp.70-38. Washington, DC: U.S. Government Printing Office.

U.S. Bureau of the Census. (1995). *The Black population in the United States: March 1994 and 1993. Current Population Reports*, pp. 20-480. Washington, DC: U.S. Government printing Office.

Walters, M. (1988).Single-parent, female-headed households. In M. Walters, B. Carter, P. Papp, & O. Silverstein (Eds.), *The invisible web: Gender patterns in family relationships* (pp. 75-91). New York: Free Press.

Wegscheider-Cruse, S. & Cruse, J. (l990). *Understanding co-dependency.* Deerfield Beach, FL: Health Communications.

Weick, A., Rapp, C., Sullivan, W. P., & Kisthardt, W. (1989). A strengths perspective for social work practice. *Social Work, 34*, 350-4.

Whitfield, C. (1989). Co-dependence: Our most common addiction: Some physical, mental, emotional and spiritual perspectives. *Alcoholism Treatment Quarterly, 6*, 19-36.

Woodruff, G. & Sterzin, E.D. (1993). Family support services for drug and AIDS-affected families. In R.P. Barth, J. Pietrzak, & M. Ramler (Eds.), *Families living with drugs and HIV: Intervention and treatment strategies* (pp. 219-37). New York: Guilford.

Young, I.M. (1994). Making single motherhood normal. *Dissent, 41* (1), 88-93.

Ziegler-Driscoll, G. (1981). The similarities in families of drug dependents and alcoholics. In D. Stanton & T. Todd (Eds.), *The family therapy of drug abuse and addiction* (pp. 19-39). New York: GuilfordPress, Inc.

Successful Interventions with Single-Parent Families

Susan S. Tebb, Ph.D., L.S.W.
and Cathryne L. Schmitz, Ph.D. ASCW

SINGLE-PARENT FAMILIES are diverse and common. At some point in their childhood, one out of three children will reside in a Single-Parent family. These households, as a group, are not deficient, deviant or dysfunctional. Households within this group run the gamut from superior to deficient as do Two-Parent families and must therefore be assessed individually. The most universal difficulty faced by female-headed, Single-Parent households–and therefore the most universal need–is money which is primarily the result of the lower income potential of females.

Because Single-Parent families are not considered the norm by most people, they are not often supported by either the media or social policies. Two-Parent households are made the norm and in doing this, Single-Parent families become *failures*. The medical model supports the deficit model of social work practice focusing on relationships as the source of the problem, the cause of Single Parentness. This model does not acknowledge the influences of our social institutions upon family life, rather it blames the victim, supporting neither the families nor the institutions around them.

The United States Commission on Children (1993) issued a report entitled *Next Steps for Children and Families: Strengthening and Supporting Families* pronouncing children need supportive homes with married parents; two adults committed to each other are best suited to provide such a home. Imagine what statements like this do to Single Parents who have discovered the hidden opportunity in their role as a Single Parent as they raise and care for happy children.

253

A study (Miller, 1987) undertaken by the National Association of Social Workers (NASW), on the other hand, found Single Parents observed themselves to be much stronger and more competent than they were perceived by a group of social workers. The strengths named by this group of parents were independence, connectedness and cohesiveness with friends and family. "A basic requisite to strengthening families whose structure is vulnerable to impoverishment is that the family, regardless of its form, be viewed as a viable unit." (Kissman, 1995, p. 153). The deficit, if there is any, is not in the family but in a society which does not acknowledge families exist in many configurations. One is not better than another.

Single-Parent families are *traditional* family structures in the sense they have existed in numbers even greater than those noted by official statistics (Kissman, 1995). We, as social workers, need to examine our own perception of Single Parents. The social work view of Single Parents frequently falls into the model provided by George Gilder in *Wealth and Poverty* (1981). Gilder, in his discussion of welfare workers, points out the most serious menace to independent functioning of families is workers who provide families with programs rather than opportunities. As social workers we can easily fall into this pattern by continuing to see the Single-Parent family as having deficits and not strengths.

> A holistic view of families is more difficult to conceptualize than is a simple cause-and-effect model based on dual and hierarchical thinking that places women and people of color at the bottom of some *normative* family structures. Such pathological perspectives result in an impasse and a preoccupation with exploring how to put families back together rather than naming families as diverse and exploring alternatives for strengthening families. (Kissman, 1995, p. 153).

All families across their many structures, deserve the status of legitimacy. Single-Parent families need to be considered as a *mainstream* family life not as *alternative*. A multidimensional view of families which includes grandparents, good friends, relatives and partners expands our perception of potential resources and strengths.

Transitions

The transition into Single Parenthood is an experience unique to each family. This uniqueness must be acknowledged, respected and allowed for in social work interventions. Hanson and Sporakowski (1986) found the differences between Single Parents are not in the life stage they or their children are in, "but in the timing, number and length of the critical transitions" (p. 5). Tebb found this to be true when she became a Single Parent through the unexpected death of her children's father, she could not predict nor be compared to any other widow in how she would respond.

Many Single Parents enter the role by way of a crisis–a failed relationship, a divorce, an unplanned pregnancy, a death. A crisis brings potential and risk as the two symbols in the Chinese word for crisis indicate–one depicts *danger* and the other *hidden opportunity*. Social workers can provide assistance and support during the adjustment phase. Practitioners need to first help by making sure the people involved are not in danger; then helping the parents look for and seek opportunities.

Social work intervention involves providing families with assistance in (a) coping with and weathering transitions positively; (b) redefining a family and (c) strengthening their unit by developing family transitions, having family times and seeing themselves as a family. As Mendes (1979) said "one of the most important tasks for counseling with Single-Parent families, regardless of their life style, is to help liberate families that are tyrannized by the two-parent family model" (p. 195).

Cashion (1982) found when socioeconomic factors were controlled, children of female-headed, Single-Parent households were no different in emotionality, school success or self-esteem than children from two-parent households. It is easier to blame family structure for difficulties exhibited by one or all family members, rather than looking at the multiplicity of complex issues affecting individuals and families including income and unrelated family conflicts. The effect of focusing on the negative facets of Single-Parent families is the continuation of negative social stereotypes. As Kiely (1995) points out, "Seeing single mothers in terms of derogatory stereotypes is probably a reincarnated form of moral prejudice" (p. 932). As a social worker, it is helpful to focus on successful Single Parents, rather than relying on myth and bias. Social workers need to keep abreast of the increasing availability of resources and the growing body of literature.

The number of resources and models for empowerment intervention available for social workers is growing. Social workers may find the following resources of help both for themselves and for the families with whom they are working. Schlesinger (1986, 1995) presented annotated lists of books written about and for Single Parents. Kimmons (1995) and Gaston (1986) developed a filmography catalog which gives social workers with an extensive list of films, videos and film-strips dealing with Single Parents. Also Julian (1995) developed a inventory of national organizations which provide services for Single Parents and their families.

Practice Models

We can work toward strengthening and empowering Single-Parent families as we move into the twenty-first century if we take heed and listen to Barbara Solomon (1985). She cautions us to understand the importance of balancing between government and family responsibility in the move to transform families. As she notes, in learning the balance, social workers develop the potential to provide assistance which can help in the "transformation of a significant number of families from powerless, unstable collectivity ties to strong, well functioning centers of identity for the members" (p. 3). In doing so, those "professionals sanctioned by society to provide assistance to families will have understood the difference between assisting problem families and empowering families to solve their problems." (p. 3).

Olson and Haynes (1993) investigated the characteristics of successful Single Parents. The twenty-six Single Parents involved in the study were middle class, had at least a high school degree, were gainfully employed or pursuing a higher degree and were not experiencing commanding money difficulties. Seven themes emerged: (a) acceptance (an internalization and integration of the parental role) of the responsibilities and challenges; (b) prioritizating her/his role as a parent; (c) consistent, nonpunitive discipline; (d) open communication; (e) the fostering of individuality within a supportive family unit; (f) recognition of the need for self-nurturance and (g) rituals and traditions. These themes can be used to help families look at and become *successful* families. These themes are characteristics of good parenting not just successful Single Parents.

Social work interventions can help a family create its own meaning. Atwood and Genovese (1993) proposed a six-stage social construction model for social workers to use in helping a family develop meaning: (a) joining the family meaning system, (b) proposing the notion of a family meaning system, (c) learning the family's meaning system, (d) challenging the family's meaning system, (e) amplifying the new family meaning system and (f) stabilizing the new meaning system. Social workers can help Single-Parent families see the difficulties experienced by family members are part of the life experiences of a family and not part of an *abnormal* family structure. The family is helped to see the normalcy of diverse family structures and to understand changes and transitions can build stronger families.

The Strengths Perspective

Because most Single-Parent households are headed by women, the social context of women must be taken into consideration when developing social work interventions for Single-Parent families. The greatest problem facing the Single Parent, especially the female head of household, is economic need (Kissman, 1991; Schmitz, 1995). Poverty continues to plague female-headed household across cultural and ethnic backgrounds (Jivanjee & Tebb, 1998; Schmitz). Society continues to view the Single-Parent household as deficient even though family-system functioning is more predictive of difficulty than family structure (Hanson, 1986; Quinn & Allen, 1989).

Social workers can help to reframe the definition of family both to the family and to the community through advocacy, educational programs and support groups. Early intervention and outreach are important in helping newly Single Parents find and use effective social supports. At points of transition, needs are intensified because social relationships are frequently strained. Short-term, solution-oriented approaches are in most instances best, emphasizing the strengths of the situation rather than the deficits.

Strengths-perspective intervention focuses on reducing the Single Parent's burden and enhancing well-being. In the health or strengths model, the social worker develops relationships by listening, exploration and caring (see Weick 1983, 1984, 1986; Weick and Freeman, 1983; Weick, Rapp, Sullivan & Kisthardt, 1989). As noted in this volume, when respect for the client is given by the workers, the client can begin to work on and develop self-knowledge and strength. One's own ability to affect positive change is essential in coping with stress and providing well-being in one's own life. Through the social work relationship, the worker assists the client in strengthening her/his belief that she/he can bring about change.

The first step involves listening (Tebb, 1990). Understanding the client knows "best", means listening is a key skill in the strengths model. The worker must understand how the client perceives the situation and her/his environment. Listening is a skillful, intellectual and emotional process integrating the physical, mental, social and spiritual environments of the social worker and client in a quest for understanding the meaning of the Single-Parent's situation. An effective listener listens to the meaning behind those words, noting body language which hints at what the parent is feeling and thinking. Improving listening skills involves suspending judgment, not responding too promptly, listening for the themes expressed, reflecting on what is said and seeking the meaning.

Kalyanpur and Rao (1991) found sharing, accepting, interpreting and conversation to be the precursors to establishing rapport and exploration. The worker needs to help the client express or learn to express her/his emotions; when emotions are expressed, the client can instinctively make decisions participating in her/his own growth. Expression of the social worker's own emotions is also part of listening and communicating with the client. Social workers, in developing their relationships with clients, need to be aware of and express their own feelings in a way which supports and defines while positively influencing and assisting in changes.

The second step in helping Single Parents make positive changes in their life is exploring the Single-Parent's environment, family structure and perception and desires (Tebb, 1990). Here the worker acknowledges the parent's strengths while helping her/him express fear, depression and feelings of being overwhelmed. The worker also notes the resources within the family's environment.

257

The third part of the intervention is that of caring and expressing concern (Tebb, 1990). In offering caring, the worker encourages the client to seek self-knowledge and make decisions and plans. When the client knows another cares for her/him, it provides her/him with the trust which incites the development of inner knowledge and the discovery of what will best enable her/him to have a good parenting experience. The caring the worker gives to the Single Parent provides self-value. Solomon (1976) provides a structure for using the strategies of enabling, linking, catalyzing and priming. Support and caring given to the Single Parent enables them to use resources more effectively. The linking strategy connects Single Parents to support group, networks, friends and family and appropriate resources.

Throughout this book the reader has been reminded of the importance of recognizing, acknowledging, understanding and incorporating the contextual placements of the families within the community(ies). Chapters two, three, four and five, in particular, frame the significance of support through community, neighborhood and group. In chapter five, Prince describes groups which share much in common with Kenya's "Harambee" projects, part of the Kenyan Department of Social Service founded to help women help themselves (described in Jivanjee and Tebb, 1998). "Harambee", meaning "Let's pull together", has been the inspiration behind Kenya's self-help development which is evident in women's groups across Africa. The value of self-help has been and is a vital part of the African tradition of neighborliness and communal assistance. Women in Kenya, as in the United States, have historically come together to help one another in daily tasks, pooling resources to meet common needs, such as at times of childbirth, funerals and farming. Group work and community building are vehicles for empowerment, occurring within a strengths focused framework. When women join with other women, they are able to increase their understanding of the systemic oppression they experience, sharing their ideas and skills in bringing about change.

Finally, change requires priming the system, providing information which helps the system respond differently. For example, a school social worker primes the system by discussing the strengths of Single-Parent families and presenting examples of successful Single Parents and their children. When the teacher looks over their class roster and notes children from Single-Parent homes they will then be able to think about the strengths each of those children have instead of the problems.

Working with Single Parents necessitates creativity and an openness to helping these parents develop methods of parenting which work for them and their families. "Strategies that mediate the negative social prescriptions of Single Parenthood and maximize the linkage to social supports–whether achieved through individual, group, or family interventions–work best" (Strand, 1995, p. 2162). Acknowledging, reframing and contextualizing obstacles can help make them manageable. Acknowledge the lack of resources, such as financial resources, as a hurdle but as one which can be overcome. Many Single Parents believe these hurdles are caused by them, when, in reality they are caused by social issues and circumstances. If a Single Parent does not have or is ineligible for resources, the social worker uses the strategy of catalyzing to develop a resource or adapt an existing one.

Single-Parent families are similar, diverse and unique. All families face challenges. Social workers are charged with helping families face difficulties in a manner which precipitates growth and healing. Creativity, respect and belief all contribute to a productive process. Single-Parent families need the same respect and hope required by all families. Approaching Single-Parent families from a base of understanding, respecting their culture and history and listening for their unique context and reality; provides a base for productive intervention. The authors/practitioners of these chapters on a diverse range of Single-Parent families hope the reader/practitioner finds ways of working with parents which will enable them to seek out and find strengths together. Such strengths are the base from which parents develop the skills and resources necessary to make their life and that of their children more enjoyable and productive.

Bibliography

Atwood, J.D. & Genovese, F. (1993). *Counseling Single Parents.* Alexandria, VA: American Counseling Association.

Cashion, B.G. (1982). Female-headed families: Effects on children and clinical implications. *Journal of Marital and Family Therapy, 8,* 77-85.

Gilder, G. (1981). *Wealth and Poverty.* New York: Basic Books.

Hanson, S.M.H. (1986). Healthy single parent families. *Family Relations, 35,* 125-132.

Hanson, S.M.H. & Sporakowski, M.J. (1986). Single parent families. *Family Relations, 35,* 3-8.

Jivanjee, P. & Tebb, S. (1998). Visions of Community: Women and Children in the Developing and Developed World. *International Social Work, 42* (1), 27-38.

Julian, D.J. (1995). Resources for single parent families. *Marriage & Family Review, 20*(3/4), 499-512.

Kalyanpur, M. & Rao, S.S. (1991). Empowering low-income black families of handicapped children, *American Journal of Orthopsychiatry, 61*(4), 523-532.

Kiely, R. (1995). Single mothers and supermyths. In Turner, F.J. (Ed.), *Differential Diagnosis and Treatment in Social Work. (4th ed)* (pp. 928-933). New York: The Free Press

Kimmons, L.C. (1995). Video/filmography on single parenting. *Marriage & Family Review, 20* (3/4), 483-498.

Kimmons, L.C. & Gaston, J.A. (1986). Single parenting: A filmography. *Family Relations, 35,* 205-211.

Kissman, K. (1991). Feminist-based social work with single-parent families. Families in Society: *The Journal of Contemporary Human Services,* 23-28.

Kissman, K. (1995). Divisive dichotomies and mother-headed families: The power off naming. *Social Work, 40*(2), 151-153.

Mendes, H. (1979). Single-parent families: A topology of life-styles. *Social Work, 24*(3), 193-199.

Miller, D. (1987). *Helping the Strong.* Washington, D.C.: National Association of Social Work.

Olson, M.R. & Haynes, J.A. (1993). Successful single parents. *Families in Society: The Journal of Contemporary Human Services,* 259-267.

Quinn, P. & Allen, K.R. (1989). Facing challenges and making compromises: How single mothers endure. *Family Relations, 38,* 300-395.

Schlesinger, B. (1995). Single parent families: A bookshelf. *Marriage and Family Review, 20*(3/4), 463-482.

Schlesinger, B. (1986). Single parent families: A bookshelf: 1978-1985. *Family Relations, 35,* 199-204.

Schmitz, C.L. (1995). Reframing the dialogue on female-headed single-parent households. *Affilia, 10,* 426-41.

Solomon, B. (1976). *Black empowerment: Social work in oppressed communities.* New York: Columbia University Press.

Solomon, B. (1985). How do we really empower families? New strategies for social work practitioners. *Family Resource Coalition Report, 4*(3). 2-3.

Strand, V. C. (1995). Single parents. In *Encyclopedia of Social Work* pp. 2157-2163.

Tebb, S. (1990). *Caregiver Manual.* Washington, DC: Department of Veteran Affairs.

United States National Commission on Children. (1993). *Next steps for children and families: Strengthening and supporting families.* Washington, DC: National Commission on Children.

Weick, A. N. (1983). Issues on overturning a medical model of social work. *Social Work, 28,* 467-471.

Weick, A.N. (1984). The concept of responsibility in a health model of social work. *Social Work in Health Care, 10,* 13-25.

Weick, A.N. (1986). The philosophical context of a health model of social work. *Social Casework: The Journal of Contemporary Social Work,* 551-559.

Weick, A.N., & Freeman, E. (1983). *Developing a Health Model for Social Work.* Unpublished manuscript, University of Kansas, School of Social Welfare, Lawrence.

Weick, A.; Rapp, C.; Sullivan, W. P., & Kisthardt, W. (1989). A strengths perspective for social work practice. *Social Work, 34,* 350-354.